Public Los Angeles

Public Los Angeles

A PRIVATE CITY'S ACTIVIST FUTURES

DON PARSON

EDITED BY

ROGER KEIL AND JUDY BRANFMAN

WITH ADDITIONAL CONTRIBUTIONS BY
DANA CUFF, MIKE DAVIS, STEVEN FLUSTY, GREG
GOLDIN, JACQUELINE LEAVITT, LAURA PULIDO,
SUE RUDDICK, TOM SITTON, EDWARD W. SOJA,
AND JENNIFER WOLCH

THE UNIVERSITY OF GEORGIA PRESS
Athens

© 2019 by the University of Georgia Press
Athens, Georgia 30602
www.ugapress.org
All rights reserved
Set in 10/12.5 Minion Pro by Classic City Composition

Most University of Georgia Press titles are
available from popular e-book vendors.

Printed digitally

Library of Congress Cataloging-in-Publication Data

Names: Parson, Donald Craig, author.
Title: Public Los Angeles : a private city's activist futures / Don Parson ; edited by Roger Keil
    and Judy Branfman ; with additional contributions by Dana Cuff, Mike Davis, Steven Flusty,
    Greg Goldin, Jacqueline Leavitt, Laura Pulido, Sue Ruddick, Tom Sitton, Edward W. Soja, and
    Jennifer Wolch.
Description: Athens : The University of Georgia Press, 2020. | Series: Geographies of justice and
    social transformation ; 45 | Includes bibliographical references and index.
Identifiers: LCCN 2019018156 | ISBN 9780820356228 (hardback) | ISBN 9780820356235 (paperback) |
    ISBN 9780820356211 (ebook)
Subjects: LCSH: Los Angeles (Calif.)—Social conditions. | Political activists—California—Los
    Angeles. | Social justice—California—Los Angeles.
Classification: LCC HN80.L7 P37 2020 | DDC 306.09794/94—dc23
LC record available at https://lccn.loc.gov/2019018156

CONTENTS

ILLUSTRATIONS

Tables

ACKNOWLEDGMENTS

We gratefully acknowledge the assistance, at York University, of Daniel Taylor, Jenny Lugar, and Zoi de la Peña at various stages of preparing this book. Roger Keil thanks York University through its York Research Chair program and the Social Sciences and Humanities Research Council for funding that assisted this project throughout. Completion was supported in part by a much-appreciated grant from the Historical Society of Southern California, with the Ahmanson Foundation.

Some material in this book has been previously published. We have received permission to reproduce this material from the sources that hold the rights to it. "City Lite" by Steven Flusty was first published in *L.A. Architect*, September 1993, pp. 8–9. Don Parson's EEK A MICKEY MOUSE! is an abridged version of a text that first appeared as a review of *Variations on a Theme Park: The New American City and the End of Public Space*, edited by Michael Sorkin (New York: Noonday Press, 1992), in *Science and Culture* 4, no. 2 (1993). A version of Dana Cuff's essay "Power Lines" was first published in *Perspecta* 50 (2017). Dana Cuff and Jennifer Wolch's interview with Mike Davis was originally released on the online media publication *Boom California* on December 16, 2016. Jacqueline Leavitt's chapter "Public Housing in Los Angeles" was first published as "Adding Space: The First and Final Frontier?" in the author's book *Defining Cultural Differences in Space: Public Housing as a Microcosm* (College Park, Md.: Urban Studies and Planning Program, University of Maryland), 3–24, and is reprinted courtesy of the publisher. Edward W. Soja's contribution "The City and Spatial Justice" was originally prepared for presentation at the Spatial Justice conference in Nanterre, Paris, March 12–14, 2008. The article was previously published as "The City and Spatial Justice" («La ville et la justice spatiale»), translated by Sophie Didier, *Spatial Justice* 1 (September 2009), www.jssj.org. Laura Pulido's chapter is an excerpt from the article "Race, Class, and Political Activism: Black, Chicana/o, and Japanese-American Leftists in Southern California, 1968–1978," which first appeared in *Antipode* 34, no. 4 (September 2002): 762–88. Greg Goldin's article "Ben Margolis and Gregory Ain: A Meeting of Radical Minds" was originally published in the *Los Angeles Times*, August 18, 2011.

We thank the publishers, editors, and authors for granting us permission to use these texts here. And many thanks to the archivists and special collections staff who were so helpful with locating, scanning, and acquiring photos and other images, in particular the Southern California Library, Getty Research Institute, and especially Molly Haigh in Special Collections at UCLA's Charles E. Young Research Library for going above and beyond. And thanks to Hunter Deckelman for the beautiful map and to Maria Jankowska, Librarian for Maps at the UCLA Charles E. Young Research Library.

Particular appreciation goes out to Special Collections at California State University, Los Angeles for taking Don's personal archive and creating the Don Parson Collection (2018.002).

We would like to thank the editors of University of Georgia Press for their support and are grateful to the reviewers for their careful reading of the manuscript and their valuable and supportive suggestions.

We started the project before we lost Jackie Leavitt (1939–2015), Edward W. Soja (1940–2015), and Kevin Starr (1940–2017). All of them dear friends of Don Parson, they enthusiastically supported this project. We were able to include contributions by the former two greats of Los Angeles scholarship posthumously. Kevin Starr was working on his contribution to this volume when he passed. He was not able to complete it. His longtime partner, Sheila Starr, wrote, "He was indeed planning to write the postscript to your volume *Public Los Angeles*. Alas, Kevin wrote for deadlines: he made most of them, just barely, but not this one."

Our biggest loss was of course Don Parson himself, with whom and around whom we had worked to get this book completed over the past years. There is more on Don from both of us in the prefatory material of this book. Let us just acknowledge that this book is mainly based on this remarkable scholar's work.

Don died on August 4, 2018, at home in Simi Valley, northwest of Los Angeles. Born February 10, 1955, Don was a native of Thousand Oaks and earned his PhD in urban planning from UCLA in 1985. As this book will underline, he was one of the major historians of metropolitan Los Angeles during the mid-twentieth century. An avid collector of books on California history and amateur photographer, Don was a lover of music (especially Irish music and the Kinks), language, and traveling the byways of Ventura County. For many years Don heroically endured the physical complications of the disease Friedreich's ataxia. Undeterred, he studied in Ireland and traveled through Europe and the United States, living life courageously and with humor. He was grateful for the loving care provided by his mother Patricia, who

predeceased him, and most recently by Ana Sandoval and Timothy Sheehan, with whom he lived.

We wish Don were here to have the final say (and a fiendish laugh); unfortunately we were on different deadlines and he left it in our hands. We are thankful he gave us this chance and hope the next generations will find his work as inspiring as we do.

Roger Keil and Judy Branfman
Toronto and Los Angeles, July 2019

Public Los Angeles

Setting the Stage

Los Angeles and Urban Archaeology

ROGER KEIL

> When cities disappear, they don't come back.

In his satirical novel *The Sellout*, set in a fictional Los Angeles, Paul Beatty has his main character involved in the following conversation:

> "Isn't there something else that would make you happy?"
>
> "Bring back Dickens."
>
> "You know that is impossible. When cities disappear, they don't come back."[1]

This is a book against disappearance. It is a statement for the celebration of a past urban commonwealth, based on popular forces that coalesced to make a better world.[2] That city is mid-twentieth-century Los Angeles, and the book focuses on the decades it took to dismantle its possibilities. As the subtitle to this book suggests, those possibilities were real outcomes of activism and social struggle and, as we will see below, were built in brick and mortar, institutions and community memory. But memory itself has been erased and other memories re-created often in a city that has excelled in "forgetting."[3] Yet perhaps more than ever, the memory of that other Los Angeles is in need of being conjured up in our collective contemporary imagination. So despite the dry humor in the quip from Paul Beatty's 2015 satirical novel, *The Sellout*, in the epigraph above, the city of the past may be kept alive as a specter that orients us today. For that we will turn to one of the foremost historiographers of that alternative Los Angeles, radical Los Angeles scholar Don Parson. This volume consists, most especially, of a collection of unpublished papers by Parson. It is, to some degree, a sequel to his highly recognized *Making a Better World: Public Housing, the Red Scare, and the Direction of Modern Los Angeles* (2005).

In that book, which has been hailed as a masterpiece by scholars of housing, planning, geography, and urban history, Parson outlines the complicated history of how public housing, once celebrated as a positive force in the struggle for better and more housing for the masses, was turned into a threat to American society as its Cold War opponents red-baited anyone and anything that had any association with the idea and the projects. Mike Willard notes that the book contrasts the community modernism of public housing advocates and the corporate modernism of urban renewal advocates. One of the many strengths of Parson's book is his emphasis on the agency of housing directors and residents who used tenant organizations and the physical space of public housing itself as important platforms for labor and civil rights struggles. Public housing developments were important places for mid-twentieth-century interracial alliance and political activism. For example, the Aliso Village housing development became a place of temporary protection for Mexican American youth fleeing vigilante violence during the 1943 zoot suit riots. After the riots, housing directors formed organizations that provided local youth with important social capital (social and political skills, recreational opportunities) that was otherwise severely limited in the working-class neighborhoods of East Los Angeles. During the 1940s, L.A. public housing was a place where pachucos were not draft dodgers but, in Parson's estimation, "colorful revolutionists."[4]

Public Los Angeles does indeed drill down more into the themes raised by the previous volume and adds detail and color to the narrative of an alternative history and geography of housing, life, and work in the Southern California metropolis. But the current political and economic context also makes Public Los Angeles a book with a different horizon. Almost ten years after the meltdown of the housing market, especially that section of the industry that contained the subprime mortgage deals that ravaged poor communities across the United States, this current book is not so much a commentary on alternative histories but more, as Sue Ruddick reminds us in her contribution, a history of the present and possible futures in an urbanized world.

For the title of the book, we take up a thought that the eminent historian of the state of California, Kevin Starr, expressed in the foreword to Making a Better World: "Los Angeles, that is, turned from public housing—and by implication, from anything resembling social democracy—and reconstituted itself as one of the most private cities in America." Parson's work as featured in this current book sees an even broader palette of popular alternatives for different ways to navigate the sedentary and mobile space that is Los Angeles. This is a bit of a stereotype, of course. The great urbanist from New York and Toronto Jane Jacobs, who was no friend of Los Angeles (as a concept and a city), bemoaned the lack of urbanity in Southern California. Her observation directly fed off the idea that "Los Angeles is an extreme example of a metropolis with little public life, depending mainly instead on contacts of a more private social nature."[5] The interplay of the private and the public is a perennial concern in Los Angeles. As it is a capitalist metropolis, this may not be a surprise. As Ed Soja wrote in his brilliant study on spatial justice, a "property blanket is the underlayer of a thick sedimentation of bounded spaces that powerfully shape our everyday life."[6] The fight over the use and meaning of public space and collective property is central to challenging capitalist hegemony in Los Angeles and elsewhere. In Soja's words, "Although seeking spatial justice should not be confined only to struggles over public space, such struggles are vital and can be extended in many different directions in the search for justice and the right to the city."[7] Soja concludes that we should "use a critical spatial perspective to open up a fresh look at the subject of public versus private space and to explore the possibilities for developing new strategies to achieve greater socio-spatial justice."[8] Taking a broad view of the meaning of the public and the private in Los Angeles, we present Parson's work as well as the commentary that follows in that critical sense.

Los Angeles: A Brief History and Geography of the "Postmodern" City

At its core, this is a book about Los Angeles, a city that has shaped the lives and careers of all contributors profoundly. Los Angeles is the main character in the diorama that is on display in this book. Los Angeles is a "real and imagined" place at the far end of the American "manifest destiny," the city from where the United States turned back east and looked at itself as a space contained, after all, by geography.[9] A generation after the LA School of urbanists appeared on the scene, even casual observers of how we talk about cities will not be surprised that the city (or more precisely the urban region) has had just about any moniker and qualification we have in the urban studies lexicon applied to it. Southern California perennially attracts strong opinions and controversial judgments. As we shall see, the archaeology of the Southland's social geography and political ecology that is subject to Don Parson's sharp and critical eye is multifold and generative of powerful ideas about where and how we live. It is an urban region that provides blueprints for urban ontologies. Or, to engage a concept recently introduced into urban studies, it is the "site multiple" of our urban imagination, which for our purposes means that we look at the "manifoldedness" of that object we call Los Angeles.[10] The purpose of this brief introduction is not to provide a comprehensive historical geography of Los Angeles but to highlight a few of its central characteristics that might help in understanding the place of the events and developments in this book.

The Imagined Los Angeles

Before we get to the "real" Los Angeles, let us acknowledge the city's influence on theorizing what the urban might mean. Talking about Los Angeles is always fraught with the problem of definition. Born disparate, dispersed, and suburban, Los Angeles grew into one of the densest carpets of urbanized humanity anywhere in the world, tied together by a federally financed and globally fueled infrastructure of the military, media, and mobility. The Southern California metropolis was at once the largest industrial city in the West and anyone's post-industrial dream, sweatshop nightmare, and postmodern phantasmagoria all in one. In the 1980s and 1990s, when Los Angeles enjoyed its moment in the sun-shine of the urban studies universe, the city and its region were rethought by the influential LA School as either a palimpsest of possibilities or a dystopian hell, depending on which one of their representatives one believed. The Southland had megacity ambitions as it outpaced most economies in the United States and elsewhere. This conversation on definition or identity ultimately leads to the question of how Los Angeles inspired "new geographies of theory" in ur-ban studies.[11] A good place to start is the awakening of Los Angeles research in the 1920s to the spatiality of Southern California as a modern prototype. As would be the case so often in the decades to follow, the city attracted the attention of visitors from afar. In fact, over the course of the twentieth century, there were two camps of Los Angeles watchers that held each other in balance: one of the native sons and one of the itinerant visitors or immigrants to South-ern California. Among the latter, the German geographer Anton Wagner set the tone in a tome published in his native German in 1935: *Los Angeles: City of Two Million in Southern California*.[12] The discovery of Los Angeles as a freak of (urban) nature in the view of outsiders became a stereotype. Much of it had to do with the extended, automobile-driven form of Los Angeles. The scale of LA suburban growth during the twentieth century was unprecedented, although today's megacities have outpaced the range and speed of Southern California's urban expansion. Wagner wrote as early as the 1930s, "Endlessly, the masses of houses expand like a giant box of toy bricks emptied across the landscape. The sea of houses surges from the inner city, via the long North-South arteries Vermont Avenue and Western Avenue, towards the West all the way to the dis-tant coast by Santa Monica. The southern suburbs push towards the horizon in even a wider manner, and through the valleys and passes and across the hills in the East, the residential suburbs penetrate the San Fernando Valley and farther into the San Gabriel basin. The highrise center of the inner city sticks out from the host of small houses and mansions. . . . In the Northeast lies the highrise center of Glendale, surrounded by the small-house-city like an army of aligned matchboxes."[13] But that it has always been suburban is really captured in per-haps the most crucial period of its existence when it became known less as an aberration and more as a model of future urban form and social structure fol-lowing the Second World War.[14] Roughly fifty years later, another outsider, the Briton Reyner Banham, took up the mantle from Wagner but noticed that Los Angeles was becoming more than an oddity but rather a leader in urban form and function. His *Los Angeles: The Architecture of Four Ecologies* (1971) revolu-tionized the way the landscape of Southern California could be viewed: Disdain was replaced by curiosity and explanation. Driving on a freeway became a more normalized urban activity, and living in a suburb was part of the overall metropolitan experience rather than a social pathology.[15] Picking out Wagner and Banham as two bookends of visiting Los Angeles observers is not accidental: the time that separates them is roughly the period that is covered in this book, especially in the chapters by Don Parson. Yet Parson, like his contemporary Mike Davis, is a native son who looks from within. Davis takes up the cues from both Wagner and Banham but views the place from the inside. His *City of Quartz* painted a much more prohibitive and dystopian picture of Los Angeles.[16]

The most far-reaching rewrite of the conceptual geography of Los Angeles was provided by the LA School toward the end of the twentieth century.[17] The city and its school also became the lightning rods of a backlash that spanned the continent from New York to Chicago and San Francisco.[18] Parson's earlier essays preceded this controversy slightly, but his teachers and contemporaries from the LA School were undoubtedly his interlocutors throughout. And in the contribution here by Steven Flusty and in the article by Edward Soja, we see glimpses of the LA School's influence. The school's writers made three important advances that contextualize our contemporary view of Los Angeles and the essays collected in this book: they discuss the (new) urban form of Los Angeles as paradigmatic for urbanism more generally; they view the center of the city differently—instead of seeing either a place of desolation or a place of eviction, they point to the post-Fordist economic districts that enliven the core; this leads finally to celebrating the alternative political possibilities resting in the immigrant post-Fordist city.

Defying the classic center-periphery dichotomy of much (eastern) urban scholarship as well as the presumed linearity of the urban-suburban continuum, LA School representatives used Los Angeles as the basis for a fundamental rethinking of urban form in general. Thus, Los Angeles gave rise to a multifaceted, contested, but widely acclaimed school of urbanism,[19] and to arguably the most important urban monograph of the late twentieth century, Mike Davis's *City of Quartz*.[20] Perhaps the most pervasive claim associated with the LA School has been that it has given birth to conceptualizing urban process and form in contradistinction to the metropolitan model of the Chicago School but, which others contend, signifies the way all cities will grow in the future. It has been noted that LA—meaning urban sprawl—is now everywhere. Beyond mere form, the Los Angeles urban model has given rise to claims about (post) modern urban society generally, where traditional scales and hierarchies of urban living are suspended in a topologically organized grid of flows that renders centers unimportant or sees them as organized from the periphery. Postsuburbia's "composite" character—with its global manifestations, divergences and mixing of land uses, less predictable geographic forms, new politics, new work-residence relations, and discordant land use—describes well the complexity of form, structure, and politics we find in Southern California.[21] It is the inverted city. Peripheral urbanization provided the main narrative of metropolitanization and beyond in the Southland. The growth of self-governing cities in Southern Californian suburbia represented a form of peripheral urbanization, which includes the concentration of jobs, factories, offices, and commercial areas in addition to residential expansion. It also structured the region's landscape of racial and class segregation.[22] Lately, Los Angeles has been one of the chief urban areas in which the fusion of neoliberalization and urbanization has created a peculiar form of privatized vulgarity that has characterized the early years of twenty-first-century American sub/urbanization.[23]

To the LA School, the geographic and political center of Los Angeles, commonly referred to as Downtown LA, became a place of two important insights. For one, while many urbanists observed the "emptying" of classical inner cities after the 1960s, the downtown of Los Angeles became a veritable magnet for new populations and activities. Site of the emergence of new post-Fordist economic districts in garments, food, jewelry, and other industries and commercial activities, the inner city of Los Angeles turned out to be one of the signature geographies of a new age after mass production and Fordism (on par with the Third Italy, the Lombard region, or Baden-Württemberg). While the spatial imaginary described above may include a sense of up and down, high and low, rich and poor, it is really the metaphors of mixity, flow, and unboundedness across an open rhizomatic landscape that allows untraded interdependencies to be exchanged freely, but in a micro-organized fashion to gel into new flexibilized economies. Such a sociospatial image of the global city region has become pervasively used and programmatically espoused in regional politics discourse. The regionally networked, often crafts-based, globally financed, and "ethnic" businesses at the basis of the global city economy in LA have become well-known tropes of global city economies everywhere. This economic change also led to a demographic shift as the populations and many workers of the inner city factories tended to be Latino or Asian rather than white or African American. But second, Downtown LA as a once central space was reconceptualized by the LA School figuratively and literally as a space dependent on the periphery. This was perhaps nowhere as succinctly put as in Michael Dear's famous quip: "Angelistas counter that the concept of an urban core organizing its hinterland is obsolete, since the urban peripheries now organize what remains of the center."[24]

Last, and based to the two preceding shifts, the LA School notes the emergence of new political possibilities. This includes, certainly, the recognition of a strong and increasingly vocal immigrant workforce but also includes the remaking of the institutional political geography in which, as Dear and Dahmann have noted, beyond the challenges of horizontality, "the altered geographies of postmodern urbanism are redefining the meaning and practice of urban politics," potentially leading to "the subordination of the local state to plutocratic privatism."[25] Yet the diffusion of power also enables certain autonomies, creative local economies, and ecological politics.[26] In addition, the suburbanized region has become the place of innovative labor and community politics.[27]

The Real Los Angeles

THE NATURE OF URBANIZATION IN LOS ANGELES. Los Angeles was born a suburban city notwithstanding the existence of a central place in its original pueblo.[28] That was the case at least since its first significant property boom in the 1880s, as the city sprawled and leapfrogged across the coastal basin and up the hills. In the 1920s, the city already defied common definitions of the urban boundary. Richard Neutra recalled that fact when, as the International Congress of Modern Architecture met in Brussels in 1930, all cities were mapped at the same scale. For Los Angeles "the chosen scale produced a monstrously oversized chart. . . . A map produced according to this established set of rules became a huge and strange jungle of misunderstandings, not possible of interpretation even by connoisseurs and experts."[29] Yet unlike the pastoral images from other parts of the United States of subdivisions moving concentrically or in checkerboard patterns across vacant and verdant agrarian land, Los Angeles faced a more inimical nature of shifting sands, crumbling mountains, and fault lines. Hedged in between a vast ocean and forbiddingly uninhabitable (so it seemed) mountains, the Southland presented a volatile landscape of floods, droughts, and earthquakes. Initially, Los Angeles did not look like it might be an easy place to live but rather foreshadowed those later forms of urban settlement we now find in cities of the Global South—where squatters squeeze wedges of land out of surroundings that are less than welcoming.

WATER WAS CENTRAL. And the government is central to providing and draining it. The city started on the river. Around it, the Spanish colonial irrigation system contributed a modicum of order to the political economy of land in Los Angeles early on. The Army Corps of Engineers concreted the river in the middle of the twentieth century. Built and refined over decades, this system has insured the region against the worst forms of flood-related risks. In combination with insurance issued through the Federal Emergency Management Agency (FEMA) for suburban home owners, the concreted spine of the river was the best foundation for the full development of the basin where suburban expansion had massed people for almost a century. While floodwaters were designed to be rushed out to sea in the most efficient way, fresh water was shipped over great distances through an elaborate and monumental infrastructure that piped the expensive good from Central California's Owens Valley through the suburban (and at that time still rural) San Fernando Valley, into the Los Angeles basin. In recent decades, the Los Angeles River has become a discursive and metabolic band along which societal relationships with nature keep being rearranged.[30] The San Fernando Valley and its particular form of settlement at the rural frontier also serves as a reminder that suburbanization continues to grow as an expression of a semirural urbanization that retains whiteness as identity in Southern California.[31] Outside of the settled region, in the peripheral suburbs, the colonization of nature persists to date as exurban developments continue to push into the desert frontier. The attempts to regulate air pollution on a super-regional basis speak to the ongoing renegotiation of urban metabolisms across the suburbanizing region.

CAPITALISM RULES! During the twentieth century, Los Angeles took shape through an amalgamation of the martial metropolis, the Keynesian conurbation, the post-Fordist region, and the global city: a dynamic mix of spatial fixes, economic restructurings, and demographic shifts. It has been the site of rampant and constant renewal and never a static and unchanging environment.[32] Both the site of fine-grain immigrant-built suburbanization and home to some of the largest builders in the nation, Southern California pioneered large builders, huge subdivisions, high automobilization rates, the scale of regional industrialization, and the embrace of the freeway as the ordering infrastructure of the landscape.[33] Today, Los Angeles, while it continues to be enigmatic, equally confirms the major trends of North American and perhaps global sub/urbanization. One recurrent theme around LA's role in redefining what cities are in the twenty-first century has been its polycentricity and overlapping job-housing mismatches.[34]

The city's fragmentation itself has been subject to much study. Already at the turn of the twentieth century, the typical fragmented landscape of suburban Los Angeles could be observed.[35] A class- and race-stratified privatization of space at the basis of the social ecology of suburbanization coincided with the rise of big industry (from oil to consumer durables) and the interventionist force of the Keynesian welfare state.[36] While residential housing tract subdivisions have been the most visible form of segregated land use, Los Angeles has also been a poster child for the development of a particular kind of suburbanization that saw industrial development as the driver of massive sprawl. Capital accumulation through employment lands has been a major driver in Los Angeles: from the early twentieth-century oil fields through the Cold War–fueled expansion of the military-industrial complex to the technopolitan hub formations of the high tech age.[37] "Los Angeles lacks a super-dense core like Manhattan. But it also lacks a very low-density suburban periphery," leading to the description of its suburbanization as "dense sprawl."[38]

The increasingly negative vision of Los Angeles as a significant, if problem-atic model of sub/urban form and structure was held most prominently in the 1960s, when the smog that had lingered over the Southland since the 1940s became unbearable (but first measures were taken to deal with it), when the nation and the world learned about a riotous suburb called Watts, and when Charles Manson's gang murdered Sharon Tate and others in the Hollywood Hills and Los Feliz. This was also the time when Italian director Michelangelo Antonioni made the film *Zabriskie Point* (1970), which introduced the limitless urban region through the depiction of "a vicious circle in which the escape from Los Angeles will always lead us back to the city."[39]

Los Angeles Today

More recently, it was in the Southern California suburbs where many of the region's foreclosures took place during the 2008 crisis. Even the often cited and incited desert frontier has now become postsuburban. In the empty ruins of the Great Recession, in places as far out as Rialto, the push has come to a halt and the inner reworkings of the suburbs have begun.[40] Not surprisingly, it is in the rapidly changing Los Angeles suburbs that social service needs have become particularly high.[41] Los Angeles has been showing features of peripheral pov-erty and diversity for a while. Before the 1970s, "segregation of minorities had been built into the structure of the city."[42] In the 1990s already, almost one-third of all new immigrants coming to the region settled directly in the suburbs,[43] and the area produced North America's first "ethnoburbs" where (typically non-European) immigrants live in a new type of middle-class suburb that is tied into both local ethnic economies and cultures and into world-market-based networks.[44] In more recent decades, the urban region has become a classical "arrival city."[45]

At the same time, Downtown LA has been the site of an aggressive gentri-fication process often celebrated in the media. One observer even wrote that "downtown Los Angeles has, on the whole, made the most impressive recov-ery of any American central city in the 21st century."[46] The "inversion" that was thrown into stark relief by the crisis in Ferguson, Missouri, has been a defining fact of the Southern California landscape for decades,[47] particularly as the mechanism of "privatizing with class" became the organizing principle of sociospatial and governmental segregation in Los Angeles County after the introduction in 1954 of the Lakewood Plan, which allowed the newly incorpo-rated municipality by that name to contract municipal service delivery from Los Angeles County and laid the roots for subsequent waves of incorporated autonomy of suburbs with weak tax bases.[48]

Globalization usually conjures up images of placelessness, flows, disjuncture, and dissolution. Defying these notions of globalization, Los Angeles has become, since the 1980s, a place where "the world becomes a city" and a visible symbol of the reemergent importance of local-to-global connectivity. Nowhere was this claim better expressed than in Edward Soja's famous passage that extolled the diversity of the LA region as emblematic of a new form of universal urbanism: "One can find in Los Angeles not only the high technology industrial complexes of the Silicon Valley and the erratic sunbelt economy of Houston, but also the far-reaching industrial decline and bankrupt urban neighborhoods of rust-belted Detroit or Cleveland. There is a Boston in Los Angeles, a Lower Manhattan and a South Bronx, a Sao Paulo and a Singapore."[49] Los Angeles remains of immense interest to urban studies today. Driven by and itself co-producing dynamic processes of globalization, neoliberalization, immigration, and regionalization, the Southern California metropolis remains today a city of multiple contradictions.

When speaking of Los Angeles, we refer to a city of four million in a county of ten million and an urban region of eighteen million in Southern California. Given its often inward-looking and conservative traditions, based on the rooted economies of land, oil, and agriculture, Los Angeles is an unlikely symbol of the global age. Although its spatial form and eccentric culture are often cited as evidence for the city's unique character in recent decades, Los Angeles rather typified a sequence of different urban models. In the early part of the twentieth century, the city was a Midwestern outpost, white, nonindustrial, and small-townish despite its Mexican heritage and gigantic size; after World War II, it was in many ways the oil-rich poster child of the consumerist American way of life. During that time, a wide swath of industrial factories—autos, aerospace, consumer durables—started to be rolled out along the region's freeways. Industrial and residential suburbs dotted a continuously urbanizing landscape spreading evenly between the mountains and deserts of the Inland Empire to the surf of the Pacific Ocean, from the vast suburbs of the San Fernando Valley to the citrus groves turned high-tech corridor in Orange County. While LA became known for its freewheeling lifestyle and easygoing, capitalist joie de vivre, it was perhaps more of a product of the federal government than was any other American city.[50] The planned and richly financed expansion of the war economy that made its home in LA complemented the ideology of unrestrained freedom and personal achievement. It was the ultimate Fordist-industrial metropolis. Eventually, Los Angeles—with its a colorful palette of urban contradictions—was a prime model for the global city network that scholars saw emerge in the 1980s.[51]

Whereas to many Los Angeles is a powerful symbol of capitalist accomplishment, a land of opportunity under sunny skies, it has also served as the prototype of a dystopian strand of urbanism that sees the place as the paradigmatic city of disaster and mayhem, and as a site of struggle over environmental and social justice.[52] The spread of either image throughout the global channels of hype, the "sunshine and the noir" to paraphrase Mike Davis, is invariably tied into the power grids of LA's most trademark industry that put LA on the mental and visual map of the globe. In Hollywood, Los Angeles has had its own strong base for globalized self-production. The other process through which LA propels itself to global significance is through the shameless boosterism of its elites. From the early settlers to the global place entrepreneurs of today, the city has always been able to create the local political conditions from which the city's insertion into the streams of global capitalism could be organized through hype and infrastructures. From the railway barons and newspaper tycoons of the late nineteenth century to the Committee of 25 and the growth machine of Mayor Tom Bradley, who brought the Olympics to LA, and the ongoing placemaking of today, LA elites have been relentless. But not all politics in LA is elite. In fact, the city has given the world some of the most pervasive images of popular politics and violent uprising, peaceful protest, and mass democracy: Watts 1965, the Chicano Moratorium of 1970, Rodney King and the LA uprising of 1992, the Bus Riders Union's Consent Degree, and the new social unionism of its immigrant labor organizations. It is from these contestations that LA has rejuvenated itself periodically to remain a leading urban center and to some "the capital of the Pacific Rim."

Los Angeles: Mega-urbanization in the Global North

Born as a colonial outpost in the Spanish and later American empires, the city had a high proportion of white, native-born Americans until World War II. The war years brought a new and more diverse population to the Southland. By the 1980s, finally, the Southern California metropolis had become the ultimate symbol of a globalized immigrant region, which, for a while, had the highest percentage of non-native-born residents in the United States.

Los Angeles also typifies many of the conundrums currently faced in urban research. It starts with the problem of scope and definition. Is it a city, a region, a city-region? Is the region of eighteen million a global city or megacity? Is it urban or suburban? As early as the 1920s, the city had grown out of scale compared to all other cities in the world. Sprawling across Southern California, with an annexed port in San Pedro to the south and a hydrocephalic San Fernando Valley to the north, the City of Los Angeles had exploded the original pueblo, fanning out along railway lines at first, and later along the emerging systems of roads and freeways into residential neighborhoods that spread from the sea to the mountains. Fed by imported water through the Owens Valley aqueduct, the city was able to sustain itself beyond its local desert metabolisms; the port and the railway kept it provisioned when there was no longer any regional wealth to be exploited once the ranchos and orange groves had receded into subdivisions. The land rush of the 1880s, which had created real estate fiefdoms out of agricultural land, laid a pattern of developer-driven, railroad-supported, media-hyped development that allowed for the highest degree of fragmentation possible. Each developable patch of land seemed to incorporate into yet another city. The founding of cities merely for functional purposes—industry, commerce, and the "black gold suburbs" in the South Bay oil fields—established a pattern of segregated land use and ultimately population that was cast in stone with the Lakewood Plan of 1954. This allowed unincorporated lands that could not provide their own services to become municipalities and have their public duties picked up by the County of Los Angeles. An incorporation boom ensued that made for a process of "privatizing with class" whereby taxpayers could theoretically live with only those neighbors that fit their social expectation and income. But it also made initially invisible those communities, like the African Americans of Watts before the 1965 riots, the Chicanos of East Los Angeles, and the gays of West Hollywood, that lived in pockets of the municipal puzzle.

Today, Los Angeles is one of the densest urban areas in North America, perpetually growing economically and demographically although not at the clipped speed of previous decades, remaining international and culturally diverse in population, although today the region's foreign-born population takes up a smaller percentage of the total than has been the case in the recent past. The region has also become a site of significant transit development based on an ultimately extensive rail network and environmental innovation, as the once smoggy air is cleaned up and its namesake river begins to be a green spine rather than a concreted flood control channel. Los Angeles remains the place where the world's dreams are produced and televised in motion pictures while it continues to provide opportunity for millions of its inhabitants as well as newcomers to help define the notion of living the urban revolution.

The suburban landscape of Los Angeles was envisioned and has been analyzed as an expression of individualism, class difference, and segregation. In its postsuburban phase, it has become something quite different: the terrain for social change. As Downtown makes its transition from redeveloped corporate citadel surrounded by skid row poverty and sweatshop industrial district to a gentrified urban playground, the diverse suburban expanses of the region gain significance as sites of everyday life and innovative civic politics.

Don Parson's Los Angeles

Let us briefly consider how things have changed in the long decade since Parson first presented his research in *Making a Better World: Public Housing, the Red Scare, and the Direction of Modern Los Angeles.*

On the bright side, we have seen America's first African American president in the White House; an encompassing Occupy movement shook the foundations of the country's creed of meritocratic justice—the myth that virtuous work will lead to individual success (now we know, of course, that the 1 percent are rarely virtuous and wealth has little to do with work regardless of how much and how good); Black Lives Matter turned the horrible bloodletting on the streets of African American communities at the hands of the police into a powerful slogan for fundamental human rights; and an outspokenly socialist presidential campaign by Vermont senator Bernie Sanders vied with a declared feminist for the candidacy of the Democratic Party for the U.S. presidential election and succeeded in changing the political discourse and dynamics in the spring and summer of 2016.

On the dark side, though, we have seen the election and taking of power of a white supremacist billionaire president who entered his tenure with a slew of reactionary executive orders; the spreading of right-wing populist movements, even openly fascist ones; the rise of racist violence across the nation and continued leniency for police who brutalize citizens of color; and the appointment of white male representatives of the 1 percent and reactionary publicists to cabinet and other government posts.

As Ananya Roy reminds us in a powerful commentary in which she channels the intellectual authority of W. E. B. Du Bois, we live in an era of reactionary reconstruction.[53] In many ways, the time we live through now is not unlike the reconstruction of capitalist power during the early years of the Cold War after the impressive popular front openings that were created at the tail end of the Depression before World War II, both subject to Don Parson's analysis in this book's chapters. Like in the period from the late 1930s to the 1950s, we are now facing a backlash against institutions and movements of collective power. Housing stood out then and stands out now in the development of political alternatives. And the relationships of race and class are once again rearticulated in Los Angeles and elsewhere as the Trump administration controls the White House. And it is not accidental at all that Trump, as a hotel mogul and developer and son of a racist slumlord, is the symbolic representative of the real-estate-driven economy of the times; he finds his local counterpart and substantial donor in Geoff Palmer, whom one article in 2016 described as "Trump's Los Angeles Money Man." Palmer, like Trump a belligerent and litigious space entrepreneur with splashy, garish tastes and exclusionary reflexes, has put his stamp on the distant suburbs and downtown alike with his preference for a demonstrative "fauxtalian" style.[54]

Things have changed dramatically since those years in the mid-twentieth century. Around the world, housing is the subject of a pitched battle over living space as dignified use value versus chips in a casino economy that sees built space as merely exchange value.[55] In fact, as Henry Grabar has observed, "Los

Angeles is not the only city with a regulation-induced housing shortage. As the . . . *Economist* attests, the problem is global: From Mumbai to the Bay Area, the magazine writes, 'the value of housing is an ever-greater store of wealth.' According to a recent argument by Matthew Rognlie, a doctoral student at Harvard, the increasing global returns to capital calculated by the French economist Thomas Piketty in his best-selling book *Capital in the Twenty-First Century* can be explained almost entirely by housing wealth."[56] In Los Angeles, while another real estate boom vies for attention with a renewed crisis of housing and homelessness, a debate on density and housing supply has ensued in which arguments of spatial justice have an important place.[57] There are, of course, some principles that don't change. As Madden and Marcuse have observed, "Housing is not produced and distributed for the purposes of dwelling for all; it is produced and distributed as a commodity to enrich the few. Housing crisis is not a result of the system breaking down but of the system working as intended."[58] But today, housing is produced in a context of hypercommodification, and "housing and urbanization are becoming more central to the global economy."[59] Deregulation, financialization, globalization, gentrification, and luxury housing are now the rules of a game that is decided more and more by the ones who own, monopolize, build, and sell housing and not by those who use housing for shelter.

Those are the current lineaments of a housing crisis that seems universal in nature, especially after the experience of the 2008 financial crisis. This book, though, reminds us of the fact that each such crisis has its distinctive roots in the class, color, and gender lines of individual places. Los Angeles, a city of majority tenants, an expanse of dense sprawl, a city of diversity and immigration, has its own troubled lines along which the permanent crisis of housing has evolved.

Los Angeles: An Evolving Urban Laboratory

The Los Angeles of the mid-twentieth century cemented the suburban feel of the urban form that most associate with the city and its region. Moving further toward a single-family-home-dominated landscape of privatism was the outcome of the industrial-style suburbanization fabricated by large builders particularly after the war. Lakewood became the remarkable symbol of this style of carpeting the Southland with hundreds of thousands of "little boxes." Yet, to be sure, as Greg Morrow reminds us, only one-third of Angelenos actually currently live in owner-occupied single-family houses, a form of living whose reputation as a cultural icon outweighs its reality even in what is considered one of the most suburban cities in the United States.[60]

While the large infrastructure projects—the LA River, the freeways, the ports, sports stadia, and so much more—were never far away, the appearance of the bourgeois utopia of the subdivisions crowded out all other representations of Los Angeles at the time. The landscape that was built during those decades also concreted the power lines of race, class, and gender in the Southland on a register of white privilege and white supremacy. As Laura Pulido has noted so perceptively when talking about the uneven distribution of environmental pollution in the Los Angeles area, "In the case of Los Angeles, industrialization, decentralization, and residential segregation are keys to this puzzle. Because industrial land use is highly correlated with pollution concentrations and people of color, the crucial question becomes, how did whites distance themselves from both industrial pollution and nonwhites?"[61] The horizontal suburbanity of Los Angeles has continuously reproduced and hidden tremendous socioeconomic and environmental inequities. A suburb in Los Angeles can be a privileged gated community or a polluted industrial district.[62]

In his chapters in this collection, Parson contributes to the detailed understanding of what was lost and what was gained in the process during those critical decades when today's Los Angeles took shape. The other voices assembled here complete and color in the blueprint Parson provides.

Today, a different Los Angeles emerges, but very similar questions continue to be asked. Erstwhile *Los Angeles Times* architecture critic Christopher Hawthorne observes, pondering the state of the city and the nation as Trump is inaugurated, "Los Angeles is in the midst of its biggest construction boom in decades. County voters just passed (with 71% approval) a sales-tax hike that will raise a staggering $100-billion war chest for the Metropolitan Transportation Authority. It's no exaggeration to say that a new Los Angeles—taller and less suburban, with a dramatically expanded transit network—is taking shape."[63] Once again Los Angeles—not the governments and elites who direct its fate but its people and activist publics—has become a focus of progressive options in a general context of retrograde politics in a nation that shuts down against all things foreign and different. Filled with hope, Hawthorne speculates, "Los Angeles is rediscovering its sense of civic ambition even as Trump seems ready to turn the country inward and exploit, if not provoke, tensions with foreign powers. L.A. is a city on the verge in a nation that may begin to feel consistently on the brink."[64] Among other things, a region often vilified as a bastion of white supremacy showed leadership in a growing municipal sanctuary movement that will defend the rights of immigrants and refugees against sanctions by the federal government under the Trump administration.[65] The progressive movement and civic culture in Los Angeles have been in the making for a generation, perhaps since the anti-plant-closing struggles of the 1970s that ultimately spawned organizations such as the Labor/Community Strategy Center and the Bus Riders Union, but at least since the uprising of 1992, after which a persistent shaping of an organizational infrastructure and an everyday politics took place that propelled labor, social justice, transit justice, and environmental organizations to the fore while neoliberalization and entrepreneurialism became the determining factors in Los Angeles' development.[66]

Los Angeles may be the most misunderstood city in North America. What, we might ask, can possibly come from La La Land, the perennial city of fake identity, make-believe, and celluloid dreams. Let us once again borrow from the literary genius of Paul Beatty to portray Los Angeles in these terms:

> There are more cars in Los Angeles County than in any other city in the world. But what no one ever talks about is that half those cars sit on cinder blocks in dirt patches passing for front yards from Lancaster to Long Beach. These not-so-mobile automobiles, along with the Hollywood sign, the Watts Towers, and Aaron Spelling's 56,500-square-foot estate, are the closest L.A. gets to approximating the ancient marvels of engineering like the Parthenon, Angkor Wat, the great pyramids, and the ancient shrines of Timbuktu. Those two- and four-door rusted pieces of antiquity stand impervious to the winds and acid rains of time, and like Stonehenge, we have no idea what purpose these steel monuments serve. Are they testaments to the bichin' and firme hot rods and lowriders that grace the covers of custom-car magazines? Maybe the hood ornaments and tail fins are aligned with the stars and the winter solstice. Maybe they're mausoleums, the resting places of backseat lovers and drivers. All I know is that each of these metallic carcasses means one less car on the road and one more rider on the bus of shame. Shame because L.A. is about space, and here one's self-worth comes from how one chooses to navigate that space. Walking is akin to begging in the streets. Taxicabs are for foreigners and prostitutes. Bicycles, skateboards, and Rollerblades are for health nuts and kids, people with nowhere to go. And all cars, from the luxury import to the classified-ad jalopy, are status symbols, because no matter how shoddy the upholstery, how bouncy the ride, how fucked-up the paint job, the car, any car, is better than riding the bus.[67]

Beatty's satire makes the private and the public, the car and the bus, the house and the apartment, stark choices of worth and insignificance.

There is no concluding verdict on what the public possibilities might have been in a private city. What the public may have been, and how it was represented in an Anglo city may have been part of the problem. As Mike H. F. Wood has recently written specifically about the story of Chavez Ravine, "Powerful bureaucratic forces and wealthy special interest groups inevitably enacted their modernized urban visions for the future of Los Angeles, at the expense of working class minorities and without regard for what the consequences would entail."[68] More work needs to be done as we continuously change our historical narratives under pressure from the often-sidelined social forces in a city that has been whitewashed all too many times. The book before you assembles some truly important voices to add to the understanding of that history. Prime among them is the voice of Don Parson himself. We are now turning to his historical studies of crucial events in the history of Los Angeles.

NOTES

This opening chapter is a composite text of fragments written by Roger Keil over two decades. They are an attempt at framing this current book in the reflection of research that has positioned Los Angeles in the maelstrom of some of the most influential urban developments and theories of the past century.

1. Paul Beatty, *The Sellout* (New York: Picador, 2015), 78.

2. Margaret Kohn, *The Death and Life of the Urban Commonwealth* (Oxford: Oxford University Press, 2016).

3. Norman M. Klein, *The History of Forgetting: Los Angeles and the Erasure of Memory* (London: Verso, 1997).

4. Michael N. Willard, "Nuestra Los Angeles," *American Quarterly* 56, no. 3 (September 2004): 807–43.

5. Jane Jacobs, *The Death and Life of Great American Cities* (New York: Modern Library, 1993).

6. Edward W. Soja, *Seeking Spatial Justice* (Minneapolis: University of Minnesota Press, 2010), 44.

7. Ibid., 45.

8. Ibid., 46.

9. Edward W. Soja, *Thirdspace: Journeys to Los Angeles and Other Real-and-Imagined Places* (Oxford: Blackwell, 1996).

10. Josh Lepawsky, Grace Akese, Mostaem Billah, Creighton Conolly, and Chris McNabb, "Composing Urban Orders from Rubbish Electronics: Cityness and the Site Multiple," *International Journal of Urban and Regional Research* 39 (2015): 189–99, DOI:10.1111/1468-2427.12142.

11. Ananya Roy, "The 21st-Century Metropolis: New Geographies of Theory," *Regional Studies* 43, no. 6 (2009): 819–30.

12. Anton Wagner, *Los Angeles: Werden, Leben und Gestalt der Zweimillionenstadt in Südkalifornien* (Leipzig: Bibliographisches Institut, 1935).

13. Ibid., 6, translation by RK.

14. Roger Keil, *Los Angeles: Globalization, Urbanization and Social Struggles* (Chichester: Wiley, 1998).

15. Reyner Banham, *Los Angeles: The Architecture of Four Ecologies* (Harmondsworth: Pelican, 1971).

16. Mike Davis, *City of Quartz: Excavating the Future in Los Angeles* (London: Verso, 1990).

17. Michael Dear and Nicholas Dahmann, "Urban Politics and the Los Angeles School of Urbanism," in *The City Revisited: Urban Theory from Chicago, Los Angeles, New York*, ed. Dennis Judd and Dick Simpson (Minneapolis: University of Minnesota Press, 2011), 74.

18. For a representative collection of papers documenting L.A. School claims and backlash, see, for example, Michael P. Conzen and Richard P. Greene, "Introduction: All the World Is Not Los Angeles, Nor Chicago: Paradigms, Schools, Archetypes, and the

Urban Process," 97–100; Michael Dear, Andrew Burridge, Peter Marolt, Jacob Peters, and Mona Seymour, "Critical Responses to the Los Angeles School of Urbanism," 101–12; Saskia Sassen, "Re-assembling the Urban," 113–26; and Richard P. Greene, "Urban Peripheries as Organizers of What Remains of the Center: Examining the Evidence from Los Angeles and Chicago," 138–53; all in *Urban Geography* 29, no. 2 (2008).

19. Allen J. Scott and Edward W. Soja, eds., *The City: Los Angeles and Urban Theory at the End of the Twentieth Century* (Berkeley: University of California Press, 1996).

20. Davis, *City of Quartz.*

21. Renaud Le Goix, *Sur le front de la métropole: Unegéographiesuburbaine de Los Angeles* (Paris: Publications de la Sorbonne, 2016).

22. Charles Hoch, "Municipal Contracting in California: Privatizing with Class," *UAQ* 20 (1985): 303–23; Edward W. Soja, "Los Angeles, 1965–1992," in Scott and Soja, *The City,* 426–62.

23. Jamie Peck, "Chicago-School Suburbanism," in *Suburban Governance: A Global View,* ed. Pierre Hamel and Roger Keil (Toronto: University of Toronto Press, 2015); Paul L. Knox, *Metroburbia, USA* (New Brunswick, N.J.: Rutgers University Press, 2008).

24. Michael Dear, "Comparative Urbanism," *Urban Geography* 26 (2005): 248.

25. Dear and Dahmann, "Urban Politics."

26. Ibid., 75.

27. Roger Keil and Derek Brunelle, "Government, Politics, and Suburbanization in Los Angeles," in *The Life of North American Suburbs,* ed. Jan Nijman (Toronto: University of Toronto Press, forthcoming); Genevieve Carpio, Clara Irazabal, and Laura Pulido, "Right to the Suburb? Rethinking Lefebvre and Immigrant Activism," *Journal of Urban Affairs* 33, no. 2 (2011): 185–208; Eric Mann, *Taking on General Motors: A Case Study of the UAW Campaign to Keep GM Van Nuys Open* (Los Angeles: Center for Labor Research and Education, Institute of Industrial Relations, UCLA, 1987).

28. Don Parson, "The Search for a Center: the Recomposition of Race, Class and Space in Los Angeles," *International Journal of Urban and Regional Research,* 17, no. 2 (June 1993): 232–40, https://doi.org/10.1111/j.1468-2427.1993.tb00478.x.

29. Richard J. Neutra, "Homes and Housing," in *Los Angeles: Preface to a Master Plan,* ed. George W. Robbins and L. Deming Tilton (Los Angeles: Pacific Southwest Academy, 1941), 189–201.

30. Gene Desfor and Roger Keil, *Nature and the City: Making Urban Environmental Policy in Toronto and Los Angeles* (Tucson: University of Arizona Press, 2004).

31. Laura R. Barraclough, *Making the San Fernando Valley: Rural Landscapes, Urban Development, and White Privilege* (Athens: University of Georgia Press, 2011).

32. Keil, *Los Angeles,* 54–75.

33. Greg Hise, *Magnetic Los Angeles* (Baltimore: Johns Hopkins University Press, 1997).

34. Ali Modarres, "Polycentricity, Commuting Pattern, Urban Form," *International Journal of Urban and Regional Research* 35, no. 6 (2010): 1193–1211.

35. Robert Fogelson, *The Fragmented Metropolis* (1967; Cambridge, Mass.: Harvard University Press, 1993).

36. Laura Pulido, "Rethinking Environmental Racism: White Privilege and Urban Development in Southern California," *Annals of the Association of American Geographers* 90, no. 1 (2000): 12–40.

37. Robert Fishman, "Foreword," in Fogelson, *Fragmented Metropolis*, xv–xvii; Robert Fishman, *Bourgeois Utopias: The Rise and Fall of Suburbia* (New York: Basic Books, 1987); Keil, *Los Angeles*; Don Parson, *Making a Better World: Public Housing, the Red Scare, and the Direction of Modern Los Angeles* (Minneapolis: University of Minnesota Press, 2005).

38. Eric Eidlin, "What Density Doesn't Tell Us about Sprawl," *Access*, Fall 2010, www.accessmagazine.org/articles/fall-2010/density-doesnt-tell-us-sprawl/.

39. Keil, *Los Angeles*, 40.

40. Reinhold Martin, Leah Meisterlin, and Anna Kenoff, "The Buell Hypothesis: Rehousing the American Dream" (New York: Columbia University, Graduate School of Architecture, Planning and Preservation, the Temple Hoyne Buell Center for the Study of American Architecture, 2011).

41. Scott Allard and Benjamin Roth, "Strained Suburbs: The Social Service Challenges of Rising Suburban Poverty" (Washington, D.C.: Brookings Institution, 2008), www.brookings.edu/research/reports/2010/10/07-suburban-poverty-allard-roth.

42. Fishman, "Foreword," xviii.

43. Enrico A. Marcelli, "From the Barrio to the 'Burbs: Immigration and the Dynamics of Suburbanization," in *Up Against the Sprawl: Public Policy and the Making of Southern California*, ed. Jennifer Wolch, Manuel Pastor Jr., and Peter Dreier (Minneapolis: University of Minnesota Press, 2004), 142.

44. Wei Li, "Anatomy of a New Ethnic Settlement: The Chinese Ethnoburb in Los Angeles," *Urban Studies* 35, no. 3 (1998): 479–501.

45. Doug Saunders, *Arrival City: The Final Migration and Our Next World* (Toronto: Knopf, 2010).

46. Colin Marshall, "The Gentrification of Skid Row—A Story That Will Decide the Future of Los Angeles," *Guardian Cities*, March 5, 2015, www.theguardian.com/cities/2015/mar/05/gentrification-skid-row-los-angeles-homeless?CMP=share_btn_tw.

47. Elizabeth Kneebone, "Ferguson, Mo. Emblematic of Growing Suburban Poverty," *The Avenue*, August 15, 2014, www.brookings.edu/blogs/the-avenue/posts/2014/08/15-ferguson-suburban-poverty.

48. Keil, *Los Angeles*, 174.

49. Edward W. Soja, *Postmodern Geographies: The Reassertion of Space in Critical Social Theory* (London: Verso, 1989), 193.

50. Wolch, Pastor, and Dreier, *Up Against the Sprawl*.

51. Keil, *Los Angeles*.

52. Mike Davis, *Ecologies of Fear* (London: Verso, 1998); Desfor and Keil, *Nature and the City*.

53. Ananya Roy, "Divesting from Whiteness: The University in the Age of Trumpism," *Society and Space*, November 28, 2016; http://societyandspace.org/2016/11/28/divesting-from-whiteness-the-university-in-the-age-of-trumpism/; W. E. B. Du Bois, *Black Reconstruction in America: An Essay toward a History of the Part Which Black Folk Played in the Attempt to Reconstruct Democracy in America, 1860–1880*, ed. L. H. Gates (1935; Oxford: Oxford University Press, 2007).

54. Matt Tinoco, "Trump's Los Angeles Money Man," *Politico*, August 4, 2016, http://www.politico.com/magazine/story/2016/08/geoffrey-palmer-trump-donor-los-angeles-214130.

55. David Madden and Peter Marcuse, *In Defense of Housing: The Politics of Crisis* (London: Verso, 2016); Robert Kaltbrunner, "Lebst du schon oder wohnst du noch?," *Frankfurter Rundschau*, January 30, 2017, www.fr-online.de/kultur/architektur-lebst-du -schon-oder-wohnst-du-noch—,1472786,35118970.html.

56. Henry Grabar, "The Incredible Shrinking Megacity: How Los Angeles Engineered a Housing Crisis," *Salon*, April 5, 2015, www.salon.com/2015/04/05/the_incredible _shrinking_megacity_how_los_angeles_enginereed_a_housing_crisis/.

57. Greg D. Morrow, "How to Make Los Angeles More Affordable and More Livable," *Los Angeles Times*, July 24, 2015, www.latimes.com/opinion/op-ed/la-oe-morrow-la-and -its-housing-density-problem-20150724-story.html.

58. Madden and Marcuse, *In Defense of Housing*, 10.

59. Ibid., 27.

60. Morrow, "How to Make Los Angeles."

61. Pulido, "Rethinking Environmental Racism," 14; see also Laura Pulido, "Geographies of Race and Ethnicity 1: White Supremacy vs White Privilege in Environmental Racism Research," *Progress in Human Geography* 39, no. 6 (2015): 809–17.

62. Christopher G. Boone and Ali Modarres, "Creating a Toxic Neighborhood in Los Angeles County: A Historical Examination of Environmental Inequity," *Urban Affairs Review* 35, no. 2 (November 1999): 163–87.

63. Christopher Hawthorne, "Building Type: Introducing a Weekly Column on Architecture," *Los Angeles Times*, January 13, 2017, www.latimes.com/entertainment/arts/la -ca-cm-building-type-hawthorne-1-2017-01-15-story.html.

64. Ibid.

65. Ruben Vives, "California 'Sanctuary Cities' Vow to Stand Firm Despite Trump Threats of Funding Cutoff," *Los Angeles Times*, January 25, 2017, www.latimes.com/local /lanow/la-me-california-sanctuary-cities-20170125-story.html?utm_source=dlvr.it& utm_medium=twitter.

66. Julie-Anne Boudreau, *Global Urban Politics* (Cambridge: Polity, 2017); Walter J. Nicholls, "Forging a 'New' Organizational Infrastructure for Los Angeles' Progressive Community," *International Journal of Urban and Regional Research* 27, no. 4 (December 2003): 881–96; Manuel Pastor Jr., "Common Ground at Ground Zero? The New Economy and the New Organizing in Los Angeles," *Antipode* 33, no. 2 (March 2001): 260–89; Laura Pulido, *Black, Brown, Yellow, and Left Radical Activism in Los Angeles* (Berkeley: University of California Press, 2006); Mark Purcell, "Politics in Global Cities: Los Angeles Charter Reform and the New Social Movements," *Environment and Planning A* 34 (2001): 23–42; Soja, *Seeking Spatial Justice*.

67. Beatty, *Sellout*, 116–17.

68. Mike H. F. Wood, "Red Scare Politics and the Post-War Racialized Vision of Chavez Ravine," *Toro Historical Review* 3 (2017), https://thetorohistoricalreview.org /2017/09/29/red-scare-politics-and-the-post-war-racialized-vision-of-chavez-revine/; see also William Deverell, *Whitewashed Adobe: The Rise of Los Angeles and the Remaking of Its Mexican Past* (Berkeley: University of California Press, 2004).

PART 1

Don Parson

FROM URBAN IDEALISM TO
REACTION—FIVE ESSAYS

Introduction

ROGER KEIL

In this first part of the book, we have assembled five unpublished chapters
by Los Angeles historian and urban intellectual Don Parson. Getting these
chapters into print has been a labor of love. From my own point of view,
they cap a long engagement with Don and with his work, which I would
like to briefly recall here. I first crossed paths with Don Parson in April 1986
when he and I were listening to speakers at a conference on green politics
at UCLA. Crossing paths is an apt expression as we actually didn't meet and
I didn't know who he was. It was a few months later, when I spent more
time in Los Angeles, that I heard of a mythical former surfer who was now
bound to a wheelchair. I knew immediately whom I had spotted way back
at the Greens conference. We crossed paths in the sense that he rolled
past me. We acknowledged each other but then went our separate ways.
Don had developed a reputation among the resident PhD students at UCLA,
where he received his degree under Ed Soja's supervision, by publishing
its chapters, ahead of assembling them in the dissertation, in prestigious
refereed journals. With recognition from such sources, what supervisory
committee would dare doubt their validity and rigor? The articles themselves became hugely influential for my own work on Los Angeles, and the
dissertation format struck me as brilliant! I still use his example occasion-
ally when I advise my own students today.

It must have been three years later, in the spring of 1989, that Mike
Davis called me up and said, "I'm going up to the Valley on Sunday to meet
this comrade of mine, Don Parson." I said, "Sure, when are you gonna pick
me up?" I had known Mike for a while and had heard the most incredible
and invaluable stories from him about LA's past and present. The drive
up Laurel Canyon and then along the Ventura Freeway to Thousand Oaks
must however have been particularly fertile ground for Mike's storytelling. As we were pushing up through the canyon's bamboo-lined hills of
brush and lush forests, we got to talk about urban wildlife. After listening
to Mike's anecdotes of boa constrictors appearing from toilet bowls and

cougars in backyards, I have never again been able to look at the verdant foliage of the Southland innocently.

Meeting Don that day in the presence of Mike was an important event in my life as a budding Angeleno. Here I was between arguably two of the most important chroniclers and cartographers of the city's working-class histories and geographies, listening in awe to their shared stories and perspectives. I wouldn't have been surprised to have seen the ghost of Carey McWilliams walk into the room. The conversation meandered between Don's and Mike's shared experiences in Europe and the state of Los Angeles. For me, it was the beginning of a friendship.

At the time, Don lived in the home where he had grown up, with his wonderful and welcoming mother caring for him. The interior design of the large suburban house, entirely dedicated to Don's physical needs as a mobility impaired person, reminded me of my childhood home in Germany, an American-style prefab bungalow, equally adept to be used by my sister who was in a wheelchair. Having spent my teenage years in an environment of multiple cyborgian machines meant to make my sister's life easier, I was nonplussed by the same assemblage of awe-inspiring metal contraptions that surrounded Don.

Like Steven Flusty, who recalls his own adventures in the vehicle in part 3 of this book, I was allowed to drive the Donmobile. Among other places, we visited bucolic hippie oasis Ojai down Ventura way on at least one occasion, one sunny spring Sunday afternoon.

This was the late 1980s. Los Angeles was buzzing with excitement musically with the post-punk culture around the iconic band X and its remnants, Concrete Blonde, and the emerging hip-hop culture in Compton. At Jesse Jackson presidential campaign events, the punk elite played country and western. I had just discovered alt and outlaw country and was thrilled to see Don's affection for Gram Parsons, one of the godfathers of that genre. Still today, whenever I hear Sin City, I think of Don's smile when he listened to the Flying Burrito Brothers. And of course Merle Haggard, another rebel soul who spoke to the core of Don's rooted romanticism. If memory doesn't fail me, I first spotted one of my all-time alt country faves, the 1994 compilation *Tulare Dust*, honoring the late Bakersfield growler, in Don's CD collection.

Sue Ruddick and I visited Don when possible. After we moved away from Los Angeles, we stayed in touch and made it a habit to look him up when we were in town. In the meantime, in the early 1990s, Don and I had embarked on a joint project. For a while we believed we could write a book on Los Angeles together and kept struggling through a few draft chapters (converting various Wordstar, Word, and WordPerfect files back and forth). I lived in LA once more for a few months in 1995 with Ute Lehrer when she worked on her PhD at UCLA. Gene Desfor and I were in Southern California for field research for our book *Nature and the City* (2004). During that time, Don and I made a final push for but then decided to abandon our joint project. It became apparent that our methodological and also political preoccupations did not match sufficiently to carry on. We divorced our project amicably and without impact on our friendship. Our separate ways led to two sole-authored books, his *Making a Better World* (2005) and my *Los Angeles* (1998).

Over time, the visits became rare and then stopped. I was fully occupied by life in my new home in Toronto, with work and family obligations in Canada and aging parents in Germany. Except for a while during my first sabbatical in 1999, Los Angeles and Don began to fade in my life. I was enthusiastic when, during the meetings of the American Association of Geographers in 2013, Sue Ruddick suggested we drive out to our old friend Don. So, once again, I found myself as a passenger in a car that made the trek up to Ventura County. Symbolically, perhaps, we started our journey in bowels of the Bonaventure Hotel and journeyed north on the 101 Freeway. Its concrete canyon, dotted with homeless encampments, was a far cry from the lush valley through which I drove up with Mike Davis thirty years earlier.

It was an important visit, the last time I saw Don. Almost immobilized and turning blind—between sips from his cappuccino that I fetched for him from a nearby corporate coffee shop—Don asked us to have a look at a few remaining unpublished manuscripts of his that he thought should see the light of day. He emailed them to us when we returned to Toronto, and after some reflection and with much help from our friends, we found the format of the current book would serve the purpose of this request best. So the chapters you see here in this part 1 of the volume are the edited versions of these diamonds in the rough that Don had meticulously researched and written over time.

These chapters are the core of the volume. They excavate a mid-twentieth-century history of the Southern California metropolis that is experiencing the convulsions of several forms of capitalist urbanization, layered, often simultaneously, in intertwined but segregated geographies that stretch the flood plains between the mountains and the sea, a desert with possibilities, where both rabid capitalist profiteering and the most utopian forms of solidarity sometimes stood side by side (or confronted each other). While, as the opening chapter argued, "when cities disappear, they don't come back," the following chapters by Don Parson develop the sense of a city under construction that lays a foundation on which today's Los Angeles still exists, although the specific places that once stood on top have long disappeared. The construction scaffolds are gone, the holes have been filled, the paint has faded, yet the tremendous contradictions between Los Angeles as a potential paradise for the working people and as a real capitalist hell hole in which no holds are barred remain. Los Angeles, like most cities in North America, never had the experience of a full-fledged municipal socialism—progressive governments in 1980s West Hollywood and Santa Monica notwithstanding (the latter often referred to by friend and foe as the "People's Republic of Santa Monica"—but its communities nonetheless were innovative and generative of social formations that still inform the way we live today. The communal and community-based forms of urban life that the city produced in the early part of the twentieth century were obliterated in the latter decades' thrust to build a Keynesian-Fordist region, to which the military-industrial complex and civil engineering projects (the LA River!) were central. It was a region acutely segregated by race and class. Parson dives deeply into the historical geography of this area that presents promise to the capitalist and the worker alike.

Parson approaches these contradictions chiefly through the lens of housing, its politics, its potential, and its people. In the chapter "A Mecca for the Unfortunate: Housing and Progressive Reform in Los Angeles," Parson dissects the geography of race and class in early twentieth-century Los Angeles and some of the contested decisions made during that time about housing form and tenure, housing reform, segregation, and so forth that would set the path along which many of Southern California's housing battles would be fought during the century.

In the following chapter, humorously titled "'Houses for the Rich Were Also for the Birds': Designing a Better World," Parson reminds the reader of the intricate relationships of planning, design, and modernism. Rather than the landscape of privatism for which LA became known in later decades, the early modernist design for the city, especially for its public housing projects, foretold a possible alternative future, one that Parson calls "Community Modernism."

This is followed by "'A New Deal Democrat Plus': The Progressive Judicial Career of Stanley Moffatt." This chapter about left-liberal justice of the peace Stanley Moffat is testament to the range of possibilities that existed for progressive individuals to make a difference in a system that became increasingly conservative during the middle of the twentieth century. Moffat's actions in defense of the poor and underprivileged are remembered here as a constitutive part of agency for social justice in LA.

Next comes a detailed examination of the changing political fortunes of the public housing movement after the 1952 Gwinn Amendment that banned groups deemed "subversive" from public housing in "Breeding Ground of Communism: The Gwinn Amendment in Los Angeles' Public

Housing." The amendment made an important part of working-class life and space subject to new forms of state harassment under the pretext of anticommunist campaigns. It resulted in a consolidation of anti-public-housing campaigns with other Red Scare politics at the time.

Last, in "Housing Is a Labor Process: Housing Policy and Housework," having dealt with race and class in previous chapters, Parson focuses on gender. Viewing sub/urbanization in post–World War II Los Angeles through the lens of struggles around housing policy and housework in an ascendant feminist movement, he brings the book on collective experiences in Los Angeles full circle.

Don Parson's insightful discussion of the personal and political fates of the architects of alternatives, the movements of change, provide some of the archaeology of the crisis of housing in Los Angeles today. Parson's essays have been amplified with carefully chosen photographs and restored and edited by Judy Branfman.

The significance of Parson's essays is twofold. In the first instance, they are a freestanding work of historical scholarship that will be appreciated by historians of mid-twentieth-century America in general and Los Angeles in particular. The detailed and careful reconstruction of specific events, personalities, and processes in the chapters Parson presents add up to a colorful diorama of a time that was markedly different from our own period. Still, the historical narratives also point beyond their specific era toward our current time. Parson identifies some of the main themes of social debate and societal conflict that echo still today: the relationships between the state and society and between the public and the private; the significance of social movements and political activism in creating policy alternatives; and the role of popular movements in challenging the status quo, even or particularly in times of adversity. This continuity will be further explored in part 3 of the book following Parson's own contributions and the biographical focus of part 2.

■ **Projects Constructed under the 1937 Housing Act**
1   William Mead
2   Aliso Village
3   Pico Gardens
4   Rose Hill Courts
5   Ramona Gardens
6   Estrada Courts
7   Pueblo Del Rio
8   Avalon Gardens
9   Hacienda Village
10 Rancho San Pedro

⬟ **Projects Constructed under the 1949 Housing Act**
1   San Fernando Gardens
2   Aliso Apartments
3   Elysian Park Heights (Never Built)
4   Rose Hill Annex (Never Built)
5   Mar Vista Gardens
6   Estrada Courts
7   Pueblo Del Rio
8   Jordan Downs
9   Nickerson Gardens
10 Imperial Courts
11 Rancho San Pedro

▨ Approximate boundaries of San Antonio Township, where Stanley Moffatt served as justice of the peace

● **Wartime and Veterans Housing Projects**
1   Basilone Homes
2   Pacific Park Annex
3   Pacific Park
4   Estrada Courts Annex #1
5   Rodger Young Village
6   Pacific Park Annex #2
7   Estrada Courts Annex #1

8   Corregidor Park Annex #2
9   Corregidor Park Annex #3
10 Corregidor Park and Corregidor Park Annex #1
11 Pueblo Del Rio Annex
12 Jordan Downs
13 Imperial Courts Annex #2
14 Imperial Courts Annex #3
15 Imperial Courts Annex #1
16 Lumina Park and Lumina Park Annex
17 Normont Terrace
18 Bataan Park
19 Keppler Grove
20 Dana Strand Annex
21 Dana Strand Village
22 Wilmington Hall #1
23 Wilmington Hall #2
24 Western Terrace
25 Portsmouth Homes and Annex
26 Channel Heights

▲ **Downtown Locations**
A   Little Tokyo
B   City Hall
C   The Plaza
D   Union Station

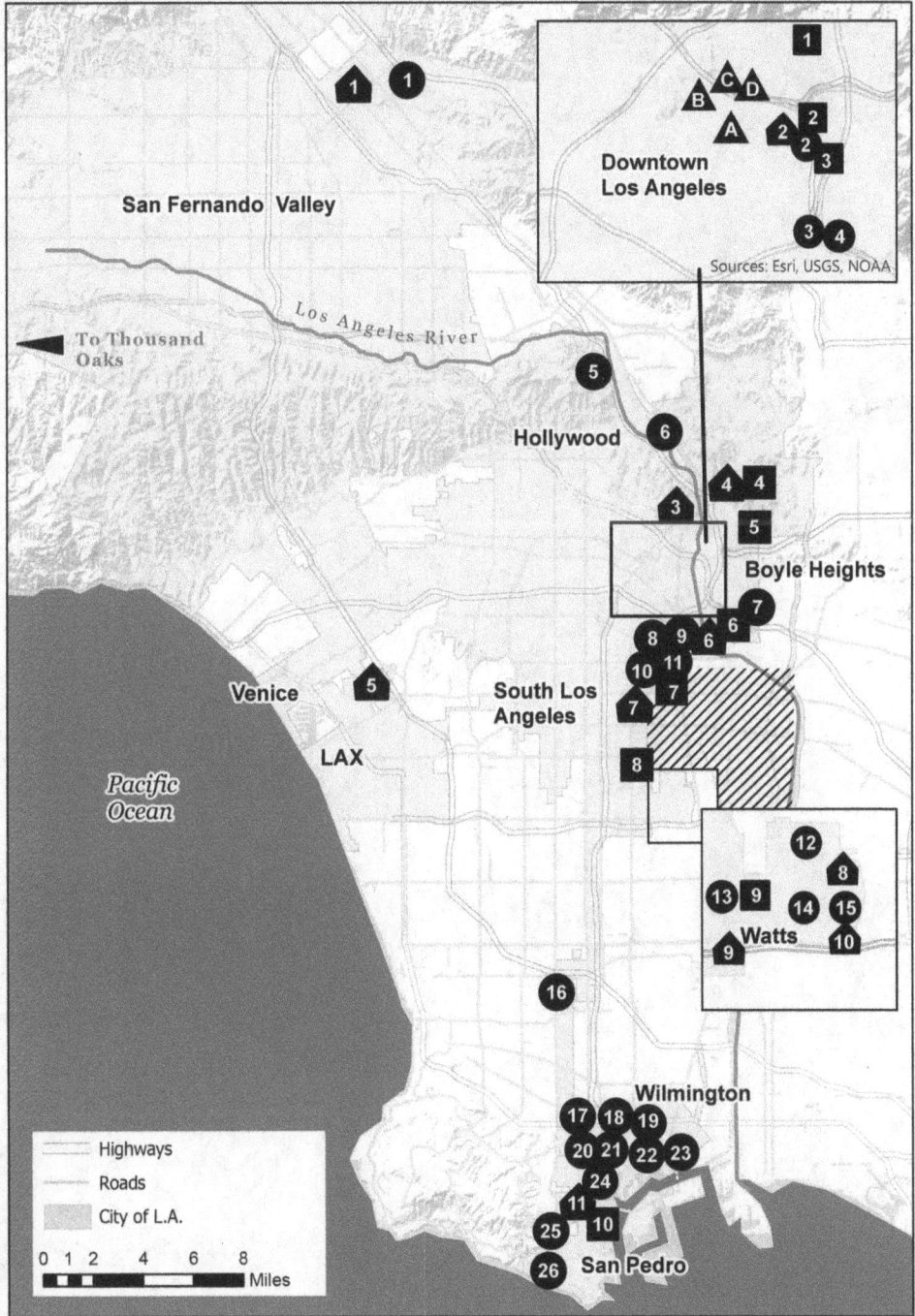

San Fernando Valley

Los Angeles River

To Thousand Oaks

Hollywood

Downtown Los Angeles

Sources: Esri, USGS, NOAA

Boyle Heights

Venice

South Los Angeles

LAX

Pacific Ocean

Watts

Wilmington

Highways
Roads
City of L.A.

0 1 2   4   6   8
Miles

San Pedro

Map created by Hunter Deckelman

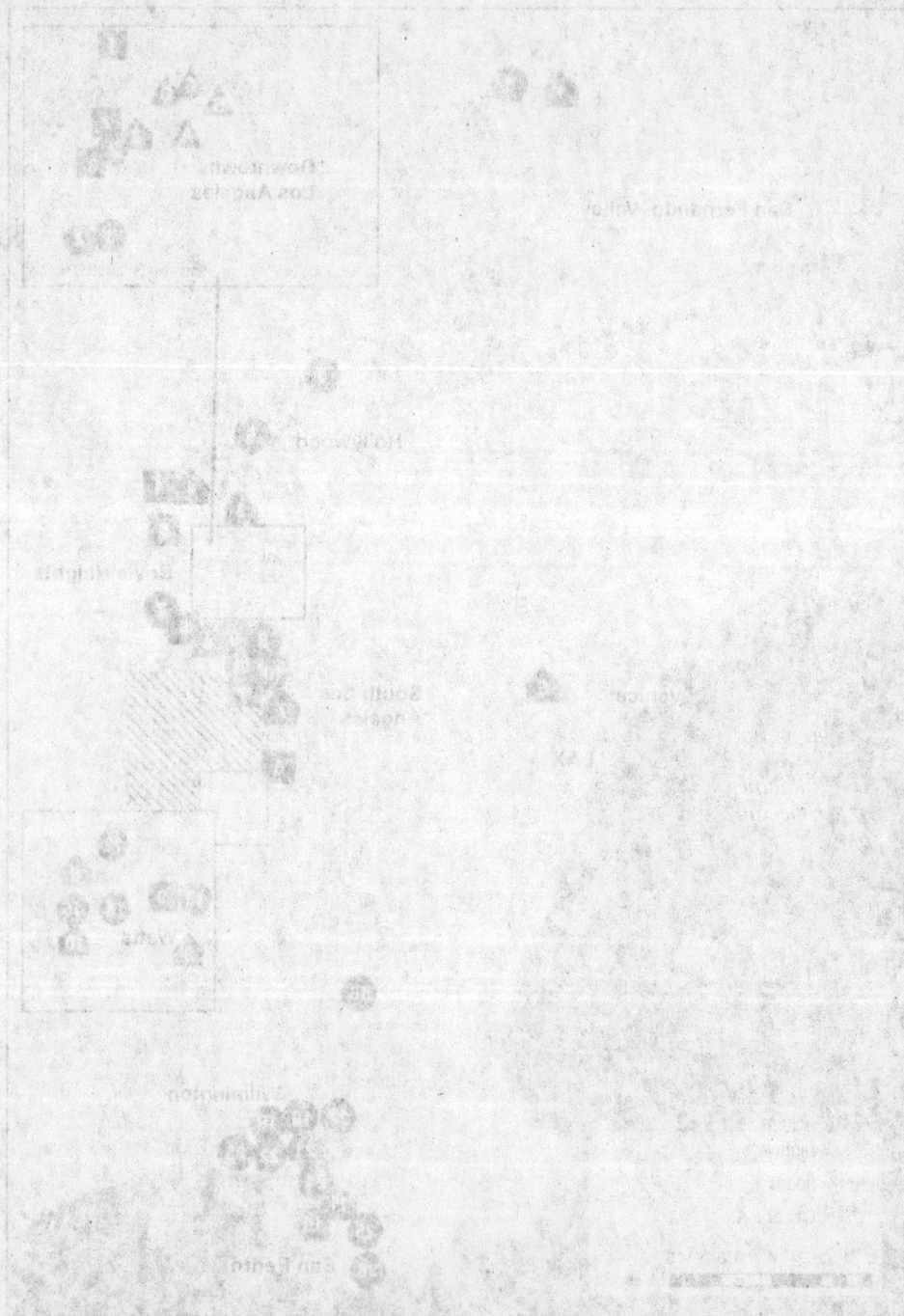

CHAPTER 1

A Mecca for the Unfortunate

Housing and Progressive Reform in Los Angeles

DON PARSON

In the early 1900s, Los Angeles presented itself to the world as a city of sunshine, orange groves, and single-family bungalows—as a municipality free from the housing problems, slum conditions, and attendant social ills that beset other American cities. "In such a climate [as that of Los Angeles] the struggle for existence will always be modified, and can never under the worst conditions be like that of other cities," wrote Rev. Dana Bartlett in his influential 1907 book, *The Better City*. "Here even the pauper lives in surroundings fit for a king."[1]

Many social reformers, however, were confronted with a reality seemingly at odds with this popular imagery. "Fortunately the sun is usually shining in Los Angeles," wrote Bessie Stoddart in 1905, "or perhaps unfortunately, for if it were not, the very unsanitary conditions of the [house] courts could not possibly be tolerated by the community at large." Jacob Riis, noted national housing reformer and author of the influential *How the Other Half Lives*, had visited the city in 1905 and declared, to the "great surprise" of affluent Angelenos, that the slums of Los Angeles were "as bad, if not as extensive, as anything to be found in New York City." The city's "uptown people are ignorant of the fact, unable to believe until they see for themselves, that the land of sunshine has any dark spots," bemoaned the Housing Commission of the City of Los Angeles in 1908.[2]

Obscured to Westside residents, Los Angeles slums were endemic to the communities where the working class, immigrants, and racial minorities lived—in Sonoratown in central Los Angeles, on the Eastside, and to the south of downtown. This geography of race and class would circumscribe and inform the development of housing reform in Los Angeles. Through the work of the Settlement Houses, the Housing Commission, and the State Commission of Immigration and Housing, attempts by reformers to come to grips with the housing conditions in Progressive-era Los Angeles set the stage for the city's subsequent housing policy.

Lopez Court, Buena Vista Street, Showing Stagnant Water.

FIGURE 1.1. Lopez Court with stagnant water, 1909–10.
Report of the Housing Commission of the City of Los Angeles 1909–10,
John Randolph Haynes Papers (1720411), Library Special Collections,
Charles E. Young Research Library, UCLA.

The Geography of Race and Class

Ethnic diversity and strong class demarcation were central characteristics of the industrial expansion of Los Angeles at the beginning of the twentieth century. Determined to prevent unions from establishing a stronghold, the business establishment declared LA an "open shop" city in the 1890s, denying workplaces the option of requiring union membership for employment, and it remained so until the 1930s. The *Los Angeles Times* ran a continuous barrage of articles about the open shop's success nationwide and the benefits of the resulting "Industrial Freedom." Los Angeles sought to attract capital by virtue of the differential between itself and heavily unionized San Francisco. An avid proponent of the open shop, Alfred Holman, wrote in 1908 that "under this policy and by it, Los Angeles has drawn to herself a prodigious power of accumulated capital with personal forces that have achieved marvels in the vast work of her development." Political dissent—as seen in a flourishing of immigrant radicalism, the growth of municipal socialism, and the bombing of the *Los Angeles Times* building—grew out of opposition to such a strategy.[3]

The city's population increased in tandem with its economic growth: from 102,000 in 1900 to 1,237,000 by 1930. The low-waged working class that was integral to the city's industrial expansion was achieved by means of immigration from Mexico, Eastern and Southern Europe, and Asia. Los Angeles was, in the words of housing reformer Bessie Stoddart, "a Mecca for the unfortunate as well as the privileged classes." The open shop industrial strategy was reflected in the segregation and social inequality of the city's residential and housing dynamics. The Los Angeles Housing Commission observed that "low wages and high rents work a hardship which is not consistent with the . . . abundant wealth found in this city."[4]

The evolution of the city's central neighborhoods exemplified this divide for reformers. After the conquest of Los Angeles by the United States in 1847, the area to the north of the central Plaza remained the residential quarter of the *Californios*, descendants of elite Spanish families who had received land grants from Spain and Mexico. With the discovery of gold in Northern California,

S. P. CARS USED AS HABITATIONS.

FIGURE 1.2. Southern Pacific Railway cars used as habitations, 1908–9.
Report of the Housing Commission of the City of Los Angeles 1908–9,
John Randolph Haynes Papers (1720411), Library Special Collections,
Charles E. Young Research Library, UCLA.

INTERIOR SALT LAKE CAR.
Child sleeping covered with flies, doors and windows not protected with screens.

FIGURE 1.3. Interior, Salt Lake Car, 1908–9.
*Report of the Housing Commission of the City of Los Angeles 1908–9,
John Randolph Haynes Papers (1720411), Library Special Collections,
Charles E. Young Research Library, UCLA.*

many Mexican miners from the province of Sonora passed through or returned
to the district (having been ejected from the goldfields), earning it the nickname of "Sonoratown." In her 1906 collection of short stories, *The Hieroglyphics
of Love*, dedicated to the author's colleagues at the Los Angeles College Settlement Association, Amanda Mathews described Sonoratown as

> detested by the citizens of Los Angeles as the last outpost against progress, and
> adored by the tourist as the last melting remnant of decayed romance. Neither
> tourist nor citizen knows much of the life of this section, which has within itself
> the widest of social gulfs. Behind the adobes occupied by the descendants of proud
> old Spanish families, poor now, but with the tradition of the halcyon days before
> the gringo invasion, are numerous courts concealed from the street and swarming
> with the despised *cholos*, imported by the railroads for cheap labor. Here the low
> life of Mexico is duplicated.[5]

Sonoratown was considered an economic and social anomaly embedded within
a modern American urbanity. Mathews went on to compare Sonoratown, "a
Mexican pueblo, dirty, peaceful, unprogressive, with [Anglo Los Angeles as] a

handsome, bustling, modern city." Bessie Stoddart, a visiting nurse and teacher from the College Settlement Association, described the unsanitary, dilapidated house courts—"nests of humanity"—that were constructed in the yards behind the adobes of the original *Californios*, and appeared a bit astonished at the contrast between the kindliness and respectability of the inhabitants and their appalling living conditions.[6]

In 1907 Dana Bartlett described the residential transformation of Sonoratown, which

> has still remnants of its original Mexican dwellers in adobe houses, crowded by the incoming Italian, Slavonians and Syrians. For these newcomers, one-story shacks were built in the rear of the old Mexican houses. As might be expected, these courts, as they were called, soon became as vicious as the tenement conditions in Eastern cities.[7]

In 1912, John Emmanuel Kienle, an inspector for the city's Housing Commission, noted the widespread dispersal of the Mexican immigrant population of Los Angeles. He observed that despite the predominance of Mexicans in Sonoratown, there was no area of the city that could be termed a "Little Mexico." Even in Sonoratown, he wrote, other groups of the immigrant and native-born working class were "rapidly crowding into that district, and it appears that the Mexicans in Sonoratown will be outclassed by other nationalities."[8]

The house courts of which Bartlett and Mathews had written were the indigenous slums of Los Angeles, defined in a 1907 city ordinance as three or more habitations situated on a single lot with vacant land held in common. In form, house courts could have their lineage traced to a modified Spanish architecture, while their purpose must be ascribed to the agglomeration of low-waged labor and the resulting demand for low-income housing. "Small spaces with huts and hovels ranged around, where misery reigns," the house courts were defined by the *Record* in 1906. In his 1916 study of house courts, Emory Bogardus observed that "in order to maintain cheap rents in spite of rise in land values the custom became common of building several cheap houses . . . upon the same lot." "The more Mexicans to the lot," the Housing Commission had written, "the more money for the owner." Bogardus estimated that there were 1,202 house courts in Los Angeles sheltering an excess of 16,000 working-class people from diverse ethnic backgrounds. Based on data from 854 courts, he extrapolated that the residents living in the 1,202 courts citywide were American (398), Mexican (298), Italian (141), Russian (73), Negro (68), Jewish (56), Slavonic (31), Japanese (24), Chinese (24), Greek (17), and Other (87).[9]

As the industrial and commercial district grew during the 1910s, the adobes and house courts of Sonoratown were supplanted by factories and warehouses. This succession of land uses was due in part to the destruction of the house courts by the Housing Commission, which could only demolish but not build housing (see below). In 1920, religious reformer Rev. G. Bromley Oxnam accurately predicted that, with the construction of Union Station adding to the transformation of land use adjacent to Sonoratown in Central Los Angeles, the Mexican population would be forced northward into Chavez Ravine, across the river to the Eastside, and to the industrial district to the south of the city limits.[10]

Bisecting the city, a residential pattern was established of immigrant and native working-class settlement on the Eastside, while American-born migrants fueled Los Angeles' westward expansion: "Class-stratified Los Angeles" notes George Sánchez, "exhibited a rigid residential separation between its core and eastern regions and the rest of the city." As a point of entry for many immigrants, Eastside working-class neighborhoods developed multicultural residential patterns. The site of the future Aliso Village public housing project, the western edge of Boyle Heights, became known as the "Russian Flats" after five thousand pacifist Molokan Russians settled there in 1905 to escape the

RUSSIAN COURT (REAR)
Showing Out-door Kitchen and Russian Oven.

FIGURE 1.4. Russian court with outdoor kitchen and oven, 1909–10.
Report of the Housing Commission of the City of Los Angeles 1909–10,
John Randolph Haynes Papers (1720411), Library Special Collections,
Charles E. Young Research Library, UCLA.

Russo-Japanese War. Pauline Young noted that "life in The Flats is a strange conglomerate of immigrant peoples living side by side though speaking a veritable babel of tongues. . . . [In addition to the Molokan Russians and Mexicans,] Negro workmen, Jewish merchants, Armenian truck drivers, Japanese gardeners, barbers, tradesmen, all contribute to the common life of The Flats." A 1908 Housing Commission report asked, "Do uptown [westside] people know that we have about four thousand Russian peasants, two thousand Slavs, and a large number of Italians, Japanese, Chinese, Syrians, not to mention the original Mexicans, the rapidly increasing colored population and other elements of a cosmopolitan whole?"[11]

The "barrioization" of the Eastside was a post–World War II phenomenon. For the first half of the century Mexican Americans shared the Eastside with both Anglo and non-Anglo working-class Angelenos. George Sánchez notes that the most marked feature of Mexican residential settlement in Los Angeles during the period 1900 to 1940 "was not intense segregation; rather, it was the widespread dispersal of Mexican homes throughout central and eastern Los Angeles." The Eastside of World War II was described by Sandro Neblo in his novel *Sacred Earth*:

> Across the wide bridges over the [Los Angeles] river, street cars, busses and crowds of pedestrians are constantly on the move. In crossing the central bridge, one finds oneself in almost another country. Everything is so different here . . . poor house construction, poor shops and old fashioned horse carriages. Life is really primitive. Many poor foreigners live here, including Greeks, Armenians, Syrians, Mexicans, and, farther down the line, apart from the rest, Negroes. The more central part of the district is occupied by Russian Molokans.

Even as late as 1955, Ralph Friedman was writing of the continuing cultural diversity of Boyle Heights, which he saw as the essence of a community democracy.[12]

"No Beauty Spots" for the Ethnic Working Class

Progressive reformers would explore the housing conditions of working-class Los Angeles, classifying their observations by ethnicity. The circumstances of the Mexican working class were the first to be analyzed. Dana Bartlett wrote of Mexican immigrants who, "being very poor and accustomed to a bare life in their own land, have chosen to live in shacks closely crowded together, thus forming the city's first housing problem. With the exception of the quick use of the knife after drinking cheap wine, they are a peaceable, hard-working people." The derogatory nickname of "cholo courts"—"the type of dwelling place built by low-class Mexicans," as defined by the *Express* in 1906—was given to the shacks occupied by the lowest rung of the immigrant working class. Such house courts were built on unimproved land, with the landlord charging a dollar fifty per month to allow tenants the privilege of constructing dwellings out of old wood, scrap iron, tin, and matting. The California State Commission of Immigration and Housing wrote in 1919 that the squalid condition of Mexican housing was a salvation in the terrible influenza epidemic of the previous year! "Their houses are so full of chinks that the fresh air fans through undisturbed, and the predilection for sunning themselves—they crawl out just as instinctively as the lizard—provided heaven-given medicine."[13]

In her 1920 study, *The Mexican Housing Problem in Los Angeles*, Elizabeth Fuller surveyed fifty Mexican homes on East Ninth Street and on Channing Street near the Los Angeles River. She declared that the "present housing conditions among the Mexicans are not intolerable, but are deplorable and a menace to Los Angeles." She described a typical house court occupied by Mexican immigrants that comprised 26 two-room units squeezed onto a lot measuring 80 by 145 feet. Each habitation had one window and was separated from adjacent cubicles by a thin board partition. Four toilets and seven faucets were the sum sanitary facilities for the entire population of the court. Fuller encouraged enlightened landlords to improve labor productivity by providing better housing: "If America is going to awake the latent power of the Mexican, she cannot offer him miserable shacks for a shelter."[14]

Infamous for its squalid housing conditions, the Ann Street district, where the William Mead Homes public housing project would be built in the early 1940s, was located to the northeast of Sonoratown. Locally known as "Dogtown," the district was bisected by the Los Angeles River and nearly surrounded by railroad tracks. When it was surveyed by Gladys Patric around 1917, the residential composition of the district was 51.8 percent Mexican, 30 percent Italian, and 18.2 percent other (Spanish, Austrian, German, French, English, Irish, and American). Rents for substandard accommodations were a high percentage of wages: the average rent was $6.37 per month for Mexicans, $9.82 for Italians, and $11.00 for others, compared to an average wage of $10.35, $12.35, and $13.60 per week, respectively. Patric determined that, after rent, $4.25 was available each month to each member of a (not atypical) family of eight for food, fuel, clothing, "and all the other necessities." However, a 1916 study by the Bureau of Labor in Washington found that an average family of five required a minimum of $7.67 per person per month for food and fuel alone.[15]

In 1904 J. B. Loving editorialized in *The Liberator* that "the Negroes of this city have prudently refused to segregate themselves into any locality, but have scattered and purchased homes in sections occupied by wealthy, cultured White people." This meant that blacks would enjoy the same quality of municipal services, police, and fire protection as their white neighbors. Indeed, J. Max Bond

FIGURE 1.5. "Dwelling occupants in their kitchen: There is a small stove,
but the windows are covered so there is very little ventilation."
Oviatt Library Digital Collections, Poor Housing Conditions in Los Angeles 1938–40.

observed that the "lack of a distinct concentration [of African Americans] in
any particular area indicates an absence of racial segregation in Los Angeles in
1900." Bond identified the following neighborhoods, though they were neither
monoracial nor slums, where African Americans were concentrated by 1910:
(1) West Temple Street to Occidental Boulevard; (2) First to Third streets, San
Pedro to Santa Fe streets; (3) Seventh to Ninth streets, Mateo to Santa Fe streets;
(4) First Street to Broadway, Evergreen to Savannah streets in Boyle Heights;
(5) Thirty-Fifth Street and Normandie; and (6) Pico and Vermont boulevards
(Pico Heights).[16]

Upon visiting Los Angeles in 1913, W. E. B. Du Bois of the National Association for the Advancement of Colored People (NAACP) wrote enthusiastically,
"Los Angeles is wonderful. Nowhere in the United States is the Negro so well
and beautifully housed." However, he cautioned in *The Crisis* that "Los Angeles
is not Paradise. . . . The color line is there and sharply drawn." Although blacks
were often relegated to the least desirable areas, such as Temple Street, satu-
rated with the stench of the oil fields, or the swampy and fever-ridden Jefferson
Street, racial boundaries were as yet not strictly defined, and African Americans were not subject to acute housing discrimination until the years following
World War I. The subsequent growth of the black population in Los Angeles,

according to J. Max Bond, led to the "formation of Negro communities" as a "result of segregation, invasion, and succession . . . accompanied by intense racial feeling."[17]

The 1920s saw a continuation of the social demarcation of the African American communities. Blacks had participated in the "bungalow boom," especially along Central Avenue in South Central Los Angeles; four- to five-room "California cottages," priced from nine hundred to twenty-five hundred dollars, were within reach of African Americans of modest means who worked in such occupations as porters and domestics. The prevalence of home ownership among blacks was more extensive in Los Angeles than in other urban areas of the United States. By 1930, over one-third of the black families in Los Angeles lived in their own home, in contrast to 5 percent in New York and 10 percent in Chicago.[18]

The in-migration of African Americans to Los Angeles during the 1920s and the expansion of the black residential districts led to white flight to the suburbs on the Westside and African American succession into older downtown neighborhoods. At the same time, the growth of racially restrictive covenants—legal and binding agreements among property owners that disallowed housing sales or rentals to minorities—attempted to hold the color line. In actions that originated in Los Angeles County Superior Court, the 1919 California Supreme Court declared that racial covenants based on occupancy were legal and the 1928 Court ruled that racial covenants were enforceable even if minorities already occupied the area in question.

In her 1929 study, *The Changing Urban Neighborhood*, Bessie McClenehan described the transformation of a middle-class Anglo residential community located near the University of Southern California (USC), just south of downtown. She found that of "universal concern to the residents is the threat of invasion by the Negroes and Japanese." The territorial expansion of the increasingly segregated and delineated African American ghetto from the east was perceived to endanger the social stability and property values of the Anglo neighborhood that was being studied. One response of the residents was to form property-owner associations to enforce restrictive covenants and stand fast against the invaders. Those who could afford to do so moved westward to more fashionable areas, leaving the old craftsman houses and bungalows to be subdivided into flats and encircled by newly constructed house courts and apartment buildings.[19]

The end result, due to both white suburbanization and racial restrictions, was the formulation of the modern ghetto, complete with chronic housing shortages and poor conditions. "By 1930," according to Lawrence Brooks de Graff, "70 per cent of Los Angeles' Negroes were concentrated in one Assembly District in the Central Avenue area, and most of the remainder lived in adjacent sections."[20]

Like African Americans, the small population of Japanese in Los Angeles at the turn of the century meant, as William Mason and John McKinstry pointed out, that there "was no tight concentration of Japanese in the city; small groups were scattered about in different wards." Little Tokyo, centered on East First and Alameda streets adjacent to Skid Row, began its development in the early 1900s. It was "no beauty spot," observed John Modell, serving as a commercial center and the location of boarding houses for single laborers, with a small amount of "generally cramped and often dilapidated housing" for families. The Japanese population increased rapidly following the 1906 San Francisco earthquake, with settlement in Boyle Heights on the Eastside and west of downtown to the West Jefferson, West Tenth Street, Pico Heights, and Washington Boulevard districts. The Japanese districts were not monoracial ghettos. Blacks, Mexicans, and foreign-born whites lived side by side in Japanese neighborhoods. In 1940, Little Tokyo, with the highest concentration of Japanese in any area of the city, contained only 36 percent Japanese.[21]

In contrast to the increasing concentration of African Americans, Japanese, and Mexican Americans was the un-ghetto of Los Angeles—Chinatown. Originally settled in the 1860s and located adjacent to Sonoratown, immediately to the east of the Plaza and across Los Angeles and Alameda streets, Chinatown was home to about 7,000 Chinese at its apex at the turn of the century. "The worst housing in the city centers is in Chinatown. The buildings were erected before there were housing ordinances and patterned after houses in China," wrote the principal of Macy Street School, Nora Sterry. Due to the effects of the Chinese Exclusion Act of 1882, its population had shrunk to 2,062 by 1920. Choosing Chinatown as the site for northward expansion of the civic center and for a new Union Station begged the question: where will the Chinese go? Throughout the 1920s, Chinese families dispersed into outlying residential districts, abandoning Chinatown to commerce and to bachelors. Constructed specifically as a tourist attraction, New Chinatown—described by Bruce Henstell as "a modern, comfortable shopping area on land that the Chinese owned"— was opened in 1938 to the north of the Plaza in Sonoratown, dispersing the multiethnic working-class population living there to the Eastside and Chavez Ravine.[22]

Progressive Housing Reform

In the sphere of urban politics, progressives often saw themselves as purveyors of a social reform motivated by a spirit of noblesse oblige. "As a non-Christian land can never become Christian except by the cooperation and leadership of the natives of that land," wrote Rev. Dana Bartlett in 1907, "so in city life, the better day will come only when those whom we sometimes call the common

A View of a Corner of the Locality in Which Over 200 of our
Chinese Vegetable Men Live and Stable Their Horses.

FIGURE 1.6. View of locality where 200 Chinese vegetable men live, 1909–10.
Report of the Housing Commission of the City of Los Angeles 1909–10,
John Randolph Haynes Papers (1720411), Library Special Collections,
Charles E. Young Research Library, UCLA.

people are inspired to cooperate with their leaders in striving after the higher civic ideals," implying that rather than resort to militant political actions that were fueled by class and race antagonisms, slum dwellers should rely on the honest, nonpartisan, and "classless" leadership that the progressives could provide. "The progressives," Ricardo Romo points out in his history of East Los Angeles, "who took an interest in municipal reform and meeting the challenge of the rise of socialism, organized labor and non-Nordic immigration, considered the barrios of Los Angeles an important experimental location for putting their ideals into practice." Yet the diversity within the progressive movement often defied a neat categorization. Maude Foster of Los Angeles' College Settlement refuted the stigma of charity and argued that progressives "must throw off the shackles of a worn-out system" in favor of a cooperative and democratic socialism. "To make way for social justice by declaring for Socialism," she wrote in 1899, "is the only path now open to the settlements."[23]

Foster's declaration was echoed in the challenge to Los Angeles' political culture taking place in its public spaces. Street speaking by diverse political groups, from the socialists to Partido Liberal Mexicano, and later the communists, increasingly engaged a broad public with issues central to poor and working-class Angelenos in the heart of the city. As Mark Wild describes it,

> The mobilization of central city residents in the streets, whether sparked by speakers or some other catalyst, posed one of the greatest political threats to middle-class and elite Anglos during the early twentieth century. . . . The specter of inter-ethnoracial, class-based protest touched off a war against street speaking that raged hot and cold from the early 1900s through the Great Depression.[24]

Despite the public dynamics of a city in the process of defining itself, for the majority of the progressives housing problems were to be identified by experts, catalyzed by social workers, and then addressed via the education of both tenants and landlords as to the moral improvement and civic virtue of better housing. Ultimately, restrictive legislation (housing code and its enforcement) might enlighten a recalcitrant landlord to the evils of poor housing. Elizabeth Fuller, a social worker from USC, placed the fault for the deplorable housing conditions of the Mexican working class squarely on the shoulders of the landlord, but structural social change was not required as the problem could be confronted with empathy and understanding:

> My personal recommendation is the immediate education of the house-owner. Give them a personal knowledge of the conditions among their tenants. . . . Were he [the landlord] made to feel his responsibility, he would be willing to better conditions. I believe that the housing problem of the Mexican can be solved by the business man.[25]

Progressive reformers would frequently press at the limits of the private housing market and prescriptions for restrictive legislation. Bessie Stoddart, a social worker with the College Settlement, saw the creation of slums as being due to landlords attempting to maximize their profit at the expense of their tenants: "The reckless zeal of a few individual landlords should not blind the community at large" to the congested housing conditions that resulted in "physical ill-health and moral depravity." Writing about the house courts, William Matthews admonished Los Angeles about the dangers of "a 'laissez faire' housing policy which ever brings forth fruits of unrighteousness." Regarding the manifestations in California of the worldwide housing shortage that began with World War I, the State Commission of Immigration and Housing noted that "private enterprise and municipal projects, while the most logical agencies to handle the construction of homes, were inadequate for the present crisis." But the commission advocated, in contrast to a program of government-constructed housing, state financial aid to private home builders for the construction of dwellings within monetary reach of the working class.[26]

Settlement Houses

The settlement houses were one or more buildings in slum areas where progressive reformers, frequently college- or university-educated, lived or worked with the intent of teaching a model way of living and diffusing the means of physical and moral improvement to the other half. A settlement, as defined by the Los Angeles Settlement Association, "is interested in the life of the neighborhood, working through the people of that neighborhood for better government, better sanitation, more intelligent citizenship, and higher intellectual and social development." Women were the driving force behind the settlement house movement and composed the active membership of the numerous civic betterment and discussion groups that served to educate the concerned citizenry about the social ills of the modern city. "Today [women] are studying unpleasant facts, looking at them straight in the face and by their combined efforts are seeking to right what is wrong," wrote Dana Bartlett. This reformist political culture of municipal housekeeping was propagated in Los Angeles by the Friday Morning Club, the Ebell Club, and the Civic Association.[27]

Following a visit to Los Angeles by Jane Addams of Chicago's Hull House, the first settlement house west of the Mississippi River was founded by the Los Angeles Settlement Association, the local branch of the College Settlement Association. In February 1894 the organization rented a room at Alpine and Cleveland streets. Requiring more space, the association moved to several rooms on New High Street and finally rented the Begon adobe in December 1895, purchasing the property in 1902. Casa Castelar (as the adobe was renamed) was situated at Castelar and Alpine streets to serve Sonoratown, where, wrote Katharine Coman, "huddled together in rapidly narrowing quarters, dwell Aztec Indians, Mexican half-breeds and people of pure Spanish blood." The settlement boasted a number of social clubs, as well as a resident nurse, the Caroline M. Severance Kindergarten, a public library branch, a night school, a clothing department, a savings bank, and a lecture program that covered a plethora of subjects from ancient history to zoology.[28]

Located on the Eastside flats at Vignes and Jackson streets was the Bethlehem Institute, a Protestant settlement that grew out of the Bethlehem Congregational Mission. In 1896, reformer Dana W. Bartlett took up residence as pastor, and the institute would offer a bath house, swimming pool, and evening classes for, as *The Commons* noted, "Japanese, Corean, Mexicans and Russians [who] . . . are crowding into this district." With a paid staff of seven and eighteen volunteers, the settlement ran a men's hotel that served seven thousand transients during the winter of 1905, a Coffee Club that served meals at cost, a free employment bureau, a free dispensary, reading rooms, music classes, concerts, and lectures. J. M. Campbell enthused that "everything about the whole establishment has a cheerful and homelike appearance."[29]

These settlements were followed by the 1901 founding of the Catholic Brownson House. Originally occupying a rented bungalow at 422 Aliso Street, it moved to new quarters erected for the community by the diocese at 711 Jackson Street in 1905. The settlement maintained a nonsectarian approach to its charitable work, cooperating freely with both Casa Castelar and the Bethlehem Institute. The Brownson House had, wrote Mary Workman, "no religious test in its work, and the religious rights of all are respected." With an attendance of about a thousand people per week, the house offered sewing workshops, a library, clubs for boys and girls, baths, a playground, and a clothing bureau—all of which were administered by three salaried workers and about sixty volunteers. In addition there was religious instruction and Mass on Sundays. A field worker would visit homes in the surrounding slums in order to offer advice for home improvement and refer hardship cases to the appropriate charities or social welfare agencies. The house maintained an orthopedic dispensary for the disabled and was given over to the city each week as a Municipal Child Welfare Station where mothers could bring their babies for medical examinations. By 1916 the settlement was also embarking on an ambitious lecture program.[30]

Bethlehem Institute lasted until 1913, when Dana Bartlett underwent financial difficulties. Casa Castelar ceased operations in 1918, while Brownson House continued into the 1920s despite the challenges posed by the reorganization of diocesan charities. As the settlement houses declined, the City of Los Angeles absorbed settlement house workers as well as many of the services that the settlements had offered. Appointed by ordinance in 1913, the Municipal Charities Commission was empowered to investigate, endorse, or encourage the formation of municipal and private charities and to secure the cooperation of these institutions. The commission's "Friendly Visitors" would collect statistical information (social, financial, physical, and work histories) of a needy family and prescribe the appropriate charity to assist them. Mary Workman wrote in 1918 that she considered the settlement to be a forerunner of the modern social movement and that those "who have been trained in the settlements are occupying the most important positions on many city, state, and national welfare commissions." Mary Chaffee's 1918 survey of social work in Los Angeles noted the city's steadily increasing demand for social workers "as the people develop a socialized public opinion which is urging more adequate provision for meeting our social needs."[31]

The Housing Commission

Pressure by social workers, housing reformers, and institutions such as the Municipal League and the College Settlement Association, who sought to institute restrictive legislation to deal with the slum problem, resulted in the founding of

INSPECTOR DOING EDUCATIONAL WORK
A Kindly Use of the "Arm of the Law" Far More Effective
Than Force.

FIGURE 1.7. Inspector doing educational work, 1909–10.
Report of the Housing Commission of the City of Los Angeles 1909–10,
John Randolph Haynes Papers (1720411), Library Special Collections,
Charles E. Young Research Library, UCLA.

the Los Angeles Housing Commission. Originally an advisory body appointed by Mayor Owen McAleer in February 1906, the Housing Commission was established by ordinance in October 1908. The mayor appointed the following commissioners: Titian Coffey, MD, Miss Elizabeth Kenney, Rev. Wm. Horace Day, George E. Bergstrom, Charles L. Whipple, and Mary A. Veeder. It saw its role as dealing with "the homes of the poorer classes which need special laws to regulate and educate them." The Housing Commission was concerned primarily with the house courts of Los Angeles, which, as Dr. Titian Coffey, president of the commission, explained, "would furnish work for all the sociological experts that we can bring to the city." Mary Veeder defined the commission's function as "educational inspection: to teach the public and the landlord that it pays in every way to give the people a fair chance; and to show the latter how to make the most of life and to rise to a better plane of living."[32]

In 1907 the commission was authorized, through the Board of Health, to inspect and issue citations to house courts that met the following criteria: were congested (at least 30 percent of the ground area was to be unoccupied); or were built of insubstantial material, had earthen floors, or were not waterproof; or had an inadequate number of privies or water closets; or had less than one hydrant for every three habitations; or had open spaces that were not covered with sand, gravel, asphalt, or concrete (to prevent dust). The commission had no powers to increase the supply of low-income housing but, in contrast, only could condemn substandard courts and thus restrict the availability of marketable units. Pedro Castillo reports that "what occurred in Los Angeles between 1906 and 1913 was an 'urban renewal' project with the Housing Commission having the power to condemn house courts, tear down buildings and have the land sold to private developers." The commission's scope was broadened in 1912 to include inspections of tenements, hotels, and boarding houses and then in 1913 was consolidated within the Department of Health, where, as the Bureau of Housing, 2,260 violations of the housing laws—more than six a day—were uncovered in 1917.[33]

Progressive feminism was strongly entrenched in the commission, which hired a woman housing inspector—Johanna von Wagner, a settlement house worker with experience in Yonkers and New York City—in order to bring a female perspective and "natural" sensitivity to the field of housing reform. Another commission member, Mary Veeder, was a worker in the Los Angeles Settlement House Association. The *Express* congratulated the "business men and philanthropic women" who worked with the commission. Its membership varied over the years, usually consisting of three men and two women; it included a social worker, a doctor, a member of the Anti-Tuberculosis League, an architect, a plumber, and a lawyer.[34]

Beyond inspections, education, and condemnation, the commission undertook two constructive programs—the model house court and the Garden City. Neither met with success. Mrs. Frances M. Norton sought, in 1906, to mobilize support for her model apartment:

> The building ought to be four stories high, with passage-ways through in both directions, making an inner court, where they intersect. Here would be the playground for the children. The top floor would be devoted to those house hold activities which the flat dwellers could with advantages perform in common. There ought to be on this floor a cooking room, a baking room, a nursery, a hospital, a library, a gymnasium, an amusement hall, and a laundry.

An architectural competition was held by the Housing Commission in order to promote the model house and "to interest the capitalist and philanthropist in the betterment of the foreigner and the unfortunate." The commission suggested that public-spirited citizens might consider forming a stock company, fashioned after the Octavia Hill Association in classes at a 4 to 5 percent rate of return on their investment. In response, a Municipal Housing Association was formed as a philanthropic housing venture, but its pledges evaporated with the severe drop in the real estate market of 1912.[35]

Commission member Dana Bartlett sought to "ruralize the city" by providing uncongested housing, primarily single-family homes, for workers in suburban locales. He was heavily influenced by the Garden City movement in Britain, maintaining that the rationality of the Garden City proposals and their benefit for society as a whole "ought to inspire many more capitalists to think of the other fellow, as well as of themselves." In 1911, the Model Village association proposed constructing a prototype in the vacant land of Chavez Ravine "to be built along strictly sanitary lines . . . and will be grouped with the idea of providing recreation centers and other sociological features." Interest in this project was initially expressed by John Ihlder, secretary of the National Housing Association, though he later criticized as politically naive the ability of the Garden City idea to address the existing housing situation, especially the growth of tenement housing, among low-waged workers.[36]

The Housing Commission had noted the ethnic diversity of the city and saw its task as one of absorbing these immigrants, by way of housing reform, so that they might perform better in the expanding Los Angeles economy: "Most of the foreigners come to us unfit for anything but manual labor. . . . [Mexicans] seem contented to do the hardest kind of manual labor. . . . The Russians show a decided improvement over the Mexicans. . . . The Japanese show still higher intelligence. . . . The Negroes are not classed as foreigners, but a large number of them live in the city. . . . The Armenians are dirty. . . . The Jews live up to their record," and so forth. Better housing, argued the commission, would result in better workers. It would also result in better politics, as evidenced by a commission slogan: "Men cannot live like pigs and vote like men."[37]

The Housing Commission was abolished in 1922 and its activities assumed by the Bureau of Housing and Sanitation of the Health Department. Los Angeles' new City Charter of 1925 reestablished the Municipal Housing Commission (MHC), to which Mayor Cryer appointed fifteen directors. The MHC was given the power to issue bonds and receive donations and gifts in order to build and operate low-rent housing for people who would otherwise live in the city's slums. The driving force behind the MHC was its president, William Mead, who obtained pledges from civic-minded citizens to underwrite a million-dollar bond issue for a municipal housing program. The MHC's first bond issue was tested in *Willmon v. Powell* when the city treasurer refused to affix the city's corporate seal on the MHC bonds, arguing that the purpose of the MHC lay outside the boundaries of the proper affairs of a municipality. California's Court of Appeals refuted this reasoning, upholding the validity of the bonds. The court victory proved hollow as the pledges vanished following Mead's death in 1927 and before the MHC constructed any housing.[38]

The California State Commission on Immigration and Housing

Established in 1913, the California State Commission on Immigration and Housing (CSCIH) was concerned with issues regarding the care, welfare, and protection of immigrants in the state. The active assimilation of the immigrant into the dominant culture—the process of "Americanization"—was advocated. Focusing explicitly on improving housing conditions for the immigrant population as a means of Americanization, the commission wrote that the "home is the basis of all civilization in all lands. The house is the concrete aspect of the home. The house, generally overcrowded and in the slums, is the first point of contact between the immigrant and his new environment. And no culture can be fostered in a miserable hovel, but ignorance, vice and crime thrive therein." Americanization could produce not only improved citizens but cannon fodder as well: during World War I, CSCIH commissioner Mrs. Frank A. Gibson congratulated the Brownson House whose "neighborhood service has won such confidence . . . in persuading the Mexicans to register and then to answer the draft."[39]

The immigrant housewife (or, more accurately, the house*worker*) was the linchpin in CSCIH's goal of Americanization through housing reform. The CSCIH incessantly bombarded immigrant women with instructions to clean, cook, and sew in order to create an American household. The song "Work," by Mrs. Ada Patten, was to be sung by immigrant women as part of English language instruction:

> We are working every day,
> So our boys and girls can play.
> We are working for our homes and country, too;
> We like to wash, to sew, to cook.
> We like to write, or read a book,
> We are working, working, working every day.
> Work, work, work,
> We're always working
> Working for our boys and girls,
> For our homes and country, too—
> We are working, working, working every day.[40]

Combined with the decline of European immigration to California in the 1920s, the post–World War I Red Scare rendered politically moot the CSCIH's advocacy of Americanization through progressive housing reform. As the progressives lost political control of California in the 1920s, conservative Republican governor Friend Richardson sharply curtailed the CSCIH, eventually dissolving it in 1927. Americanization was a dead issue as many Mexican immigrants were deported during the repatriation program of the early 1930s. The commission was reborn in 1939 as part of California's New Deal when Democratic governor Culbert Olson appointed activist writer Carey McWilliams as its director. Concerned primarily with housing for the state's farmworkers and dust bowl refugees, the CSCIH garnered the enmity of the powerful Associated Farmers, who branded McWilliams as "Agricultural pest No. 1." The commission was dissolved once more by the unsympathetic Republican governor Earl Warren in 1942.[41]

◻ ◻ ◻

The economic boom of the 1920s dissipated the immediacy and energy behind the progressive agenda. At the outset of the Depression, the general problem of housing had been marginalized into a "Mexican problem," a "Japanese problem," or a "colored problem." Mexican Americans, along with their African American and Japanese American cohorts, were seen as invaders who could subvert middle-class Anglo residential land uses into ethnically diverse working-class communities. In 1930 Emory Bogardus, a prominent social ecologist at USC, explained, "As rents become cheaper in some American quarters, there is a tendency for the more wide-awake Mexicans to break into an American community."[42]

The deflation of progressivism can be seen in relationship to the parallel transformation of academic paradigms: the moral outrage that had motivated progressive housing reformers during the first two decades of the twentieth century was recast into a dispassionate, scientific urban sociology that emphasized the irreproachable spatiality of the capitalist city. For example, Bessie Mc-Clenehan, in her aforementioned 1929 study of the University district, stressed that her inquiry was not motivated by a "reform movement" but was instead a factual survey of a Los Angeles neighborhood employing the principles of social ecology and the Chicago School of Urban Sociology.[43]

The progressives' work on housing reform in Los Angeles helped establish the direction for the local public housing program of the 1930s and beyond. A multiethnic and working-class Eastside and an African American ghetto to the south of downtown counterpoised to a Westside Anglo suburbanization would define the geography of the city's public housing program. Issues that were delineated by progressive reformers—of race, class, architectural design of housing, women's work, and the paternalism of housing reformers—were to become central concerns of the public housing movement. Finally, the inadequacy of social ecology to conceptualize, or even recognize, housing reform efforts would lead public housing advocates to be more open to political conflict and struggle than conventional urban theory had heretofore allowed.

While the racial aspects of the slums combined with the class-stratified housing market may have offended the sense of social justice of the early progressive reformers, or may have been implicitly accepted by social ecologists, they were to be focal points for the mobilization of popular support in the realization of a public housing program proposed by the Keynesian left in the late 1930s. Moreover, national legislation that directly challenged the principles of free-market housing would be needed to address the crisis of the Great Depression. The restrictive legislation of the progressives would eventually give way to the constructive policy of public housing.

NOTES

1. Laura Chase, "Eden in the Orange Groves: Bungalows and Courtyard Housing in Los Angeles," *Landscape* 25, no. 3 (Fall 1981): 29–36; Dana W. Bartlett, *The Better City: A Sociological Study of a Modern City* (Los Angeles: Neuner Company Press, 1907), 20. Bartlett's observations of specific housing conditions in Los Angeles from his standpoint as an active housing reformer and settlement-house worker are invaluable, yet he presented the overall "housing question" in a way to de-emphasize social conflict and class struggle, perhaps so as not to alienate the monied philanthropists who were central to progressive housing reform.

2. Bessie B. Stoddart, "The Courts of Sonoratown: The Housing Problem as It Is to Be Found in Los Angeles," *Charities and the Commons* 15 (December 2, 1905): 298; Housing Commission of the City of Los Angeles, "Report of the Housing Commission," February 20, 1906, to June 30, 1908 (Los Angeles, n.d.), 6, 3. To understand the magnitude of Riis's comparison, see Jacob A. Riis, *How the Other Half Lives: Studies among the Tenements of New York* (1901; New York: Dover, 1971).

3. Frederick Palmer, "Otistown of the Open Shop," *Hampton's Magazine* 26 (January 1911): 29–44; Alfred Holman, "In the Calcium Light: Harrison Gray Otis and His Fight for the Open Shop," *Overland Monthly* 51 (March 1908): 293; Paul Greenstein, Nigey Lennon, and Lionel Rolfe, *Bread and Hyacinths: The Rise and Fall of Utopian Los Angeles* (Los Angeles: California Classics Books, 1992). In an open shop, employees can choose not to join or pay dues to the union at their workplace, but they still get the benefits of union agreements that dues-paying members negotiate.

4. Stoddart, "Courts of Sonoratown," 299; Housing Commission of the City of Los Angeles, "Report of the Housing Commission," June 30, 1908, to June 30, 1909 (Los Angeles, n.d.), 10.

5. Amanda Mathews, *The Hieroglyphics of Love: Stories of Sonoratown and Old Mexico* (Los Angeles: Artemisia Bindery, 1906), 67.

6. Mathews, *Hieroglyphics of Love*, 19–20; Stoddart, "Courts of Sonoratown."

7. Bartlett, *Better City*, 72.

8. John Emmanuel Kienle, "Housing Conditions among the Mexican Population of Los Angeles" (MA thesis, University of Southern California, 1912), 5, 6.

9. Ordinance 14113, February 4, 1907, Ordinances, book 383, p. 63, City Archives; "Frightful Overcrowding Found on Aliso Street," *Record*, July 2, 1906, clipping in John Randolph Haynes Collection, box 76; Emory S. Bogardus, "The House-Court Problem," *American Journal of Sociology* 22 (November 1916): 392, 398; Housing Commission of the City of Los Angeles, "Report of the Housing Commission," February 20, 1906, to June 30, 1908 (Los Angeles, n.d.), 8. For more on house courts, please see Stoddart, "Courts of Sonoratown," and William Matthews, "The House Courts of Los Angeles," *Survey* 30 (July 5, 1913): 461–67.

10. G. Bromley Oxnam, *The Mexican in Los Angeles: Los Angeles City Survey, 1920* (San Francisco: R and E Research Associates, 1970).

11. George J. Sánchez, *Becoming Mexican American: Ethnicity, Culture and Identity in Chicano Los Angeles, 1900–1945* (New York: Oxford University Press, 1993), 77; Mary Hudson Bulen, "Molokan Colony in Los Angeles," *Los Angeles Saturday Night* 5 (June 24, 1933): 5; Lillian Sokoloff, *The Russians in Los Angeles*, Sociology Monograph 11 (Los Angeles: Southern California Sociological Society, 1918); Pauline V. Young, *The Pilgrims of Russian-Town*, University of Chicago Sociological Series (Chicago: University of Chicago Press, 1932), 19; Sophie Spalding, "The Myth of the Classic Slum: Contradictory Perceptions of Boyle Heights Flats, 1900–1991," *Journal of Architectural Education* 45, no. 2 (February 1992): 107–19; Housing Commission of the City of Los Angeles, "Report of the Housing Commission," June 30, 1908, to June 30, 1909 (Los Angeles, n.d.), 4.

12. Sánchez, *Becoming Mexican American*, 76; Wendy Elliott, "The Jews of Boyle Heights, 1900–1950: The Melting Pot of Los Angeles" (paper, California American Studies Association, San Diego, May 6–8, 1994); Ricardo Romo, "Mexican Workers in the City: Los Angeles, 1915–1930" (PhD diss., University of California, Los Angeles, 1975), chap. 4; Sandro Neblo, *Sacred Earth* (Hollywood, Calif.: Oxford Press, 1948), 88; Ralph Friedman, "U.N. in Microcosm—Boyle Heights: An Example of Democratic Progress," *Frontier* 6 (March 1955): 11–14.

13. Bartlett, *Better City*, 78; "Housing Problem Too Much for Volunteers," *Los Angeles Express*, October 16, 1906, John Randolph Haynes Collection, box 76; *A Community Survey Made in Los Angeles City* (San Francisco: Commission of Immigration and Housing of California, 1919), 34.

14. Elizabeth Fuller, *The Mexican Housing Problem in Los Angeles*, Sociological Monograph 17 (Los Angeles: Southern California Sociological Society, USC, 1920), 10, 7.

15. Gladys Patric, *A Study of the Housing and Social Conditions in the Ann Street District of Los Angeles, California* (Los Angeles: Los Angeles Society for the Study and Prevention of Tuberculosis, ca. 1917). According to Sidney Green, a former manager of William Mead Homes, the district acquired the nickname of "Dogtown" due to the custom of the many railroad workers living there to keep watchdogs to guard their property during their absence (Sidney Green interview, July 8, 1982). Rudy Acuña pointed out that the city's first animal shelter was located here, and this fact may also account for the origin of the nickname.

16. J. B. Loving, "Refused to Segregate," *The Liberator*, January/February 1904, 14, quoted in Charlotta Bass, *Forty Years: Memoirs from the Pages of a Newspaper* (Los Angeles: California Eagle, 1960); J. Max Bond, "The Negro in Los Angeles" (PhD diss., University of Southern California, 1936), 26, 24.

17. As quoted in Lonnie G. Bunch III, *Black Angelenos: The Afro-American in Los Angeles, 1850–1950* (Los Angeles: California Afro-American Museum, 1988), 9; W. E. B. Du Bois, "Colored Californians," *The Crisis* 45 (1913): 193–94; Bond, "Negro in Los Angeles," 33.

18. Lawrence B. de Graff, "The City of Black Angels: Emergence of the Los Angeles Ghetto, 1890–1930," *Pacific Historical Review* 39 (August 1970): 351.

19. Bessie Averne McClenehan, *The Changing Urban Neighborhood: From Neighbor*

to Nigh-Dweller, Social Science Series 1 (Los Angeles: University of Southern California, 1929).

20. *Los Angeles Investment Co. v. Gary*, 181 Cal. 680 (1919); *Wayt v. Patee*, 205 Cal. 46 (1928); Lawrence Brooks de Graff, "Negro Migration to Los Angeles, 1930 to 1950" (PhD diss., University of California, Los Angeles, 1962), 21.

21. William M. Mason and John A. McKinstry, *The Japanese of Los Angeles*, Contribution in History No. 1 (Los Angeles: L.A. County Museum of Natural History, 1969), 7, 29; John Modell, *The Economics and Politics of Racial Accommodation: The Japanese of Los Angeles, 1900–1942* (Urbana: University of Illinois Press, 1977), 55, 71–75.

22. Nora Sterry, "Housing Conditions in Chinatown, Los Angeles," *Journal of Applied Sociology* 7 (1922): 71; the houses in Chinatown, Sterry wrote, were "for the most part of red brick, built flush with the street, two stories in height . . . [with no] division between properties . . . [and] wooden balconies painted in brilliant hues." Bruce Henstell, *Sunshine and Wealth: Los Angeles in the Twenties and Thirties* (San Francisco: Chronicle Books, 1984), 93; "Second Annual Report of the Commission of Immigration and Housing of California" (Sacramento: California State Printing Office, 1916), 262–66; J. M. Scanland, "Quaint Chinese Quarter Doomed by Civic Center," *Los Angeles Times*, May 9, 1926, 9–11; William Mason, "The Chinese in Los Angeles," *Los Angeles County Museum Alliance Quarterly* 5 (Fall 1967): 20; Ivan Light, "From Vice District to Tourist Attraction: The Moral Career of American Chinatowns, 1880–1940," *Pacific Historical Review* 43, no. 3 (1974): 367–94.

23. Bartlett, *Better City*, 170; Ricardo Romo, *East Los Angeles: History of a Barrio* (Austin: University of Texas Press, 1983), 130; William Deverell, "The Varieties of Progressive Experience," in *California Progressivism Revisited*, ed. William Deverell and Tom Sitton (Berkeley: University of California Press, 1994), 1–11; Maude B. Foster, "The Settlement and Socialism," *The Commons* 4 (May 1899): 3–5.

24. Mark Wild, *Street Meeting: Multiethnic Neighborhoods in Early Twentieth-Century Los Angeles* (Berkeley: University of California Press, 2005), 152–54.

25. Fuller, *Mexican Housing Problem*, 10.

26. Stoddart, "Courts of Sonoratown," 299; Matthews, " House Courts of Los Angeles," 467; Commission of Immigration and Housing of California, "A Report on Housing Shortage" (Sacramento: California State Printing Office, 1923), 5.

27. Mary J. Workman, "Underlying Principles of Social Settlement Work Are Explained," *Los Angeles Examiner*, May 16, 1915, sec. 8, 6; Los Angeles Settlement Association, "First Report" (Los Angeles: B.R. Baumgardt, 1897), 3; Bartlett, *Better City*, 97; Judith Raftery, "Los Angeles Clubwomen and Progressive Reform," in Deverell and Sitton, *California Progressivism Revisited*, 144–74.

28. "A Settlement in Adobe: Interesting Phases of Work in the 'Casa de Castelar' at Los Angeles," *The Commons* 2 (May 1897): 3–4; Los Angeles Settlement Association, "First Report"; Katharine Coman, "Casa Castelar," *The Commons* 7 (January 1903): 12; Los Angeles Settlement Association, "The College Settlement" (Los Angeles, 1905).

29. "From Social Settlement Centers: Los Angeles," *The Commons* 10 (September 1905): 526; Rev. J. M. Campbell, "A Type of the Socialized Mission," *The Commons* 10, no. 8 (August 1905): 463; Mary E. Stilson, "Dana Bartlett: The Modern Mission Father," *Out West* 3 (1912): 222–26.

30. Mary J. Workman, "Brownson House: A Catholic Social Settlement," *Queen's Work* 1 (November 1914): 299–303; Mary J. Workman, "Brownson House, Los Angeles, Cal.," *St. Vincent de Paul Quarterly* 20 (August 1915): 175–77; Michael E. Engh, S.J., "Mary Julia Workman, The Catholic Conscience of Los Angeles," *California History* 72 (Spring 1993): 8–10.

31. Ordinance 27, 510, May 6, 1913, Ordinances, book 653, City Archives; Joseph Auerbach, *A Guide to Friendly Visiting* (Los Angeles: Municipal Charities Commission, ca. 1913); Mary F. Workman, "A California Social Settlement," *Queen's Work* 8 (February 1918): 31–32; Mary Chaffee, *Social Work as a Profession in Los Angeles*, Studies in Sociology Monograph 9 (Los Angeles: University of Southern California, 1918), 10. "In a tactful way," wrote Auerbach, the Friendly Visitor would "teach the woman to become a more efficient home-maker and make the home more attractive to the husband as well as the children" (10).

32. City of Los Angeles Records, vol. 76, pp. 536, 591, City Archives (note: the corresponding ordinance number was never entered); Housing Commission of the City of Los Angeles, "Report of the Housing Commission," June 30, 1908, to June 30, 1909 (Los Angeles, n.d.), 6; "Housing Problem Too Much for Volunteers"; Mary A. Veeder, "The Working of a Housing Commission," *California Outlook* 13, no. 12 (September 14, 1912).

33. Ordinance 14113, Ordinances, vol. 383, p. 63, City Archives; "Council Passes Slum Ordinance," *Los Angeles Express*, February 4, 1907, clipping in John Randolph Haynes Collection, box 76; Pedro G. Castillo, "The Making of a Mexican Barrio: Los Angeles, 1890–1920" (PhD diss., University of California, Santa Barbara, 1979), 104; *Community Survey Made in Los Angeles City*, 21.

34. Housing Commission of the City of Los Angeles, "Report of the Housing Commission," June 30, 1908, to June 30, 1909 (Los Angeles, n.d.), 8; "Council Passes Slum Ordinance," *Los Angeles Express*, February 4, 1907, clipping in John Randolph Haynes Collection, box 76.

35. "Takes Up Flat Study," *Record Herald*, April 6, 1906, clipping in John Randolph Haynes Collection, box 76; Housing Commission of the City of Los Angeles, "Report of the Housing Commission," July 1, 1910, to March 31, 1913 (Los Angeles, n.d.), 10; "Second Annual Report of the Commission of Immigration and Housing of California," 275; Housing Commission of the City of Los Angeles, "Report of the Housing Commission," June 30, 1908, to June 30, 1909 (Los Angeles, n.d.), 6, 8, 12, 22–24; "Move to Form Corporation and House City Poor," *Los Angeles Express*, April 2, 1912, clipping in John Randolph Haynes Collection, box 76; Tom Sitton, *John Randolph Haynes: California Progressive* (Stanford, Calif.: Stanford University Press, 1992), 108–9.

36. Bartlett, *Better City*, 198; *Los Angeles Examiner*, June 5, 1909, clipping in the John Randolph Haynes Collection, box 76; Housing Commission of the City of Los Angeles, "Report of the Housing Commission," June 30, 1909, to June 30, 1910 (Los Angeles, n.d.), 14; "Model Village Interests," unidentified newspaper (August 1911), clipping in John Randolph Haynes Collection, box 76; John Ihlder, "Housing at the Los Angeles Conference," *National Municipal Review* 2 (January 1913): 68–75.

37. Housing Commission of the City of Los Angeles, "Report of the Housing Commission," July 1, 1910, to March 31, 1913 (Los Angeles, n.d.), 24–26; Housing Commis-

sion of the City of Los Angeles, "Report of the Housing Commission," June 30, 1908, to June 30, 1909 (Los Angeles, n.d.), 26.

38. Council File 5174 (1925); *Willmon v. Powell*, 91 Cal App. 1; 266 Pac. 1029 (1928); Housing Authority of the City of Los Angeles, *Handbook of Information* (Los Angeles, 1962), 3–4; Walter Wright Alley, "A Brief History of Public Housing Activities in Los Angeles" (unpublished paper, Los Angeles Housing Commission, 1936), 5–6; please see also "Public Housing in Los Angeles during the Past," *Public Housing and Slum Clearance News*, October 19, 1939, 1, 3.

39. David George Herman, "Neighbors on the Golden Mountain: The Americanization of Immigrants in California" (PhD diss., University of California, Berkeley, 1981), 322–32; "Report of the California Commission of Immigration and Housing" (Sacramento: California State Printing Office, 1921), 8; Mary J. Workman, "Brownson House," *Catholic Charities Review* 2 (September 1918): 213.

40. Commission of Immigration and Housing of California, "Report on an Experiment made in Los Angeles in the Summer of 1917 for the Americanization of Foreign-Born Women" (Sacramento: California State Printing Office, 1917); Commission of Immigration and Housing of California, "Primer for Foreign-Speaking Women," pt. 2, compiled under the direction of Mrs. Amanda Matthews Chase (Sacramento: California State Printing Office, 1918), 5.

41. Herman, "Neighbors on the Golden Mountain," 481–89; "Olson Names McWilliams," *Peoples' World*, January 20, 1939, 1.

42. Emory S. Bogardus, "The Mexican Immigrant and Segregation," *American Journal of Sociology* 36 (July 1930): 75.

43. McClenehan, *Changing Urban Neighborhood*, 10.

CHAPTER 2

"Houses for the Rich Were Also for the Birds"

Designing a Better World

DON PARSON

Public housing architecture in 1930s and 1940s Los Angeles sought to embody design principles that might provide a template for the Modern City—what I refer to as Community Modernism. Socially planned as well as physically designed, public housing projects provided space for human interaction in the forms of recreation, play, shared interests, neighborhood politics, housework, shopping, leisure, and a common sociability. As modern communities, the projects provided the skeletal framework within which a social and personal everyday life might fully flourish, reflecting the social-democratic aesthetic of a planned civic culture. Through the architecture of public housing, one could glimpse a humanitarian vision for modern Los Angeles. At the same time, however, the rapidly expanding city was moving in a fundamentally different direction.

The Architecture of Modern Communities

By the 1920s, the model tenements and restrictive legislation of nineteenth-century housing reform were seen as inadequate by progressive housers due to the speculative nature of the real estate market combined with an outmoded urban form. The tremendous social pressures generated by those poorly or inadequately housed could not be addressed by understanding low-income housing as philanthropy but rather as a public utility that required state intervention in its conception, construction, and management. Both Edith Elmer Wood, in her 1923 *Housing Progress in Western Europe*, and later Catherine Bauer, in the 1934 *Modern Housing*, presented European case studies to demonstrate that government agencies could build and maintain quality, healthful, and efficient low-income housing in an economically feasible manner.[1]

For some American architects, the design of housing was being transformed from stylistic, monumental, and individualistic works of art for a well-to-do clientele into the concern of a humane and social profession directing its expertise to people who could neither afford nor conceive of utilizing their services. Critically examining their profession, a group of architects saw their role as moving beyond the functional nuances of formal design to embodying the broad social, economic, and technical aspects of mass housing. Los Angeles public housing architect Robert Alexander wrote that, after his graduation from Cornell University in 1930, he was "out of work and had plenty of time between ditch digging and an occasional movie set design to think about my 'practice.' I decided that houses for the rich were also for the birds and that 'housing' was a vast social and economic problem that might be solved by technology and economic manipulation and that my professional life work would be more effective tackling these problems."[2]

Catherine Bauer, among others, envisioned housing as part of an international movement aimed at increasing the standard of living for workers in the industrialized countries through both architectural modernism and emerging trends in urban and regional planning. Reporting for the *New Republic* on a 1932 architectural exhibition of recent housing at the Museum of Modern Art, Bauer posed the question: what "is so specifically and unexceptionably un-American

FIGURE 2.1. Urban Redevelopment Commission members tour a slum area to build support for public housing, April 26, 1949.
Getty Research Institute, Los Angeles (2002.M.42), © J. Paul Getty Trust.

about all this modernity?" After ridiculing fears of "the socialism of German housing" and "radical" and "extreme" architecture, she concluded that despite the benefits of the environmental and structural amenities highlighted by the exhibition, ongoing claims of the un-Americanism of this trend in design were rooted in opposition to viewing housing as a positive program of popular wants and needs that were being addressed and affirmed through Modern Architecture. Modern housing, according to Bauer in her book of the same title, was to be implemented not by a patchwork of housing "reform," but within a comprehensive, rational, and planned "new form" of cities. Government intervention in the housing sector was not really socialism, maintained Bauer, but more an enlightened form of municipal capitalism.[3]

The architects of public housing in Los Angeles were influenced by the trends of the Regional Planning Association of America (RPAA) as well as those of the Modern Movement. At its apogee in the 1920s, the RPAA consisted of a loose-knit group of architects, housers, urbanists, and planners that included Charles Whitaker, Clarence Stein, Henry Wright, Robert Kohn, Benton MacKaye, Catherine Bauer, Edith Elmer Wood, Stuart Chase, and Lewis Mumford. Politically liberal, the RPAA thought it desirable to forgo parts of the private market in favor of a planned economy. The conception of the "residential superblock" in Stein and Wright's 1928 design for the new town of Radburn, New Jersey, was seen as the architectural infrastructure of the new spatial order of the Modern City. The superblock concept was characterized by a site plan that embodied the principles of curvilinear streets, common courts, open green space, community centers, and separate pedestrian and vehicular circulation.[4]

The architecture of the Modern Movement was characterized by an austerity of structural form and lack of ornamentation ("form follows function"), concern with material and techniques of construction, and viewing housing as a "machine for living." The Great Depression infused an explicit political awareness into the nuances of Modern design, producing a technological progressivism not dissimilar to that of Marxism. Modern Architecture "was to be a democratic answer to social crisis," according to Robert Hughes. The overt politicism of the Modern Movement was described by Peter Blake as "politically left, anti-capitalist, and dogmatically so." In public housing design, the Modern Movement influence was strongest on structural architecture, while the RPAA inspired site planning; urban design goals and social concerns were common to both schools.[5]

As a liberal and anticapitalist architecture in the service of the welfare state, public housing design embodied the common theme, shared by the RPAA and adherents of Modernism, of community. Modern architects, writes Blake, were "concerned with the creation of a democratic, egalitarian social order: they were concerned with problems of . . . planning humane and healthy communities for all." The community planning synthesis of the RPAA was defined by Roy Lubove as the search for the "urban structure best suited to the satisfaction of human biological and social needs." The RPAA drew upon the Progressives' equation of community with neighborhood democracy as modeled in the settlement houses. For Catherine Bauer, the essential unit for the planning, construction, and administration of modern housing, as well as the social unit for living, was that of the neighborhood. With the construction of the socially planned communities of a better world, the residents themselves would provide the basis of their own politicization and self-government. From the days of its New Deal inception, wrote Albert Mayer, architects and planners had "seen in public housing the chance of creating . . . brave new communities—uncluttered, throbbing with new life and vigor, beacons of urbane living."[6]

In an essay published in 1941, modern architect Richard Neutra put his faith in the opportunities offered by the incipient public housing program of the Los Angeles City Housing Authority (CHA) "to establish new living standards compatible with that longing for informal beauty and comfort which we have found traditional in Southern California." The housing standards that Neutra advocated were the use of new materials and construction techniques leading to the abandonment of historical style; a rationalized floor plan; the integration of indoor and outdoor space; and a compact, practical, and modern kitchen to minimize the unnecessary toil of housework. Separating vehicular and pedestrian traffic, modern housing would be sited to provide a neighborhood with "social gathering space" and "communal play areas for children." By the end of the war Neutra's forethought had become reality. Drawing on previous successful project designs, the National Housing Agency's 1946 "Public Housing Design" virtually endorsed the above housing standards for future consideration. For site planning, the review praised the fact that the majority of public housing projects had been based on the superblock concept and called for the retention of this principle in forthcoming developments.[7]

The impact of RPAA-influenced site planning waned as high-rise public housing—akin to the Modernism of Le Corbusier's "tower in the park"—was promoted by the Public Housing Administration in the 1950s and 1960s. The most spectacular outcome of the high-rise vision was the well-publicized 1972 demolition of the St. Louis Housing Authority's Pruitt-Igoe project, opened in 1954 and designed by the firm of Leinweber, Yamasaki & Hellmuth. The high-rises were assumed to be architectural disasters for their tenants, and Modernism is often viewed as the root of the poisonous tree of bad design. In contrast, Katherine Bristol convincingly argues that political, economic, and social factors—much more than architecture—were decisive in the failure of Pruitt-Igoe. High-rises, according to Brad Hunt, "were a policy choice driven by bureaucratic cost concerns" as the PHA sought to maximize the number of public housing allocations and minimize development expenditures.[8]

Los Angeles was scheduled to have thirty-four 13-story (the municipal height limit at the time) high-rises at three of the projects authorized by the 1949 contract: Elysian Park Heights, Rose Hill Courts Extension, and Aliso Apartments. Because of this plan, Councilman John Holland became the first councilmember to oppose the local public housing program. He testified to Clare Hoffman's Subcommittee on Government Operations that he, upon becoming aware of the high-rise designs in 1951, was reassured by CHA executive director Howard Holtzendorff that "they have been tried in the East. They are all right." "When I learned of the 13-story buildings," Holland then claimed, "I became an opponent of public housing." The plans were canceled when Mayor Fletcher Bowron modified the 1949 contract in August 1952, eliminating the most controversial aspects of the proposed public housing construction. With the defeat of the program in Los Angeles, the era of high-rise public housing never materialized—and neither did the specter of a future high-rise fiasco.[9]

This chapter outlines an inventory of the public projects either constructed or managed (or both) by the CHA. Two of the projects in the 1949 contract that were canceled are also appraised. Such an accounting will allow for the systematic exploration and evaluation of the characteristics of Community Modernism—site planning, architectural form, and the creation of community as a framework for everyday life—in order to design a better world.

Prototypes for Public Housing

The Committee on Community Planning of the American Institute of Architects had, in the 1920s, broadcast to design professionals the RPAA's site planning principles. A number of developments, such as Sunnyside in Queens, New York (1924), and Radburn (1928), demonstrated the viability of these precepts. Prior to the commencement of the CHA's public housing program, two private housing projects were under way in Los Angeles that anticipated the future form of LA's public housing. In addition, several of the architects involved in designing these projects would subsequently have their talents employed by the CHA.

Wyvernwood Village, built in 1939 and located on seventy-two acres in East Los Angeles, was designed by David Witmer and Loyall Watson. The existing city grid was discarded in favor of gently curving streets that followed the contours of the terrain and discouraged through traffic. Community shops were provided for on site, as were recreation centers, playgrounds, and sequestered parking areas. Its 1,102 dwellings—ranging in size from three to six rooms—were arranged in 142 two-story buildings that faced large, landscaped spaces, rather than the street.

Wyvernwood advertisements highlighted its modern conveniences: "There is no chance for housework becoming drudgery—nor is there any time for

FIGURE 2.2. Wyvernwood Garden Apartments, showing the site design and relationship to the city. Architectural Forum, *May 1940.*

MORE TIME TO

Relax and Play

There is no chance of housework becoming drudgery—nor is there any time for boredom in these new and modern Wyvernwood apartments. Housework is fun and it's done in a flash—the outdoors constantly beckons.

Badminton courts invite those who are energetic, and there are lots of little spots throughout the spacious gardens for "just lazin' in the sun". Meanwhile, the children are either in one of the many little nearby playyards or just a bit farther down the lane enjoying supervised play under the watchful eye of an experienced instructor.

When you live in these brand new modern apartments there is lots of time for pleasant relaxation. All outdoors invites you to come enjoy the sunshine.

NUMEROUS BADMINTON COURTS, LIGHTED FOR NIGHT PLAY, OFFER PLEASANT RECREATION

CHILDREN ARE SAFE IN THE MANY WELL PROTECTED AND WELL EQUIPPED PLAY YARDS

FIGURE 2.3. A page from "Life in Wyvernwood," promotional brochure, ca. 1941. *Courtesy of Los Angeles Conservancy and Nathan Marsak.*

boredom in these new and modern Wyvernwood apartments. Housework is fun and it's done in a flash—the outdoor constantly beckons." The kitchens, with two sinks, mahogany work surfaces, a Frigidaire in place of an icebox, a range, and plenty of drawers and cupboard space, were "as modern as tomorrow." The design of Wyvernwood was very attractive to the proponents of public housing; however, the project was expected to attract young professionals, junior executives, and businesspeople. Rents in Wyvernwood would be prohibitive for low-income, working-class families. "The rub:," wrote *People's World*, "rents will range from $30.25 to $50 per month."[10]

Baldwin Hills Village, located in southwestern Los Angeles, was originally conceived in 1938 but not completed until late 1941. Its design team consisted of Reginald Johnson, Robert Alexander, Lewis Wilson, Edwin Merrill, landscape architects Fred Barlow and Fred Edmondson, and consulting architect Clarence Stein. The project was composed of a sixty-five-acre residential superblock containing 627 housing units, whose living room windows looked out upon either a central village green or the smaller garden courts. An administrative building, serving as the point of contact between tenants and landlord, and a club house, consisting of a ninety-foot-long social hall adjoined by a kitchen, a darkroom, and a small lending library, were located on the formal garden court at the western edge of the development. The superblock design, the separation of pedestrians and autos, and the village green that served as the communal heart and spine of Baldwin Hills Village reflected the orientation of the RPAA. "The Radburn Idea," Clarence Stein acknowledged of the development, "was given the most complete and most characteristic expression." The unassuming architectural style of the one- and two-story frame-and-stucco buildings shared the severe simplicity of Modernism. Robert Alexander recalled that the "external appearance [of Baldwin Hills Village] is rather bland and not typed as to style."[11]

The Original Public Housing Projects Constructed under the 1937 Housing Act

Between 1939 and 1942, the CHA built ten permanent low-income projects—Ramona Gardens, Pico Gardens, Estrada Courts, William Mead Homes, Pueblo del Rio, Hacienda Village, Avalon Gardens, Rancho San Pedro, Rose Hill Courts, and Aliso Village—under the auspices of the 1937 Housing Act. With the exception of Ramona Gardens, retained for low-income tenants, the nine remaining projects were converted to housing for war workers and their families following the entry of the United States into World War II.

Constructed on a vacant thirty-two-acre site, Ramona Gardens was completed in January 1941 as the premier project of the CHA. Its 610 dwelling units—128 one-bedroom, 356 two-bedroom, and 126 three-bedroom apartments—were

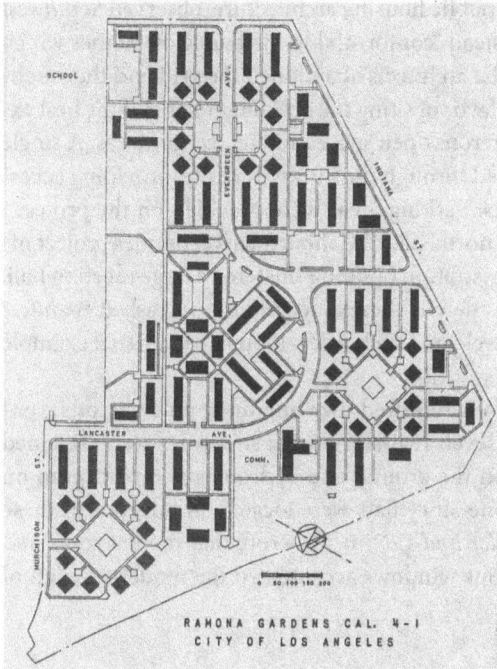

FIGURE 2.4. Site plan for Ramona Gardens.
"Public Housing—Los Angeles Area—Analysis and Report—May 1950," Housing Research Council of Southern California, 1950, from the collection of Don Parson.

contained in 112 buildings. These two-story structures, of five different types containing four, six, or eight families, were unassuming flat-roofed concrete boxes: "The monotony of the large group of structures," wrote the *Southwest Builder and Contractor*, "has been relieved by painting the exterior walls in soft, warm colors in varied combinations . . . giv[ing] the whole project a cheerful aspect." Selection of warm gray, yellow, old rose, and pale green exterior tones "accentuated the proportions in the architectural design of the buildings which in its extreme simplicity is highly pleasing."[12]

The project's sloping site was divided into four superblocks, connected by curving streets and pedestrian paths. "Every effort has been made," wrote Ramona Gardens architect Eugene Weston Jr., "to reduce public streets and increase the number of walks and play areas that are distinctly separated from the hazards of automobile traffic." In addition, a one-story T-shaped administration center contained management offices, a tool shop for project maintenance, a social room, a kitchen, and accommodations for a day nursery and playroom. Adjacent were outdoor playgrounds for children as well as a recreation area for adults.[13]

Avalon Gardens was the first CHA project to be completed following Pearl Harbor. The project's sixty-two buildings contained dwellings for 164 families. All but fourteen were one-story, including eight single-family houses. The design was not typical of most public housing architecture, observed *Southwest Builder and Contractor*, but instead "conform[s] to the bungalow homes which predominate in the district." The architects abandoned the grid and thorough-fares of private subdivisions in favor of siting the buildings to obtain the best ex-posure to the sun as well as generous open spaces and recreation areas. A single street—Caliburn Drive—looped through the fifteen-acre site, providing access and egress for project residents. Parking areas were provided on the project's southern boundary and on the north side of Caliburn Drive. Besides project of-fices and shop space, the administration building sheltered a large meeting hall, a craft room, and a kitchen. "Where is there a neighborhood," asked *Architect and Engineer*, "that would not welcome such a development as a visual example in community planning?"[14]

Pueblo del Rio contained four hundred dwelling units on a site of seven-teen and a half acres. Its fifty-seven two-story brick structures were designed with kitchen and living area on the ground and bedrooms and bathroom on the second floor. Eighty-two one-story flats were located on the ends of these buildings. The *Southwest Builder and Contractor* wrote that the flat roofs and wide overhangs shading spacious windows accentuated the modern design of

FIGURE 2.5. Pueblo del Rio housing, ca. 1948.
Getty Research Institute, Los Angeles (2002.M.42), © J. Paul Getty Trust.

FIGURE 2.6. Kitchen in a Pueblo del Rio apartment, ca. 1948.
Getty Research Institute, Los Angeles (2002.M.42), © J. Paul Getty Trust.

the buildings, and "a very pleasing effect has been produced by simple lines and good architectural proportioning." "Architecture is modern," observed *California Arts & Architecture* of the project, "lines are simple, and fenestration is unusually good due to careful planning on the part of the architects." The exterior walls were variously painted with shades of tan and off-white, highlighted with a chocolate dado treatment. While Pueblo del Rio's site planning was somewhat restricted by the grid of the existing street pattern, all of the buildings faced pedestrian courts, with parking confined to two areas located at opposite corners of the project. The one-story administration building contained a community hall, machine and woodworking shops, nursery facilities, and the project manager's office.[15]

Pico Gardens' thirty-six frame-and-stucco buildings contained 260 two-story row houses on a fourteen-acre site. With 59 one-bedroom, 45 two-bedroom, 70 three-bedroom, and 86 four-bedroom dwellings (there were four times as many four-bedroom units in Pico Gardens than in all of the other contemporary projects put together), the result was, fondly recalled by the postwar manager of Pico Gardens Oliver Haskell, "a real city-built slum—highest concentration of humanity in the whole city." Project Architect John C. Austin thought the project, designed for larger families and "the ever-growing and

FIGURE 2.7. Inside the nursery school at Pueblo Del Rio, ca. 1948.
Getty Research Institute, Los Angeles (2002.M.42), © J. Paul Getty Trust.

teeming population of children," would prove to be one of the CHA's most practical. Two central courtyards were used as play space. Only one street bisected
the project, while, located at the corners of the four superblocks, motor courts
provided convenient parking. Walkways linked the motor courts to the housing
and provided pedestrian circulation throughout the project. The community
building, used extensively by both project residents and the adjacent neighborhood, was situated on Pico Gardens' eastern periphery, where it was criticized
as not being readily accessible to a majority of tenants.[16]

With a design team that included Robert Alexander, architect of Baldwin
Hills Village, and David Witmer and Loyall Watson, architects of Wyvernwood,
Estrada Courts articulated the connection between public housing projects
and their private prototypes. The project's thirty wood-frame structures had
originally been designed to be built of reinforced brick and concrete but, in
order to eliminate the metal—a critical war material—used in this process,
they were redesigned following the outbreak of the war. The buildings contained 214 apartments—two-bedroom and four-bedroom units were designed
as row houses, while the 74 one-bedroom units and 26 three-bedroom units
were planned as flats. Twenty-three of the latter were purposely located on the

lower level, often as a wing to a two-story block of flats, in order to situate families with the greatest number of children on the ground. Second floor flats were
furnished with balconies to provide outdoor living space, while an outdoor sitting area—an extension of the entrance porch—was featured for the first-floor
apartments.[17]

Three alleys and two streets were removed from the 9.75-acre site of Estrada
Courts, creating a traffic-free superblock. At the center was a large recreation
area, containing playground equipment, a spray pool, and benches, for use not
only by project residents but those from the surrounding neighborhoods as
well. A one-story L-shaped administration building, overlooking the central
recreation area, contained project offices, a repair shop, a kitchen, recreation
rooms, and a nursery yard. Estrada Court's neutrally designed buildings and
careful site planning combined with spacious landscaping provided, wrote the
Times, "the maximum amount of lawn and recreational area . . . to permit the
greatest privacy."[18]

The fifteen-acre site of William Mead Homes was located adjacent to Chinatown and the Ann Street School in the neighborhood known locally as Dogtown.
The project's twenty-four residence buildings—"very simple and functional"
according to Southwest Builder and Contractor—contained 132 one-bedroom,
235 two-bedroom, 72 three-bedroom, and 10 four-bedroom dwelling units, for
a total of 449 units. With two exceptions, the L-shaped structures fit together
to form continuous esplanades throughout the grounds. Three-story buildings
were composed of flats on the ground floor with two-story row houses above,
while two-story buildings were planned with flats on both floors. The living
rooms of all units opened onto either a terrace or a balcony. A varied color
scheme was selected, according to project architect Herbert J. Powell, "to give
character and individuality to each of the apartments."[19]

Not a "classical" superblock site plan, William Mead Homes' three trans-
versing streets were designed not as thoroughfares but to provide residential
parking and access. Play areas for small children and "sitting out" spaces for
adults were provided for each group of four buildings. At the southeast corner
of the site, a large playground was located next to the administration building,
which contained administrative offices, a community hall, craft rooms, and a
kitchenette.[20]

Rancho San Pedro held 285 dwellings—93 one-bedroom, 144 two-bedroom,
and 48 three-bedroom apartments—in thirty-three concrete and frame-and-
stucco structures. Located on twelve and a half acres, the project was arranged in
a modified grid design. One of the two preexisting streets from the three-block
site was closed to through traffic. Eight smaller blocks of four buildings each
were grouped around an interior court, which could be utilized as play areas.
Parking courts were found at the corners of each small block. Centrally located,

the 2,348 square-foot community building with social hall and an adjoining 45,900 square-foot playground were easily accessible to a majority of the tenants, despite the rectangular pedestrian circulation and the bisection of the project by First Street.[21]

Hacienda Village was composed of 72 one-story frame-and-stucco structures. On the 17.63-acre site there were 52 one-bedroom, 96 two-bedroom, 28 three-bedroom, and 8 four-bedroom apartments—a total of 184 dwellings. Two streets made semicircles through the project, giving access to well-landscaped courts for auto parking. Asphalt walkways carried pedestrians throughout the project. A 21,600 square-foot playground and a small community center, combined with a management/maintenance building, were placed near the center of the project.[22]

Containing 100 living units, Rose Hill Courts was the smallest project constructed by the CHA. Praised as "typically Californian," the project's sixteen buildings held 28 one-bedroom, 48 two-bedroom, 20 three-bedroom, and 4 four-bedroom apartments. Similar to Estrada Courts, the concrete and brick masonry of Rose Hill Courts' original design was bypassed in favor of

FIGURE 2.8. Outside housing units at Hacienda Village, 1950.
Housing Authority of the City of Los Angeles Photograph Collection, Southern California Library, Los Angeles.

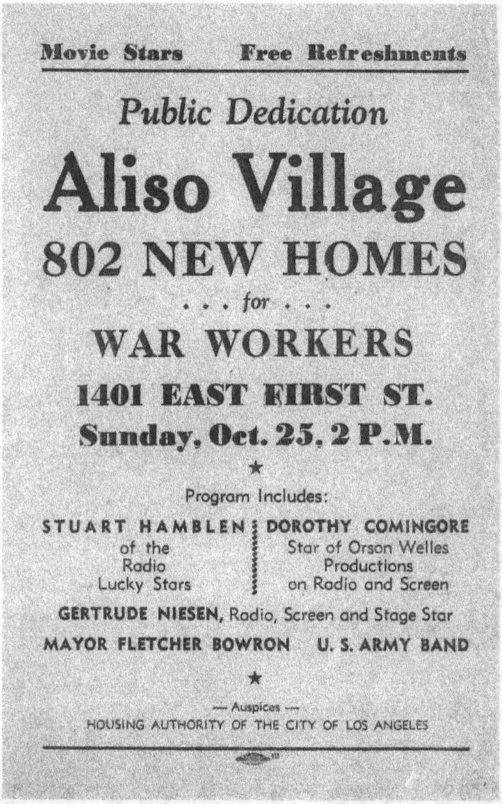

Movie Stars   Free Refreshments

Public Dedication
Aliso Village
802 NEW HOMES
. . . *for* . . .
WAR WORKERS
1401 EAST FIRST ST.
Sunday, Oct. 25, 2 P.M.
★

Program Includes:

STUART HAMBLEN ┊ **DOROTHY COMINGORE**
of the   ┊   Star of Orson Welles
Radio   ┊   Productions
Lucky Stars   ┊   on Radio and Screen

GERTRUDE NIESEN, Radio, Screen and Stage Star

MAYOR FLETCHER BOWRON   U. S. ARMY BAND

★

— Auspices —
HOUSING AUTHORITY OF THE CITY OF LOS ANGELES

FIGURE 2.9. Flyer for the public dedication of Aliso Village, 1942. *From the collection of Don Parson, from an uncited collection at the Huntington Library, San Marino, Calif.*

wood-frame construction due to defense priorities for materials. In addition to the large play area for children and outdoor sitting spaces for adults located near the administration building, ample yards were provided for each apartment. Sharing the building with the administrative office, the project's assembly room could be divided—for varying concurrent activities—by accordion doors.[23]

Dedicated on October 25, 1942, Aliso Village was the final, and largest, of the CHA's ten Wagner Act projects. On the project's thirty-one acres were sited 802 dwelling units: 218 one-bedroom, 378 two-bedroom, 156 three-bedroom, and 22 four-bedroom apartments. Cost limitations resulted in a highly simplified and stripped-down design so that architectural expression was represented by, according to project architect Lloyd Wright, "the structural arrangement of the dwelling units within the apartment blocks." Utilizing prefabricated walls, stairways and partitions, the thirty-four buildings of Aliso Village comprised 12 three-story U-shaped types containing 28 apartments each, 9 two-story buildings with 32 apartments each, and 11 two-story C-shaped types

FIGURE 2.10. Aerial view of Aliso Village, ca. 1949.
Getty Research Institute, Los Angeles (2002.M.42), © J. Paul Getty Trust.

FIGURE 2.11. Aliso Village
green, ca. 1948–49.
*Getty Research Institute,
Los Angeles (2002.M.42),
© J. Paul Getty Trust.*

FIGURE 2.12. The nursery school at Aliso Village, the first integrated public housing project in Los Angeles, ca. 1948–49. *Getty Research Institute, Los Angeles (2002.M.42), © J. Paul Getty Trust.*

FIGURE 2.13. A luncheon at Aliso Village during the Negro Leaders Tour, building support for public housing, May 8, 1952. *Housing Authority of the City of Los Angeles Photograph Collection, Southern California Library, Los Angeles.*

TABLE 2.1. Original Public Housing Projects Constructed under the 1937 Housing Act

Project Name and Location	Region	Units	Area (acres)	Dilapidated Units Previously on Site	Date Completed	Architects
Ramona Gardens: Ramona Blvd. & Indiana St.	East	610	32	0	1/2/41	Housing Architects Associated: George J. Adams,* Walter S. Davis, Ralph Flewelling, Eugene Weston Jr., Lewis Eugene Wilson, Lloyd Wright
Rose Hill Courts: Mercury St. off N. Huntington Dr.	East	100	5.23	42	6/1/42	Rose Hill Architects: W. F. Ruck,* Claud Beelman
Estrada Courts: 8th St., east of Soto	East	214	9.73	125	6/15/42	Robert E. Alexander, Winchton L. Risley, David J. Witmer, Loyall F. Watson; Associated Architects
Pico Gardens: Santa Ana Fwy. & 4th St.	East	260	14	222	8/1/42	Project Architects Associated: John C. Austin,* Sumner Spaulding, Earl Heitschmidt
Aliso Village: 1st St. & Mission Rd.	East	802	34.3	350	12/1/42	Housing Group Architects: Ralph C. Flewelling,* George J. Adams, Eugene Weston Jr., Lewis E. Wilson, Lloyd Wright
William Mead Homes: N. Main & Ann Sts.	Central	449	15.2	101	10/1/42	Housing Associates: P. A. Eisen,* Norman Marsh, Herbert Powell, Armand Monaco, A. R. Walker, David D. Smith
Avalon Gardens: 88th Pl. & Avalon Blvd.	South	164	14.9	0	5/12/42	California Housing Architects: Carleton W. Winslow,* Roland E. Coate, Samuel E. Lunden
Pueblo Del Rio: 55th St. & Long Beach Ave.	South	400	17.5	182	5/15/42	Paul R. Williams,* Richard Neutra, Adrian Wilson, Wurdeman & Beckett, G. B. Kaufman
Hacienda Village: 104th St. & Compton Ave.	South	184	17.6	19	5/15/42	Planning Associates: Paul R. Williams,* Weldon Beckett, Adrian Wilson, Richard Neutra, Walter Wurdeman
Rancho San Pedro: 3rd & Center Sts., San Pedro	Harbor	285	12.5	29	8/15/42	Reginald Johnson, A. C. Zimmerman, H. Roy Kelley, James R. Friend

*Chief architect.

including 14 apartments each. The structures were arranged in court groups with sixty-foot passages—which included shade-giving "ramadas"—from one court to another. Chief architect Ralph Flewelling wrote that the arrangement of families within the court groups "should provide a means of healthy co-operative effort." Vehicular and pedestrian traffic was segregated. A continuous *paseo* walkway circled through the project, while one-way lanes and motor court parking accommodated autos.[24]

In addition to housing the project's management offices, an assembly room, craft rooms, and kitchen, the administration building held the headquarters of the CHA. Aliso Village surrounded the Utah Street School, adjacent to which was the project's nursery school, provided with rest rooms, play rooms, kitchen, nurse's room, and an outdoor playground with equipment. Additional play areas for children—swings, slides, sandboxes, and wading pools—were located in the courts so as to allow parental supervision from apartment windows, while tennis courts, baseball diamonds, and adult exercise equipment were to be found in the center. Landscape architects Fred Barlow and Katherine Bashford envisioned the *paseos* to be lined with shade trees; the project's three hundred vines, six hundred trees, and fourteen hundred shrubs would, according to the *Times*, "lend a park-like atmosphere to the new community." "In recognition of modern trends," which stressed "convenience, sanitation and time and labor saving devices," Aliso Village kitchens were equipped with a stove, a refrigerator, a water heater, tile sinks, built-in cabinets, and washable walls.[25]

Public War Housing

Public war housing was seen by many designers as a practical means to vindicate the theories of Modern Architecture by demonstrating its applicability to the accelerated pace of life brought about by the war. Production bottlenecks, caused by the massive rehousing of industrial workers, were to be addressed by new building technologies that would reduce construction time. Sanitary and healthful housing would be the foundation for a vigorous, more productive workforce, while social planning, cooperative living, and minimal housework would allow more free time for public housing inhabitants. "War housing can be an example of our war aims," wrote architect Joseph Allen Stein, "a constant reminder of the meaning and promise of democracy." Financed by the federal government under the Lanham Act and managed by the CHA were five permanent public war housing projects, all located near the wartime plants in the harbor area. After the war, they were to be either transferred or sold to local, state, or federal government agencies; transferred or sold to the CHA as low-rent public housing projects; or sold for private residential purposes.[26]

Permanent Public War Projects Managed by the CHA

The most noteworthy project completed during the war years was Richard Neutra's Channel Heights project. Located on 150 acres of hilly topography in San Pedro overlooking Los Angeles Harbor, six hundred housing units were arranged in three superblocks with a ravine running down the center. Cul-de-sacs provided vehicular access to the housing, while pathways, including pedestrian underpasses at road crossings, segregated the foot traffic. Instead of bulldozing and leveling the site, it was treated like a garden. Drayton Bryant, manager of Channel Heights during the war, bought fifty dollars' worth of wildflower seeds to spread in the canyon to produce "the best wildflower show in Los Angeles." For three years afterward he received protests from federal authorities about his unauthorized purchase of flower seeds.[27]

The project included 222 residential structures, composed of one-story duplexes alternating with two-story, four-family units. Integrated into the landscape, the housing expressed, as *Architect and Engineer* pointed out, "Neutra's philosophy that the immediate surroundings of a home are as much a part of it

FIGURE 2.14. View of Channel Heights, designed by Richard Neutra, with the harbor in the distance, 1950.

Getty Research Institute, Los Angeles (2002.M.42), © J. Paul Getty Trust.

FIGURE 2.15. Inside a Channel Heights apartment, with the boomerang chair
Richard Neutra designed for residents and later turned into a do-it-yourself kit, ca. 1943.
© *J. Paul Getty Trust. Getty Research Institute, Los Angeles (2004.R.10).*

as the interior." Providing dramatic views of the harbor, living rooms included large sliding glass windows, and all second-story homes had balconies. Tenants who so desired could purchase, at low cost, Neutra-designed furniture for their apartments. Along with a community center, Channel Heights contained a market, a garden and craft center, and a nursery school.[28]

Channel Heights tenants were pleased with the project but rejected aspects of Neutra's romanticism. His Hispanic names were replaced, as tenant, organizer, and writer Henry Kraus recounts, with more manageable counterparts for the Anglicized tongue:

> The girls in the office reported that half of the people couldn't remember their court name to speak it and hence the expedient was adopted of always asking them for their "back door number." Eventually utility triumphed over poetry however and in the project jargon "Tobago Court" was known only by the more humble yet serviceable "Tobacco Road" while "Patzcuaro" became "Paddy's Square."

Neutra would meet with the project's tenants and management to iron out design problems and oversights. With materials salvaged from the nearby naval yards, Channel Heights tenants built a volunteer fire company, a carpentry shop, and a nursery school by themselves, which Neutra designed without payment. When later asked by federal inspectors how he could account for the three extra structures not on the blueprints, Drayton Bryant replied, "I've never tried." As architectural historian Esther McCoy pointed out, Channel Heights "was perhaps the only war housing development that was not handled as a drawing board problem."[29]

Located on a 37.6-acre site in LA's Harbor City neighborhood, the 80 two-story structures of Normont Terrace contained 400 housing units, of which 60 had one bedroom, 240 had two bedrooms, and 100 had three bedrooms. With wood frame construction, redwood siding, flat roofs, and overhangs, the buildings were of the modern style. Replacing the previous partial grid street pattern, two new streets now curved through the project forming a Y—dividing the project into three superblocks—while a system of walkways provided pedestrian access. In addition to the spacious lawns that surrounded the project,

FIGURE 2.16. The market nearing completion. Channel Heights won an Honor Award from the Southern California Chapter of the American Institute of Architects in 1947.
Photo by Julius Sherman. Richard and Dion Neutra Papers (Collection 1179), Library Special Collections, Charles E. Young Research Library, UCLA.

TABLE 2.2. Permanent Public War Housing Projects Managed by the CHA

Project Name and Location	Region	Units	Area (acres)	Architects
Normont Terrace: 990 W. 256th St.	Harbor	400	37.6	Winston Risley & Stanley Gould
Dana Strand Village: Wilmington Ave. & C St.	Harbor	384	21.17	George J. Adams & Graham Latta
Portsmouth Homes and Annex: 2323 Portsmouth Rd.	Harbor	128	22.2	?
Wilmington Hall: Cottages	Harbor	26	2.42	?
Channel Heights: Western Ave. & 25th St.	Harbor	600	149.65	Richard Neutra

there were four play areas, a baseball diamond, and a volleyball court. One wing of the L-shaped community building—comprising a large assembly room, a kitchen, and two meeting rooms (which functioned as a nursery school)—was used for social functions. The other wing contained the administrative functions of management offices, storage, and services, while a shaded porch and terrace adjoined them.[30]

Dana Strand Village was a 384-unit development housed in sixty-eight frame-and-stucco structures. The project contained 72 one-bedroom, 212 two-bedroom, 92 three-bedroom, and 8 four-bedroom dwellings. It was built on five city blocks—twenty-four acres—in Wilmington, adjacent to the harbor, and existing streets were used to provide access to five central parking lots, around which the buildings were grouped. "The basic superblock scheme," wrote the Housing Research Council of Dana Strand Village, develops "star-like around the centrally located parking area." Throughout the project were scattered six small play areas. Across a perimeter street was located the community building with social hall, lounge, and administrative offices. Added subsequent to the housing, the center was built to serve both Dana Strand Village as well as its temporary annex.[31]

Temporary Public War Housing Projects Managed by the CHA

In addition to the permanent projects, there were twenty-two temporary public war housing projects managed by the CHA. Termed a "war-time auto court" by Harrison Stephens, Banning Homes was designed by William Allen and W. George Lutzi for highly mobile war workers and their families. Located on a 156-acre site, the project's 218 single-story buildings—containing 2,000 one-bedroom and two-bedroom furnished family apartments—were arranged around a natural amphitheater. "Architectural design is uncluttered and the

FIGURE 2.17. Construction of Banning homes in San Pedro, 1943.
Getty Research Institute, Los Angeles (2004.R.10), © J. Paul Getty Trust.

buildings and their arrangement conform pleasantly with the rolling, hilly nature of the site," wrote *California Arts & Architecture*. "The wide area over which the project is spread avoids any semblance to 'barracks.'" At the center of the project were located five community buildings that accommodated "practically every facility found in a small town." The frame-and-stucco structures contained a gymnasium, auditorium, administrative offices, library, barber and beauty shops, drug store, game room, and infirmary.[32]

With 2,126 double and single rooms, Wilmington Hall was a "dormitory city" constructed for unattached war workers on a twenty-four-hour production day. Residents at Wilmington Hall, staffed by 185 service and maintenance workers, were furnished with, according to the CHA, "everything but toothbrushes and soap." The forty-acre site comprised two projects, both designed by the same architect, Lewis Eugene Weston. Cal. 4109 consisted of 62 one-story buildings and Cal. 4301 had 5 two-story structures. "Despite dormitory arrangement," observed *California Arts & Architecture*, "the project is not unpleasant to the eye." The extensive community center—containing a theater and gymnasium building, music room, cafeteria, library, lounge, barber shop, laundry and cleaning facilities, community store, and infirmary—was not only a response to the immediate demands of war housing but, as Whitney Smith wrote, "forms a splendid nucleus for a post-war neighborhood."[33]

Composed of temporary dwelling units (TDUs), portable family dwellings (PFDs), and portable shelter units (PSUs), trailers, and dormitories, the majority of the temporary projects were of an easy- and cheap-to-build wood frame and plywood construction. Their function was to provide housing units for war workers as quickly and cheaply as possible. Carey McWilliams contended that "consultation with defense workers would have been the proper functional approach to the problem; it would, also have been the democratic procedure. . . . Instead, housing has been 'handed out' in a rather hit-or-miss fashion." While site planning and community facilities of the "temporaries" may have been more than adequate, they did not live up to the architectural standards for a modern community envisioned by the Keynesian left. The Lanham Act called for the demolition of the temporary projects within two years of the war's end. Fearing a progenitor of postwar slums, progressive architects concurred with the Lanham Act while urging the retention of the community centers as the foundation for postwar modern housing.[34]

FIGURE 2.18. Community entertainment at Corregidor Park with housing behind, April 7, 1948.
Housing Authority of the City of Los Angeles Photograph Collection, Southern California Library, Los Angeles.

TABLE 2.3. Temporary Public War Housing Projects Managed by the CHA

Project Name and Location	Region	Units	Type
Pacific Park: 910 Rio Vista	East	200	Trailers
Estrada Courts Annex #1: 3300 Glenn Ave.	East	100	PSUS
Estrada Courts Annex #2: 1280 Rio Vista	East	60	PSUS
*Pacific Park Annex #2: 2059 Perlita Ave.	Central	24	Trailers
Corregidor Park: 1700 E. 48th Pl.	South	110	PSUS
Corregidor Park Annex #1: 1700 E. 48th Pl.	South	44	PSUS
Corregidor Park Annex #2: 4066 1/2 S. Compton St.	South	44	PSUS
Corregidor Park Annex #3: 2746 Staunton Ave.	South	120	PSUS
Pueblo Del Rio Annex: 5525 Long Beach Ave.	South	88	TDUS
Jordan Downs: 2151 Century Blvd.	South	512	TDUS
Imperial Courts: 2200 E. 114th St.	South	100	TDUS
Imperial Courts Annex #1: 112th & Mona	South	40	PSUS
Imperial Courts Annex #2: 1256 E. 109th St.	South	80	PSUS
Imperial Courts Annex #3: 2200 E. 114th St.	South	22	PSUS
Lumina Park: 20210 S. Western Ave.	South	75	Trailers
Lumina Park Annex: 20210 S. Western Ave.	South	50	Trailers
Banning Homes: 801 Cabinet Dr.	Harbor	2,000	War Apartments
Wilmington Hall (Cal 4109 & 4301): 700 W. "E" St.	Harbor	2,126	Dormitories
Dana Strand Annex: 401 Hawaiian Ave.	Harbor	260	PSUS
Bataan Park: 1601 Fries Ave.	Harbor	240	PSUS
Western Terrace: 1655 Seaport Dr.	Harbor	998	PFDS

*Directly operated by the Federal Public Housing Authority.
TDUS: temporary dwelling units; PFDS: portable family dwellings; PSUS: portable shelter units.

CHA Public Housing Projects for Veterans

The CHA initiated five temporary projects for veterans—Rodger Young Village, Basilone Homes, Keppler Grove, Pacific Park Annex, and Wilmington Hall.

Located on a 112-acre site in Griffith Park, 1,500-unit Rodger Young Village was constructed from surplus quonset huts from the naval base at Port Hueneme. A total of 750 huts, measuring twenty by forty-eight feet, were divided into two housing units with a floor space of 480 square feet. Each dwelling contained a living room–kitchen and two bedrooms, with two clothes closets and a linen closet, and was furnished with an icebox and stove. The project's architects, William Allen and W. George Lutzi, organized the site so that an internal loop road linked the shopping center, the school, and community and administrative buildings with thirty residential blocks of twenty-five huts each. Eight fully equipped playgrounds were spaced throughout the site. With a capacity of about six thousand residents, the project was serviced by a supermarket, pharmacy, newsstand,

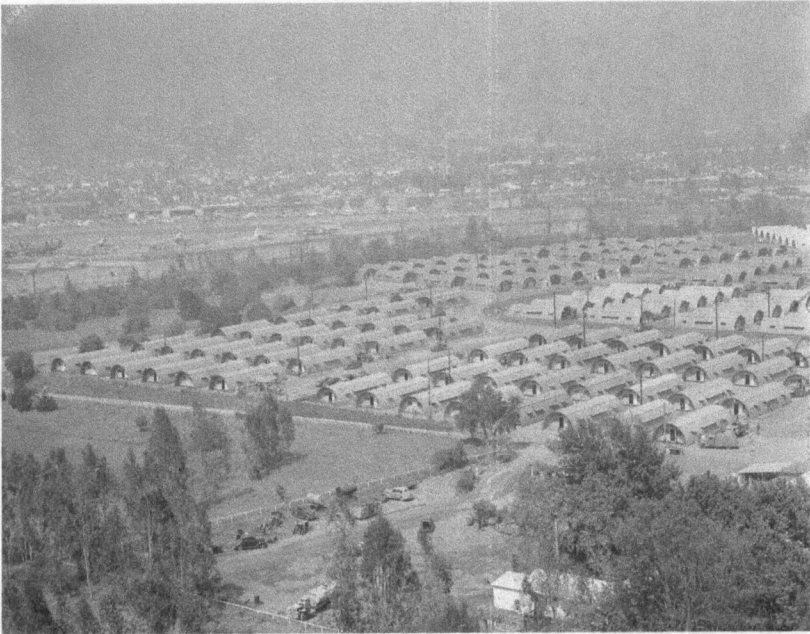

FIGURE 2.19. Rodger Young Village seen from a Griffith Park hillside, 1946.
Los Angeles Times *Photographic Archives (Collection 1429), Library Special Collections,*
Charles E. Young Research Library, UCLA.

FIGURE 2.20. Woman posing in front of her quonset hut unit in
Rodger Young Village, constructed from surplus war materials, ca. 1947.
Housing Authority of the City of Los Angeles Photograph Collection,
Southern California Library, Los Angeles.

FIGURE 2.21. Dedication of Rodger Young Village, April 27, 1946.
Housing Authority of the City of Los Angeles Photograph Collection,
Southern California Library, Los Angeles.

doctor and dentist offices, a pool hall, an ice cream parlor, and a baby shop. The
village contained its own school (twenty-eight buildings with an enrollment
of 977 in 1949), a community hall, a social hall, a public library branch, a post
office, adult education classes, a well-baby clinic, a volunteer fire brigade, and
offices for veterans' organizations. An elected Resident Council was integrally
involved in community life and project management. With the abatement of the
acute wartime housing crisis, Rodger Young Village was terminated in 1954.[35]

Basilone Homes was located in the northern San Fernando Valley on a 112-
acre site near Hansen Dam. The project's 1,500 units consisted of 420 units
of reassembled surplus war housing from Port Orchard, Washington, with the
balance being two-story army barracks from Gardner Field and Lemorre Field,
both north of Los Angeles. The design of Basilone Homes was attributed to
architect Armand Monaco. Built with conventional materials, the project contained one-, two-, and three-bedroom units, furnished with a gas range, heater,
and cooler. As with Rodger Young Village, social and community facilities were
integrated within the project. Seventeen school buildings housed the project's

1,029 pupils in 1949. The adjacent community of Roscoe donated plants, seeds, and other gardening supplies to Basilone tenants for landscaping. Manager Sidney Green thought that the project was a very good example of people acting in the face of a perceived need and then doing the best they could to make it work. Basilone Homes was terminated in 1954.[36]

Keppler Grove, located in Wilmington's Banning Park, was originally designed as a hundred-unit WAC barracks of thirty-one buildings. Redesigned by Armand Monaco, Keppler Grove consisted of 84 one-bedroom, two-bedroom, and three-bedroom units. The project's lease expired in 1949. Pacific Park Annex was a hundred-unit trailer park located on land leased from the Union Pacific Railroad at Third and Anderson on the Eastside. Each trailer could accommodate four people, with cooking and heating by gasoline pressure and kerosene, respectively. Wilmington Hall was a 2,126-unit temporary dormitory development for defense workers that was converted by the Red Cross into 486 light housekeeping units for veterans and their families, owned and operated by the CHA. The project was terminated in 1949.[37]

FIGURE 2.22. Keppler Grove, ca. 1940s.
Housing Authority of the City of Los Angeles Photograph Collection,
Southern California Library, Los Angeles.

TABLE 2.4. CHA Public Housing Projects for Veterans

Project Name and Location	Region	Units	Type
Rodger Young Village: Griffith Park	Central	1,500	Quonset huts
Pacific Park Annex: 3rd & Anderson	Central	100	Trailers
Basilone Homes: Hansen Dam	North	1,500	Surplus military housing
Keppler Grove: 307 East M St.	Harbor	84	Converted WAC barracks
Wilmington Hall: 435 Neptune St.	Harbor	486	Converted war worker dormitory

Public Housing Projects Constructed under the 1949 Housing Act

Nine of the eleven public housing projects that had been scheduled as part of the 1949 Housing Act—Jordan Downs, Nickerson Gardens, Estrada Courts Extension, Aliso Apartments, Pueblo del Rio Extension, Rancho San Pedro Extension, Imperial Courts, Mar Vista Gardens, and San Fernando Gardens—were completed during the period 1953 to 1955. The two largest projects of the 1949 contract—Rose Hill Courts Extension and Elysian Park Heights—were canceled by Mayor Poulson in July 1953.

Despite the war against public housing that raged from 1951 to 1953, work on the sites selected for the 1949 contract did proceed, albeit slowly. Under intense political attack, these projects did not receive the extensive coverage by the contracting or architectural presses as did those constructed prior to the end of World War II. As employment opportunities for professional architects blossomed during the postwar years, architects' support for the public housing program correspondingly withered. The Modern Architecture/RPAA synthesis, a heretofore characteristic of public housing design in Los Angeles, began to unravel. Aghast that federal tax dollars were being used to hire name architects to design "simple" houses for the poor, one congressman at the Subcommittee on Government Operations hearings in 1953 queried, could not "any competent architect . . . qualify for that type of job"? The fiscal wisdom of providing playgrounds in the projects and allowing two bathrooms in a four-bedroom unit were similarly scrutinized.[38]

Four of the nine completed projects were annexes to projects that had already been built under the Wagner Act. Estrada Courts Extension's eleven-acre site contained 200 units housed in 37 two-story frame-and-stucco buildings. The nine-acre site of Rancho San Pedro Extension was composed of 194 apartments in 26 two-story frame-and-stucco structures. Pueblo del Rio Extension held 270 units in 52 concrete block and frame-and stucco buildings on a fifteen-acre site. And occupying a little over nine acres, the 336 units at Aliso Apartments were accommodated within 22 three-story concrete block structures. (Before the contract modification of August 1952, Aliso Apartments was to have four 13-story buildings containing 520 units.) Architecturally, the buildings were indistinguishable from the original projects. Neither Rancho San Pedro Extension nor Estrada Courts Extension had their own community center or central play area (though smaller play areas were provided on the sites). Tenants and their children were expected to use the facilities in the parent project.[39]

Three of the largest projects were built in the community of Watts. William Nickerson Jr. Gardens was the largest CHA project—and the largest public housing project west of the Mississippi River, containing eleven hundred housing units. On the fifty-five-acre site were 162 two-story apartment buildings, some with one-story wings, which held 106 one-bedroom, 667 two-bedroom, 254 three-bedroom, 78 four-bedroom, and 5 five-bedroom apartments. With flat roofs, wide overhangs, and wide windows, the frame-and-stucco structures were described as "typically Californian." Radiating outward from the community center, the curving concentric streets allowed an observer a view of only six to eight buildings from any given point. Located throughout the project were eight play areas averaging almost 3,000 square feet each. The result, according to the *Journal of Housing*, was "the feeling of small neighborhoods." At the center of the project was a park-like 136,600-square-foot playground, a management-maintenance building, and a 12,200-square-foot community building consisting of meeting and craft rooms, a kitchen, a snack bar, and a 8,260-square-foot assembly hall.[40]

A modified grid design characterized the twenty-nine-acre site of Imperial Courts. The project's 498 dwelling units were composed of 51 one-bedroom, 318 two-bedroom, 70 three-bedroom, 56 four-bedroom, and 3 five-bedroom units. Existing streets divided the 86 two-story concrete block structures into six distinct superblocks, each containing off-street parking areas. In addition to the obligatory management-maintenance building, there was a centrally located community building/social hall and a 74,500-square-foot play area. Seven other play areas, averaging 2,105 square feet each, were scattered throughout the project.[41]

On forty-three acres, Jordan Downs held 700 dwelling units—81 one-bedroom, 257 two-bedroom, 276 three-bedroom, 62 four-bedroom, and 24 five-bedroom apartments—housed in 103 two-story concrete block and frame-and-stucco buildings. The irregular-shaped site was composed of four elongated superblocks whose borders were determined by existing east-west streets. Parking and vehicular access were available both on the street and in small parking areas. A management-maintenance building, a 4,080-square-foot community building that contained a 1,230-square-foot social hall, and a 70,000-square-foot central play area were located in the more than four-hundred-foot gap between the upper superblock and the lower ones. This was supplemented by four additional play areas averaging 1,500 square feet each.[42]

In West Los Angeles, Mar Vista Gardens, situated on thirty-nine acres, contained 601 dwelling units composed of 62 one-bedroom, 246 two-bedroom, 221 three-bedroom, 62 four-bedroom, and 10 five-bedroom apartments. A classic superblock site, the conjoined Marionwood Drive/Allin Street looped through the project, providing vehicular ingress and egress for the 62 two-story residential structures of concrete block and frame-and-stucco construction. A management-maintenance building, a community building with a social hall, and a 120,000-square-foot play area were centrally located. In addition, five other play areas, with an average space of 2,600 square feet each, were located throughout the project.[43]

Completed in October 1955, San Fernando Gardens was to be the final project constructed by the CHA. A total of 312 housing units were originally planned on the thirty-three-acre site, which would have, according to *Progressive Architecture*, "preserved the site's semi-rural character." Due to "economic adjustments," however, the number of units was increased to 448. In all, 42 one-bedroom, 152 two-bedroom, 180 three-bedroom, 50 four-bedroom, and 24 five-bedroom apartments were located in 81 concrete-block structures composed of one- and two-story row houses, interspersed with two-story duplexes. To maximize the

FIGURE 2.23. Community meeting at Jordan Downs, December 1953.
Housing Authority of the City of Los Angeles Photograph Collection,
Southern California Library, Los Angeles.

TABLE 2.5. Public Housing Projects Constructed under the 1949 Housing Act

Project Name and Location	Region	Units	Area (acres)	Depilated Units Formally on Site	Date Completed	Architects
Estrada Courts Extension: Olympic Blvd. & Lorena St.	East	200	10.9	43	3/31/54	Paul Robinson Hunter, Carl Louis Easton (associate)
Aliso Apartments: 1st & Clarence Sts.	East	336	9.2	242	6/30/54	W. F. Ruck
Jordan Downs: 103rd St. & Alameda St.	South	700	49.48	117	12/31/53	James R. Friend
Imperial Courts: Imperial Hwy. & Croesus Ave.	South	498	36.1	112	8/9/54	Spaulding-Rex & DeSwarte
Nickerson Gardens: Imperial Hwy. & Central Ave.	South	1,110	68.6	345	3/21/55	Paul R. Williams
Pueblo del Rio Extension: 55th St. & Long Beach Ave.	South	270	15	94	8/31/55	Theodore Criley Jr. & Henry C Burge; Robt. E. Faxon, Associate
Rancho San Pedro Extension: 1st & Beacon Sts.	Harbor	194	8.7	83	7/10/53	Armand Monaco
Mar Vista Gardens: Inglewood Blvd. & Braddock Dr.	West	601	43.2	23	4/15/54	Albert Criz
San Fernando Gardens: San Fernando Rd. & Van Nuys Blvd.	North	448	33.5	157	10/31/55	Arthur B. Gallion & Victor D. Gruen, Associated Architects

space between buildings, the architects mixed straight and angled buildings, resulting in a project "arranged in an orderly though informal fashion, with pleasant vistas and private terraces for all." Painted in subdued colors, the buildings "achieve a feeling of unity without monotony, and a sense of spaciousness and lightness." Two curving streets, connected by an access road divided the site into five superblocks, each with ample parking areas. The CHA listed no community facilities for San Fernando Gardens save five playgrounds, averaging 2,390 square feet each, corresponding to the superblocks.[44]

Unbuilt Projects

Two remaining projects, Elysian Park Heights and Rose Hills Court Extension, were included in the 1949 public housing contract but were never built. Both

FIGURE 2.24. View of Chavez Ravine, ca. 1950.
Housing Authority of the City of Los Angeles Photograph Collection,
Southern California Library, Los Angeles.

went through a complete design process and then faced attacks by real estate interests and adjoining communities claiming incompatibility of scale. The passage of anti-public-housing Proposition B and defeat of pro-housing mayor Bowron in 1952 put the final nail in the coffin of public housing in Los Angeles.

Having solidly supported the public housing program as a planning commissioner from 1945 to 1950, architect Robert Alexander was offered his choice of the sites selected for the 1949 contract on which to be architect by councilmember Howard Holtzendorff. Alexander, wanting a small project that he could undertake by himself, chose the Pacoima site (San Fernando Gardens), which was intended to house some of the Mexican American population in the San Fernando Valley. But Holtzendorff informed Alexander that he wanted him to work on the Chavez Ravine project, the apple of his eye, because he both trusted Alexander and liked his work at Baldwin Hills Village and Estrada Courts. But with a project the size of Chavez Ravine, a prestigious co-architect would be required. Alexander suggested Richard Neutra since they had worked together before.[45]

Designed by Richard Neutra and Robert Alexander, the never-built Elysian

Park Heights project at Chavez Ravine was to contain 3,364 housing units for 17,000 people on a 278-acre site. A total of 481 one-bedroom, 1,922 two-bedroom, 742 three-bedroom, 202 four-bedroom, and 18 five-bedroom apartments were to be arranged in 24 thirteen-story towers and 163 two-story buildings facing garden plots or finger parks. Incorporated within the project were to be sites for three churches, three schools, kindergartens, nurseries, a community hall, a fifteen-hundred-person auditorium, a commercial center, and a managerial building. Rather than bisect the site, major roads would remain on the periphery of the project, while interior streets, providing access for residents, were to be cul-de-sacs.[46]

The Elysian Park Heights design, as Tom Hines observed, did not resemble Neutra's Channel Heights nor the prototype of Alexander's Baldwin Hills Village. Instead it was more closely related to Neutra's 1920s modernist utopia "Rush City Reformed," a conceptual plan for a million-person metropolis with high-rises predominating. Neutra saw high-rise housing as a design solution to the problems of population density and open space. "However romantic it may be to dream of retaining the present charm of rural backwardness," he wrote, "the area cannot be redeveloped even with suburban bungalows. A realistic use

FIGURE 2.25. The model for Elysian Park Heights, ca. 1952.
Richard and Dion Neutra Papers, Department of Special Collections,
Charles E. Young Research Library, UCLA.

of the site by any developer will require an urban housing solution to suit the location and to take advantage of the beautiful but very hilly terrain." He proposed that small families requiring one- or two-bedroom apartments be placed in tall buildings where they would share the advantages of view windows, spectacular vistas, and access to a recreation area on each floor. "It is not hard to imagine that under such conditions these apartments will be easily the most popular in the program," wrote Nicholas Cirino, development director of the CHA, to Neutra and Alexander. He warmly praised "the basic concept for the design for the thirteen-story buildings as evolved by your office," a design that, wrote Cirino, other architectural firms were studying and emulating at Rose Hill Courts extension and Aliso Apartments.[47]

In contrast, former RPAA members Clarence Stein and Catherine Bauer were strongly opposed to the project's site plan. Stein asked the project's site planner, Simon Eisner, how he could morally and ethically justify taking people used to living on the ground with gardens, chickens, and small animals and placing them in high-rise buildings. Eisner recalled Neutra convincing the principal of Palo Verde School—a Mrs. Slavin—that the public housing project in Chavez

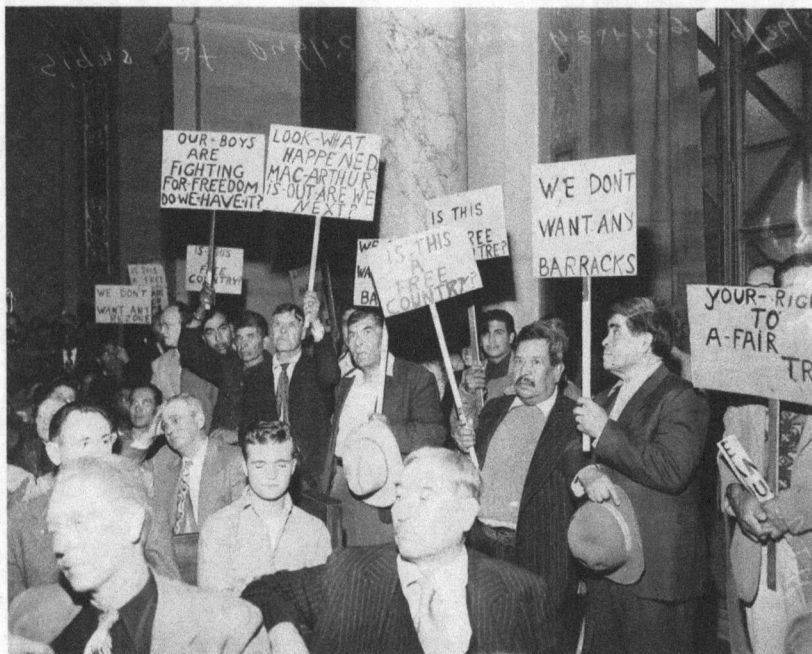

FIGURE 2.26. Residents of Chavez Ravine protest at the hearing on public housing in Los Angeles City Hall, 1951.
Courtesy of University of Southern California, on behalf of the USC Libraries Special Collections.

FIGURE 2.27. Richard Neutra testifying at a hearing on
LA's public housing program in City Hall, 1951.
*Courtesy of University of Southern California,
on behalf of the USC Libraries Special Collections.*

Ravine would preserve the lifestyle and culture of the district. "I sat there thinking in the back of my mind of those twenty-four thirteen-story buildings and didn't know whether to choke or what." In 1982 Alexander reflected on the proposed project not being humanistic and, if built, becoming a potential disaster like Pruitt-Igoe in St. Louis. His comments on the construction of the baseball stadium in Chavez Ravine instead of Elysian Park Heights were pointed: "Dodger Stadium is a blessing compared to the housing project we designed, and I'm glad we lost."[48]

The other canceled project, Rose Hill Courts Extension in the northeast LA neighborhood of El Sereno, was to be located on a hilly 201-acre site, on which there were just 167 existing dwelling units (of which 76 were substandard). Designed by William Allen and W. George Lutzi, the proposed project was to have 2,099 dwelling units, consisting of 228 one-bedroom, 1,195 two-bedroom, 523 three-bedroom, 142 four-bedroom, and 10 five-bedroom units. There were to be 6 one-story and 191 two-story garden apartments of masonry and/or frame-and-stucco construction, as well as six 13-story elevator apartment buildings of reinforced concrete. The 13-story buildings consisted of one-

and two-bedroom units for use by couples or families with older children. The buildings were well spaced, oriented to allow plenty of light and air, and sited to be integrated with the larger community by placing one-story buildings along the eastern project boundary, adjacent to the existing neighborhood, and by placing the high-rise buildings low in the valley. There was a community recreational building of approximately twenty thousand square feet and additional "tot lots" for small children. The project's recreational and cultural facilities were designed to serve not only the residents of Rose Hill Courts Extension but also those of the adjacent neighborhood.[49]

▢ ▢ ▢

Public housing architects in Los Angeles had successfully blended elements of RPAA site planning and the Modern Movement's structural design with a shared quest for community to conceive and plan housing projects distinguished by their human scale. They had provided a template for a new spatial order for Los Angeles—that of a Community Modernism. Such experimentation with architecture and design came to an abrupt halt following the public housing war of the early 1950s. Under Mayor Poulson, Modernism would forsake low-income housing in favor of the commercial and monumental glorification of the central city. Liberated from its anticapitalist origins, Modernist form would not follow function so much as it followed dollars.

The "dreary deadlock" of public housing architecture on the national level was caustically commented on by Catherine Bauer in 1957 as dragging along "in a kind of limbo, continually controversial, not dead but never more than half alive." In 1962 Albert Mayer surveyed the "arrested development" of contemporary public housing project design, calling for a reinvigorated commitment to public housing architecture. He saw architectural talent and resources directed toward "the famous monuments in the city center." Instead he called for a decentralization of architectural accumulation so as to benefit the neighborhoods and communities of daily life: "If we are achieving architectural excellence in what may be called the 'fancy' buildings and dullness or architectural poverty in the workaday areas, the record is bad: a record not in accord with our democratic professions."[50]

Since 1955, there have been no public housing projects built in Los Angeles embracing the Community Modernism envisioned by the Keynesian left prior to the McCarthy era. San Fernando Gardens, completed in October 1955, was the last project to be both constructed and managed by the Housing Authority of the City of Los Angeles. The agency has instead utilized federal programs established in the 1960s that have provided tenant subsidies for private housing and the leasing of privately constructed units. Under the Department of Housing and Urban Development's HOPE VI program (HOPE is an acronym for Homeownership Opportunities for People Everywhere) begun in 1992, which provided grants to "eradicate severely distressed public housing" and build mixed-income housing, the CHA has been upscaling and downsizing its projects. Utilizing both public funds and private investment, Normont Terrace (now called Harbor Village) and Pico Gardens and the Aliso Apartments (the Pico-Aliso complex) have become mixed-income communities that feature for-sale homes and Section 8 rental assistance as well as conventional public housing. In contrast to the Community Modernism of yore, the revamped projects have a "New Urbanism" imagery that emphasizes not a design for living that facilitates human interaction and sociability, but an integration into and acceptance of the anomie of the existing built environment.

NOTES

1. Gail Radford, *Modern Housing for America: Policy Struggles in the New Deal Era* (Chicago: University of Chicago Press, 1996), chaps. 2 and 3; Langdon W. Post, *The Challenge of Housing* (New York: Farrar and Rinehart, 1938), 118, 247, 277; Edith Elmer Wood, *Housing Progress in Western Europe* (New York: E.P. Dutton, 1923); Catherine Bauer, *Modern Housing* (Boston: Houghton Mifflin, 1934).

2. Robert Alexander to Don Parson, January 13, 1982, in possession of Don Parson. The once commonly used expression "for the birds" implies worthless, uninteresting, and/or undesirable; a slightly older definition is "full of crap."

3. Radford, *Modern Housing for America*, 83; Catherine Bauer, "Are Good Houses Un-American?," *New Republic* 70 (March 2, 1932): 74; Post, *Challenge of Housing*, 118, 247, 277; Bauer, *Modern Housing*.

4. Carl Sussman, ed., *Planning the Fourth Migration: The Neglected Vision of the Regional Planning Association of America* (Cambridge, Mass.: MIT Press, 1976); Mark Luccarelli, *Lewis Mumford and the Ecological Region: The Politics of Planning* (New York: Guilford, 1995), 123, 151–53; Edward K. Spann, *Designing Modern America: The Regional Planning Association of America and Its Members* (Columbus: Ohio State University Press, 1996).

5. Robert Hughes, *The Shock of the New* (New York: Knopf, 1981), 167; Peter Blake, *No Place Like Utopia: Modern Architecture and the Company We Kept* (New York: Knopf, 1993), 13.

6. Blake, *No Place Like Utopia*, 5; Roy Lubove, *Community Planning in the 1920's: The Contribution of the Regional Planning Association of America* (Pittsburgh: University of Pittsburgh Press, 1963), 1; Luccarelli, *Lewis Mumford and the Ecological Region*, 115; Bauer, *Modern Housing*, xv, 147, 247; Albert Mayer, "Public Housing Architecture Evaluated from PWA Days up to 1962," *Journal of Housing* 19 (October 15, 1962): 450.

7. Richard J. Neutra, "Homes and Housing," in *Los Angeles: Preface to a Master Plan*, ed. George W. Robbins and L. Deming Tilton (Los Angeles: Pacific Southwest Academy, 1941), 194, 197–200; National Housing Agency and Federal Public Housing Authority, "Public Housing Design: A Review of Experience in Low-Rent Housing" (Washington, D.C.: Government Printing Office, June 1946).

8. Katherine G. Bristol, "The Pruitt-Igoe Myth," *Journal of Architectural Education* 44 (May 1991): 163–71; D. Bradford Hunt, "What Went Wrong with Public Housing in

Chicago? A History of the Chicago Housing Authority, 1933–1982" (PhD diss., University of California, Berkeley, 2000), 274, 303–9.

9. U.S. Congress, House, Special Subcommittee of the Committee on Government Operations, *Hearings on Investigation of Public Housing Activities in Los Angeles*, 83rd Cong., 1st sess. (Washington, D.C.: Government Printing Office, May 13, 18, 19, 20, 21, 27, 1953), 414. For a rich history of Mayor Bowron's tenure, please see Tom Sitton's book, *Los Angeles Transformed: Fletcher Bowron's Urban Reform Revival, 1938–195* (Albuquerque: University of New Mexico Press, 2005).

10. "Case Studies: 1102-Apartment Development. Wyvernwood Village Housing Project," *Architectural Record* 86 (September 1939): 101–7; Life in Wyvernwood, advertisement brochure (Los Angeles: Wyvernwood Rental Office, n.d.); "Nation's Greatest Home Job Starts Here Soon," *Los Angeles Times*, July 14, 1938, pt. 1, 1, 3; "Huge L.A. Housing Project to Open," *People's World*, July 27, 1939, 2.

11. Richard D. Berry, "Baldwin Hills Village—Design or Accident," *Arts and Architecture* 81 (October 1964): 18–20+; Clarence S. Stein, *Toward New Towns for America, 1951* (Cambridge, Mass.: MIT Press, 1989), 189; Robert Alexander, oral history transcript, 98.

12. "Ramona Village Housing Project to Contain 610 Dwelling Units," *Southwest Builder and Contractor* 94 (September 29, 1939): 12–13; "Paint Styling Gives Glamour to Buildings in Ramona Gardens Low-Rent Housing Project," *Southwest Builder and Contractor* 97 (February 21, 1941): 8–11.

13. Eugene Weston Jr., "Ramona Gardens Housing Project," *California Arts & Architecture* 57 (December 1940): 34–35.

14. "Avalon Gardens: A Defense Housing Project," *California Arts & Architecture* 59 (April 1942): 32; "Avalon Gardens, First City Housing Project Completed for War Workers," *Southwest Builder and Contractor* 99 (June 19, 1942): 8–11; "Avalon Gardens: A Los Angeles Housing Project of Unusual Interest," *Architect and Engineer* 148 (January 1942): 15–20.

15. "Pueblo Del Rio Housing Project Notable for New Construction Features," *Southwest Builder and Contractor* 99 (April 17, 1942): 8–12; "Pueblo Del Rio: A Low Rental Housing Project," *California Arts & Architecture* 59 (May 1942): 32; Frederick W. Jones, "Pueblo del Rio: Los Angeles' Most Recent Housing Project," *Architect and Engineer* 150 (September 1942): 11–21.

16. Housing Authority of the City of Los Angeles, *Handbook of General Information* (Los Angeles, December 1953), 13; Oliver Haskell interview, October 3, 1982; J. C. Austin, "Housing Project Constructed as Buildings Were Being Moved from the Site," *Southwest Builder and Contractor* 101 (January 15, 1943): 7–10; Housing Research Council of Southern California, *Public Housing: Los Angeles Area: Analysis and Report* (Los Angeles, 1950), 13.

17. Robert E. Alexander, Winchton L. Risley, David J. Witmer, and Loyall F. Watson, "Ground Broken for Estrada Courts Low-Rent Housing Project as War Begins," *Southwest Builder and Contractor* 98 (December 14, 1941): 8–9; Robert E. Alexander, Winchton L. Risley, David J. Witmer, and Loyall F. Watson, "Estrada Courts Dedicated to Housing Man Behind Production Line," *Southwest Builder and Contractor* 100 (July 17, 1942): 12–15.

18. "Housing Project Ceremony Set," *Los Angeles Times*, December 7, 1941 pt. 2, 6;

Alexander et al., "Ground Broken for Estrada Courts," 8–9; Alexander et al., "Estrada Courts Dedicated," 12–15.

19. "William Mead Homes All Brick Masonry and Concrete Construction," *Southwest Builder and Contractor* 100 (October 16, 1942): 8–12; Herbert J. Powell, "William Mead Homes Housing Project Finished, Is Opened to Families of War Workers," *Southwest Builder and Contractor* 101 (April 16, 1943): 8–10.

20. "William Mead Homes All Brick Masonry and Concrete Construction," 8–12; Powell, "William Mead Homes Housing Project Finished," 8–10.

21. "The Housing Authority of the City of Los Angeles Presents a Solution," *California Arts & Architecture* 60 (May 1943): 47–66; Housing Research Council of Southern California, *Public Housing*, 17; Housing Authority of the City of Los Angeles, *Handbook of General Information*, 15.

22. "Housing Authority of the City of Los Angeles Presents a Solution," 47–66; Housing Research Council of Southern California, *Public Housing*, 29; Housing Authority of the City of Los Angeles, *Handbook of General Information*, 21.

23. "Rose Hill Courts Typically Californian Housing Project in Foothills," *Southwest Builder and Contractor* 100 (October 16, 1942): 14–16; "Rose Hill Courts," *California Arts & Architecture* 59 (August 1942): 32–33.

24. "Aliso Village, Los Angeles," *Architect and Engineer* 152 (January 1943): 13–21; Lloyd Wright, "Aliso Village Group Housing Project Result of Coordinated Planning," *Southwest Builder and Contractor* 101 (May 21, 1943): 12–17; "Prefabrication and Precision Expedite Construction of Aliso Village," *Southwest Builder and Contractor* 100 (August 21, 1942): 12–14; Ralph C. Flewelling, AIA, "Group Planning Features Aliso Village Housing Project on East Side," *Southwest Builder and Contractor* 97 (May 16, 1941): 12–13.

25. Wright, "Aliso Village Group Housing Project," 12–17; "Developed Community to Be Christmas Gift," *Los Angeles Times*, October 23, 1942, pt. 1, 17; "Landscaping Plans Made," *Los Angeles Times*, October 23, 1942, pt. 1, 16; "Convenience Featured in Kitchens," *Los Angeles Times*, October 23, 1942, pt. 1, 20.

26. Joseph Allen Stein, "Blueprint for War Housing," *California Arts & Architecture* 59 (May 1942): 18–20, 38; Housing Authority of the City of Los Angeles, *Preliminary Report on the Disposition of Public War Housing in Los Angeles* (Los Angeles, September 27, 1945).

27. Thomas S. Hines, *Richard Neutra and the Search for Modern Architecture: A Biography and History* (Berkeley: University of California Press, 1982), 179; Esther McCoy, *Richard Neutra*, Masters of World Architecture Series (New York: George Brazillier, 1960), 24; Drayton Bryant interview, August 20, 1982.

28. Hines, *Richard Neutra*, 179–80; "Channel Heights," *Architect and Engineer* 154 (September 1943); McCoy, *Richard Neutra*, 25; "Channel Heights Housing Project," *Architectural Forum*, March 1944, 65–74.

29. Henry Kraus, *In the City Was a Garden: A Housing Project Chronicle* (New York: Renaissance Press, 1951), 74; Drayton Bryant interview, August 20, 1982; McCoy, *Richard Neutra*, 25.

30. "Worthy Ideas from Wartime Housing," *Architectural Record* 94 (November 1943): 55–60.

31. Harrison Stephens, "LA Completes 5 Lanham Act Projects," *Architect and Engi-*

neer 154 (September 1943): 18–25; Housing Research Council of Southern California, *Public Housing*, 37; Housing Authority of the City of Los Angeles, *Handbook of General Information*, 32.

32. Stephens, "LA Completes 5 Lanham Act Projects," 18–25; "Banning Homes," *California Arts & Architecture* 59 (November 1942): 42–43; "Banning Homes, 2,000-Unit War Housing Project at San Pedro Completed," *Southwest Builder and Contractor* 101 (19 March 1943): 8–10, 36.

33. Stephens, "LA Completes 5 Lanham Act Projects," 18–25; "Housing Project Cal-4109," *California Arts & Architecture* 59 (November 1942): 40–41; Whitney R. Smith, AIA, "Wilmington Hall, Prototype for a Neighborhood Center," *California Arts & Architecture* 61 (December 1944): 34–35, 39; "Duration Dormitories for Three Thousand War Workers at Wilmington," *Southwest Builder and Contractor* 100 (July 17, 1942): 8–11.

34. Housing Authority of the City of Los Angeles, *Preliminary Report on the Disposition of Public War Housing in Los Angeles*; Carey McWilliams, "Labor Plans for Defense Housing," *Arts and Architecture* 59 (March 1942): 22; Henry S. Churchill, "War Housing Remainders—Post-war Slums," in *New Architecture and City Planning*, ed. Paul Zucker (New York: Philosophical Library, 1944), 308–10.

35. "Erection of Quonset Huts Continues at Park Despite Suit of Donor's Heir," *Western Construction News* 21 (April 1946): 109; Housing Authority of the City of Los Angeles, *Los Angeles Cares for Its Veterans* (Los Angeles, 1949), 4–11; Mike Eberts, *Griffith Park: A Centennial History* (Los Angeles: Historical Society of Southern California, 1996), 245; "List of Architects Employed in the Construction of Housing Developments Built by the Housing Authority of the City of Los Angeles," Bowron Collection, box 49, folder: Housing Authority; Dana Cuff, *The Provisional City: Los Angeles Stories of Architecture and Urbanism* (Cambridge, Mass.: MIT Press, 2000), pt. 4; Dick Turpin, "Big Rodger Young Village Vanishing," *Los Angeles Times*, April 4, 1954, pt. 2, 1–2.

36. Housing Authority of the City of Los Angeles, *Los Angeles Cares for Its Veterans*, 11–12; "New 1500-Unit Veterans Housing Project Planned," *Los Angeles Times*, June 17, 1946, pt. 2, 1; "List of Architects Employed"; Sidney Green interview, July 8, 1982; "4,500 Vet Homes Ordered Emptied," *People's World*, July 30, 1953, 3.

37. "List of Architects Employed"; "Veterans Move into 1st Conversion Project," *Western Housing* 28 (February 1946): 9; "Vet Housing Project Opens," *Examiner*, June 11, 1946; Housing Authority of the City of Los Angeles, *Los Angeles Cares for Its Veterans*, 12–15.

38. Art White, "L.A. Public Housing Quietly Goes On," *Los Angeles Mirror*, January 7, 1953, 16; *Hearings on Investigation of Public Housing Activities in Los Angeles*, 29, 193, 445.

39. Housing Authority of the City of Los Angeles, *Handbook of General Information*, 23, 24, 26, 28; Housing Authority of the City of Los Angeles, "Summary of General Information of All Housing Projects," June 13 1951, Fletcher Bowron Collection, box 50, folder: Reports from Housing Authority.

40. "Nickerson Gardens: Big Project of Small Neighborhoods," *Journal of Housing* 11 (December 1954): 426–27; Housing Authority of the City of Los Angeles, *Handbook of General Information*, 22.

41. Housing Authority of the City of Los Angeles, *Handbook of General Information*, 27.

42. Ibid., 25.

43. Ibid., 29.

44. "Housing Project: Los Angeles, California," *Progressive Architecture* 35 (February 1954): 72–75; "General Practice: Housing Project," *Progressive Architecture* 37 (April 1956): 120–23; Housing Authority of the City of Los Angeles, *Handbook of General Information*, 30.

45. Alexander, oral history transcript, 335–36. On June 3, 1952, Los Angeles voters defeated Proposition B, 378,000 to 259,000, voting to overturn the city's 1949 contract with the federal government that would have provided $110 million to build 10,000 units of public housing.

46. Richard Neutra, "Report upon Inspection and Analysis of Chavez Ravine," May 5, 1950, p. 8, Neutra papers, box 47; Thomas Hines, "Housing, Baseball, and Creeping Socialism: The Battle of Chavez Ravine, Los Angeles, 1949–1959," *Journal of Urban History* 8 (February 1982): 132–33.

47. Hines, *Richard Neutra*, 229; *Elysian Park Heights: A Project of Urban Reconstruction*, n.d., Richard Neutra Collection, box 47; Nicholas Cirino to Neutra and Alexander, April 25, 1951, Richard Neutra Collection, box 47.

48. Simon Eisner oral history transcript, 67, 70; Robert Alexander oral history transcript, 337, 342; Alexander to Parson, January 13, 1982.

49. Housing Authority of the City of Los Angeles, "Summary of General Information of All Housing Projects."

50. Catherine Bauer, "The Dreary Deadlock of Public Housing," *Architectural Forum* 106, no. 5 (May 1957): 140; Albert Mayer, "Public Housing Architecture," 452, 453.

CHAPTER 3

"A New Deal Democrat Plus"

The Progressive Judicial Career of Stanley Moffatt

DON PARSON

From 1938 to 1950 Stanley Moffatt was a justice of the peace for San Antonio Township in Los Angeles County. With a left-liberal perspective—which he described to the *People's World*, the daily newspaper of the Communist Party on the West Coast, as being "a New Deal Democrat plus"—Moffatt's legal actions were praised by the left of the Los Angeles area and condemned by the region's conservatives. Yet despite the controversies in which he was embroiled, he is scarcely remembered. After his death, he cremated. He left no papers save two ledgers dealing with the time he was a practicing attorney in Fresno, donated to the Southern California Library for Social Studies and Research.[1]

I had come across Stanley Moffatt's name several times while doing research on various subjects and was impressed by his legal judgments and the way they were handled by the press. He was swept up in several contentious proceedings during the Cold War era in Los Angeles that would have long-lasting reverberations in the region's policy making and politics. A political biography of Stanley Moffatt seemed an important undertaking as he was a person whose ideas and actions should be remembered. In this chapter I focus on Moffatt's judicial career, tracing the themes of the cases he handled—and reactions to them—during his twelve-year tenure as justice of the peace. I will consider the way in which the developing Cold War shaped his career, illustrated by several cases, and examine his contentions with the California Un-American Activities Committee (CUAC) and his involvement with the Independent Progressive Party (IPP).

Stanley Moffatt was born August 4, 1885, in Mansfield, Florida, the son of Charles W. and Fannie Louise (Jones) Moffatt. He received a bachelor's degree from the University of Chicago in 1912 and a doctorate in jurisprudence from Stanford University in 1914. In 1922, he married Doris Drummond of Wisconsin. The couple had one child, Doris Margaret, before Mrs. Moffatt's premature death in 1928. Moffatt's legal career consisted of private law practice in Los Angeles (1914), Fresno (1916–28), and South Gate (1930). He was elected judge of San Antonio Township in Los Angeles County in 1938 and reelected in 1942 and

1946. He served as the first vice-chairman of the Los Angeles County Democratic Central Committee from 1944 to 1948, when he resigned in order to run for a congressional seat with the IPP in 1948.[2]

Starting with his arrival in South Gate from Fresno, the news coverage of Stanley Moffatt as a public figure reveals a civic-minded individual, embroiled in a variety of political and social causes. He would represent police officers seeking reinstatement to the South Gate Police Department, become a director of the newly established South Gate Kiwanis club (Kiwanis clubs were and are business-oriented, community-minded civic organizations dealing with issues of relevance to children and youth), and represent the South Gate Better Government Association in filing a complaint of intervention in Superior Court seeking a special election to recall the mayor and a councilman from South Gate.[3]

During the interwar years, the politics of suburban South Gate were characterized by struggles over development. Merchants sought to promote local economic growth, while working-class home owners tried to insulate themselves from the ups and downs of market-centered capitalism. By 1930, the working-class home owners had gained political ascendancy in South Gate. Becky Nicolaides, in her history of the working-class suburbs of Los Angeles, attributes this in part to the "savvy leadership" of their organizational base:

FIGURE 3.1. Judge Stanley Moffatt, justice of the peace in Huntington Park (San Antonio Township), ca. 1940s.
Los Angeles Daily News *Negatives (Collection 1387),*
Library Special Collections, Charles E. Young Research Library, UCLA.

"Attorney Stanley Moffatt, in particular, armed them with legal expertise to counteract the questionable tactics of the city council."[4]

Stanley Moffatt's first foray into electoral politics appears to have been in the 1932 state primary when, as a progressive Republican, he stood for a seat in the Sixty-Ninth Assembly District. He did not win the seat, and at some point during the following two years Moffatt changed his party affiliation from Republican to Democrat. In September 1934, the *Los Angeles Times* reported that Stanley Moffatt was a County Central Committeeman for the Democratic Party in the Sixty-Ninth District, elected during that year's primary. The paper noted "a strange intermingling of Socialists and Democrats," with over one-half of the Democratic committee men supporting Upton Sinclair for governor. Indeed, Nicolaides notes that South Gate heavily supported Sinclair and his program to End Poverty in California (EPIC), returning 61 percent of its votes for Sinclair in the 1934 gubernatorial election. Enthusiastic involvement in the movement led to the formation of an EPIC club, which was closely allied with local Democrats. Stanley Moffatt emerged as a leader of both the EPIC club and Democratic Party, providing a direct link between the two. He pronounced that the EPIC club would "be forced to take an active part in all matters of civic and political importance in South Gate."[5]

In 1934, Moffatt ran for justice of the peace for San Antonio Township in a close, but losing, race with Edward H. Miller. Standing for superior judge, office number 12, in 1936, Moffatt was reprimanded by the *Times* for distributing campaign literature that identified his Democratic principles and affiliations in his play for a nonpartisan office. In 1938, Moffatt was successful in his electoral bid for San Antonio Township's justice of the peace. He was given the oath of office on December 1, beginning the first of three 4-year terms that he would serve in that office.[6]

Justice of the Peace

San Antonio Township was located in the area between the boundaries of the old Spanish land grant of Rancho San Antonio to the north and the city of Downey on the south, abutting the City of Los Angeles to the west and the old San Gabriel River on the east. The township was a Los Angeles County Judicial District composed of working-class cities like Huntington Park, Bell, South Gate, Vernon, and Maywood as well as heavily industrialized unincorporated county land. Ultimately deriving their authority from the 1849 State Constitution and subsequent legislative acts, townships were created in every county (save San Francisco) in order to establish the foundation of a justice system. First established in Los Angeles County in 1851, the original six townships would provide a justice court (justice of the peace) and constables for areas

FIGURE 3.2. Judge Moffatt decries using chains on minor offenders as "un-American and unnecessary," 1942. Los Angeles Times *Photographic Archives (Collection 1429), Library Special Collections, Charles E. Young Research Library, UCLA.*

of the county that were not incorporated by the cities of Los Angeles or Long Beach. With the new county charter of 1913, the constables were merged into the Sheriff's Department, leaving the popularly elected justice of the peace as the primary remaining function of the township. There were roughly forty-six townships by 1950, when a voter-approved constitutional amendment would eventually rationalize all city and county inferior courts, including the township system, into new municipal court districts.[7]

Throughout his judicial career in the Huntington Park courtroom, Moffatt would preside over many "human interest" cases and make judgments that had popular appeal. He wrote to Los Angeles County sheriff Eugene Biscaluz, criticizing the practice of bringing minor law violators to court in chains as being un-American and unnecessary. "Our young Americans should not carry the memory of once being in a 'chain gang' for possibly ... disobeying the traffic law." He also ruled that a popular marble game could not be classified as gambling and therefore not subject to confiscation on the part of the Sheriff's Department. The judge often sided with motorists who were caught speeding, claiming that existing speed laws were a "racket" and "archaic." He was accused of under-fining those he saw as victims of the system. The judge sentenced the Vernon chief of police Ernest F. Giles to sixty days in jail for physically assaulting a defendant in a traffic case. Moffatt presided over a 1949 court battle that pitted the Society for the Prevention of Cruelty to Animals against a woman who had bought a beheaded rooster—miraculously still alive—at a local market.[8]

One can see Moffatt's judicial style in the marriage ceremony he conducted for Frank Wilkinson and Jean Benson in 1939. Wilkinson would become a central figure during the 1950s Los Angeles Red Scare as a prominent employee of the Los Angeles City Housing Authority (CHA). Frank recalled arriving for the ceremony directly after his day's work as a laborer—tired, dirty, and dressed in his work clothes—and Moffatt performed the ceremony while he, Frank, and Jean remained seated. As Frank had little money to spare for the ceremony, Moffatt asked, instead of money, that Frank tell him of his trip to Europe, North Africa, and the Holy Land several years before.[9]

Moffatt would act on his passion for justice within and outside of the courtroom. In a 1945 letter to his friend, California attorney general Robert Kenny, he explains how he "saw a picture of a 19 year-old white boy—fugitive [in California] from a Georgia Chain Gang" where he had already served twenty months for stealing between fifty and eighty dollars. Moffatt immediately found a co-counsel, lodged protests with the governors of California and Georgia, and got a "Writ of Habeas Corpus . . . to prevent the boy being surreptitiously taken out of the state" and extradited back to Georgia.[10]

Speed Limits, Traffic Enforcement, and Fair Play

California's speed law was a major issue to the judge. His view on traffic citations was that it was illegal for the police to arrest drivers for speeding unless they were driving in an improper or reckless manner, with certain exceptions such as the proximity of schools. It was his contention, according to Sections 510 and 511 of the Vehicle Code, that California had no absolute speed law and that motorists could not be fined for speeding alone. He took issue with traffic enforcement methods in a letter to the Los Angeles County Board of Supervisors. Moffatt demanded that the supervisors investigate "why only the poor motorists, mostly working men, or even the unemployed, are haled into my court and not the rich ones." "I feel quite sure," the justice continued, "that well-dressed and prosperous motorists drive as fast as the poor." The *Times* editorialized its opposition to Moffatt's standpoint. While an examination of the language of the state speed law "lends support to Justice Moffatt's views," the paper seemed more concerned with, rather than social justice, the fiscal effects that would be incurred should fines be modified, the extra burden of proof that would be placed on traffic police, and the increased workload of the judiciary system.[11]

In a July 26, 1943, letter to the Los Angeles City Council, Los Angeles mayor Fletcher Bowron, and Los Angeles Police chief C. B. Horrall, the judge registered his protest of new speeding ordinances. The recent legislation, in contrast to the previous speed limit of thirty-five miles per hour, prohibited driving in excess of twenty-five at night or thirty by day, "without regard to whether this speed creates any hazard as provided in the basic speed law of California." Moffatt outlined his views on the state's basic speed laws, which, according to Section 510 and 511 of the Vehicle Code, had no absolute limit but one that called for "reasonable and prudent" speeds on the highway. As such, attempts to enforce a lower speed law were illegal. Moffatt outlined some of his cases regarding speeding violations in San Antonio Township and their reception in higher courts. "I therefore file formal protest with your Honorable Sirs against this proposed illegal action, on behalf of the hundreds of thousands of defense workers who haven't the time or money to retain lawyers to defend them in court on these illegal citations." The judge, also a practicing attorney, offered free defense to a war worker who was cited under the new law but did not exceed the former limit of thirty-five. Wrote Moffatt, "In the interest of justice and fair play and correct administration of the traffic laws, I am volunteering to act as attorney without compensation for the first defense worker who is cited in violation of the law." "I feel that," the judge concluded, "the war effort will suffer if workers are required to slow down to a dog trot in getting to work."[12]

Anticipating legal challenges to the new law, the council's Public Safety Committee recommended that the matter be filed. Indeed, the primary legal challenge was to come from Moffatt himself; however the justice lost this test case. Peter Cipriano made good on Moffatt's offer of a free defense after he was cited for speeding on Western Avenue near Adams Boulevard on September 8 at one thirty in the morning. He was fined five dollars in Municipal Judge Roberta Clifton's traffic court. Cipriano was found guilty when Clifton ruled that excessive speed alone was always "a potential hazard." Two years later Moffatt noted in a letter to Attorney General Robert Kenny, that an assembly member "whom we don't care for politically" had successfully amended the Vehicle Code to ensure that police provided the same information on the tickets handed to motorists that they wrote on their own copies. He noted, "This is almost the same reform you and I tried to get through a few years ago."[13]

Moffatt would maintain his views on California's speed laws throughout his judicial career. In 1950 he testified before a State Senate interim committee investigating traffic violations that the California Highway Patrol "is continuously filing illegal citations in the courts of California, paying no attention to the so-called prime facie speed law." The judge claimed that "the law sets forth no exact speed limits in California," but law enforcement put the burden of proof on the motorists to demonstrate that his speed was prudent under the law. "I rule that the burden is on arresting officers to prove that the motorist caused a hazard to some other person by his speed." A commissioner of the California Highway Patrol complained that the "only court we know of in California where we don't get reasonable co-operation is Judge Moffatt's."[14]

Under the slogan of "your judge with a heart," Moffatt won reelection as the township's justice of the peace in 1946 quite handily, with 17,918 votes for Moffatt and 8,960 for his opponent, a police judge from Bell. Red-baiting loomed large in the race: "The speed ticket citation business is one of the biggest rackets in California," he claimed. "When I broke that up here, that's when they started calling me a Communist." But Moffatt had coalesced a classic popular front coalition of business, civic, and church groups, along with both houses of labor, the American Federation of Labor (AFL) and Congress of Industrial Organizations (CIO), which ensured his final victory. "I'm a radical," he explained. "I'm a New Deal Democrat plus." Moffatt had attributed his success to his policies as well as the personalized treatment that was enjoyed by those who passed through his courtroom. He boasted of "levying small fines on the poor, but large ones against well-to-do lawbreakers." The judge sent a prominent merchant to jail for fifteen days for selling rotten meat to working people. He claimed that he had saved the people a hundred thousand dollars in illegally imposed traffic fines. Speculated Moffatt, "They say a man is radical in his youth and conservative in his old age. I must be getting younger every day because I'm getting more radical all the time."[15]

Moffatt was definitely a prolabor judge, having been prominently supported by the AFL during his 1938 and 1942 judicial campaigns, as well as both houses of labor in the 1946 election. His handling of charges that the General Motors Corporation violated the state labor code by being tardy in paying wages due to striking workers at the South Gate plant demonstrated both his sympathies and his ability to maintain a balanced judicial demeanor. When General Motors presented evidence that the delay was due to striking pickets refusing to allow payroll employees to enter their office building, the jury voted ten to two in favor of acquittal. The judge dismissed the jury and announced that the case would be continued after he determined whether further action should be taken. In the meantime, the prosecuting assistant district attorney phoned the judge, requesting that the charges be dismissed as it would be a waste of taxpayer money to continue. The following year, Moffatt's judgments against two men arrested for unemployment insurance fraud brought cheers from both employers and organized labor. He sentenced the two men to jail and fined them for their role in fraudulently claiming funds from the veterans' readjustment allowance. Moffatt declared, "I will give a jail sentence in every case of this kind appearing before me."[16]

A white working-class suburb, Huntington Park had the reputation of being a Ku Klux Klan town where racial minorities were officially harassed by local officials. LaRue McCormick, who had known the judge since the early 1930s, had campaigned in favor of his judgeship as a member of the Florence Democratic club and would appear before Moffatt as a defendant in the Communist Registration Ordinance. She recalled in her oral history, "The occasion of a black man who was arrested in a rickety old car, traveling through Huntington Park. Judge Moffatt told the arresting officer that if anyone brought in any more of these cases which were just obviously and patently anti-black arrests, someone was going to go to jail, and it wasn't going to be the defendant."[17]

Robert Miller, twenty-eight, was accused of running a lottery because he collected one dollar each from sixteen "Pyramid club" members for the purpose of forwarding the money to a club member higher on the progression ladder. Collections were made on the promise of eventual cash rewards. Thomas W. Cochran, the prosecuting deputy district attorney, his stenographer, and two investigators left the proceedings in disgust after Moffatt chided Cochran for his failure to produce expert witnesses to testify as to the mechanics of the pyramid plan. "We can continue without those fellows," said Moffatt. "I'll ask the questions." When Moffatt ruled, following a noisy, five-hour trial, that the immensely popular Pyramid Friendship clubs were not lotteries, the *Times* observed that "women rushed to kiss the bald jurist and men pumped his hand." Moffatt explained his ruling: "I've been asked if it (the Pyramid plan) is legal. I said I didn't know and I thought there should be a test case. If that be illegal, let the District Attorney make the most of it." "As far as I'm concerned," District Attorney William Simpson claimed the next day, "the trial proves nothing." Simpson and Sheriff's Captain Carl Pearson vowed, as did LAPD assistant chief Joseph Reed, to continue with the arrest and prosecution of those involved with the Pyramid clubs. Simpson commended his deputy, Thomas W. Cochran, for walking out of Moffatt's courtroom in the middle of the Miller trial. "I'd have done the same thing if I had been there under those conditions." Cochran spoke of his exit from Moffatt's courtroom. The trial "was a cross between a three ring circus and a musical comedy—the worst farce I've seen it in 22 years of law practice. It was a disgrace to the legal profession. . . . That's why I left."[18]

The controversial Pyramid club decision became a spearhead for a movement on the part of conservatives to unseat Moffatt as a justice of the peace. Addressing the Los Angeles Lawyers Club, Rollin L. McNitt asserted that Judge Moffatt should be removed immediately from the bench "either through grand jury or legislative action." Moffatt issued a reply: "I have informed Mr. McNitt that I know of no offense that I have committed under the law and that I know of no law against the filing of a case to test the law on a particular subject." "I still feel," he concluded, "that there must be more major crime in the county then holding of Pyramid clubs. I wish the officials would get after it." "As far as I know," later claimed the judge, "the only grounds on which I might be removed would involve my conviction on charges of bribery or extortion. And no such charges have ever been made." Moffatt claimed that in the previous two and a half years he had decided 2,444 civil cases, with only 44 appeals and one reversal of decision. He called McNitt's demand for his removal "a personal campaign of slander and defamation against me."[19]

Moffatt appeared to have a fondness for the "test case" as a means for determining the legality of regulations ordained by the legislative branches of government. In April 1949, William Dickey, a clerk in a drug store at 7735 Atlantic Boulevard, was arrested for selling a comic book to a thirteen-year-old boy. Dickey was the first person arrested for violating a county ordinance, approved the previous September, that prohibited the sale to minors of publications depicting methods of committing crimes of force, violence, and bloodshed. Questioning the scope of the legislation, Moffatt dismissed all charges against Dickey. The county counsel's office, however, vowed to carry the issue to a higher court. The appeal to the appellate department of the Los Angeles County Superior Court upheld Moffatt's dismissal of the charges with a two-to-one decision. The county ordinance may have gone too far, held the court, as it could be applied to areas outside of the intended object of popular comic books. The court used the example of school history textbooks that might cover Lincoln's assassination or the assassination of Archduke Ferdinand at Sarajevo, the event that touched off World War I. "It may be doubted that the ordinance hits the evil at which it is aimed, but it cannot be doubted that it strikes down many things at which it is not aimed and which are constitutionally immune from its attacks."[20]

In January 1950, a motion by Supervisor Leonard Roach to enlarge the area of the Lynwood justice court at the expense of the jurisdictional boundaries of San Antonio Township was being considered by the Los Angeles County Board of Supervisors. Moffatt's spirited protests were cut short and ignored when board chairman William A. Smith told Moffatt, "If this was a court of law I could cite you for contempt." Moffatt did opine, however, that the motivation for the proposal was that the Lynwood court was far more efficient in getting money out of the public than was his own. He also called for a public hearing on the matter. A lawsuit by James H. Crum, which asserted the new boundaries of the township would remove him from the jurisdiction of Judge Moffatt (for whom he had voted), claimed that the proposed cuts in San Antonio Township were "arbitrary, capricious, without legal basis," and unconstitutional. Crum's suit was tossed out of court by Superior Judge W. Turney Fox, leaving Crum within the new Lynwood court boundaries and Moffatt with a smaller jurisdiction.[21]

The Judge and the Cold War

Stanley Moffatt's judicial career was defined by the Cold War. With his willingness to include communists in the political and judicial processes, rather than exclude them, Moffatt was definitely outside the developing Cold War consensus. He was seen as such by the California Un-American Activities Committee (CUAC), also known as the Tenney Committee after its chairman, State

Senator Jack Tenney. Two cases in particular, one providing legal counsel to communist-affiliated public housing tenants and the other presiding over legal proceedings that brought a Los Angeles Police Department (LAPD) officer to court for the slaying of Augustín Salcido, illustrate the type of legal independence that Moffatt practiced. His judicial independence was to have political ramifications as the Democratic Party became less and less willing to embrace the liberalism that Moffatt espoused. As described previously, attempts to quash Moffatt's legal independence by limiting his judicial power were made several times. His final major decision as justice of the peace was his refusal to recognize the validity of Los Angeles County's Communist Registration Ordinance.

The Cold War politics that increasingly defined Moffatt's judicial career were in large part circumscribed by Ed J. Davenport's parallel tenure on the Los Angeles City Council (1945–53). Davenport's reputation was as controversial as Moffatt's; to confirm his increasingly conservative leanings he changed his political affiliation from Democrat to Republican in 1949. But he had the City Council chambers from which to launch his attacks and often had the will of the *Los Angeles Times* and the political elite behind him. He was a leader in the fight against public housing and the proposed Fair Employment Practices Commission and introduced LA's Communist Registration Ordinances, which put him at direct odds with Moffat, who successfully overturned the county's registration policy. But while Davenport has long been remembered as an iconic figure of Cold War politics, the events of Moffatt's life have largely been ignored or forgotten.[22]

FIGURE 3.3. Los Angeles City Council member Ed Davenport speaking during debate on his proposal to require communists to register, 1950.
Los Angeles Daily News *Negatives (Collection 1387), Library Special Collections, Charles E. Young Research Library, UCLA.*

The Tenney Committee

Moffatt had been in the sights of CUAC since 1941. That year its chairman, Jack Tenney, in testimony before the State Assembly, accused all of the organizers of a dinner honoring left-wing attorney Leo Gallagher, including Stanley Moffatt, of being communists, fellow travelers, or innocents being used to glorify the radical attorney. Moffatt received numerous citations from Tenney's CUAC due to his support or sponsorship of left-wing organizations (e.g., American Youth for Democracy, Joint Anti-Fascist Refugee Committee, and the Lawyers Guild), his friendship with or admiration for contemporary activists like Leo Gallagher, and his subscription to the *People's World* newspaper. Interrogated by the Tenney Committee in 1946 as to his affiliations with the Democratic Party, Moffatt turned the table on his inquisitors and demanded, "May I ask if this is a campaign against the Democratic Party, or what is this?" "It is an investigation of subversive activities," was the reply. "Is the Democratic Party supposed to be subversive?" replied Moffatt, with a question that went unanswered. "Stanley Moffatt is a self-avowed, if somewhat frenzied admirer of Stalin and the Red dictatorship. He not only lends his name to Communist causes and organizations, but hurls himself into activities with a vigorous abandonment that is almost incredible," the Tenney Committee described him in 1948. "To say that Moffatt has disgraced the justice's court is to make an understatement."[23]

Moffatt would be pursued by the Tenney Committee as the Cold War continued. In a 1950 trial where Frank Zaffina, a "militant naval reservist," was accused of battery during the course of an "anti-Communist riot" at the Chrysler auto plant in Maywood, Zaffina filed an affidavit that, citing the Tenney Committee, questioned Moffatt's ability, given his left-wing sympathies, to conduct a fair and balanced trial. The defense attorney, Samuel Rummel, announced that he would question each prospective juror if they were members of the Communist Party because "Communism will be an issue in this case." When Moffatt asked for a definition of communism, Rummel suggested that Jack Tenney of CUAC would be the ideal person to provide such a definition: "How about getting Sen. Tenney down here: he's the man who investigated your honor?" Moffatt replied. "He's the last man I'd want to define it." The case came to an end with a negotiated settlement in Moffatt's court, in which Zaffina pled guilty to a charge of battery and was fined.[24]

Defending Communist Public Housing Tenants

In October 1946, Sidney and Libby Burke lived in Rodger Young Village, a temporary veterans housing project in Griffith Park managed by the Los Angeles' City Housing Authority (CHA). Requested to move by Mayor Fletcher Bowron, the couple was transferred to Channel Heights, another CHA-managed project thirty-four miles to the south in San Pedro. Then the Los Angeles City Council voted to evict Sidney and Libby Burke from their new public housing domicile. Claiming Burke was a "non-veteran" (he had served in the Merchant Marine and not in the armed forces), the Burke family was not, according to the Federal Public Housing Authority (FPHA), qualified to occupy veterans' housing. But the underlying motive for their eviction was the couple's self-acknowledged Communist Party membership (Sid was the Los Angeles editor of the *People's World*). The Burkes declared that they would legally challenge the eviction notice from the Channel Heights project though the Office of Price Administration (OPA). On October 20, Judge Moffatt, working with the Civil Rights Congress, announced that he would serve without fee as the Burkes' attorney. Moffatt volunteered his labor, he stated, "in the interests of justice and American principles of fair play." The *Hollywood Citizen-News* editorialized that "Judge Moffatt [is] placing the rights of communists ahead of the rights of American war veterans."[25]

On October 31, Judge Moffatt and attorney John T. McTernan filed an appeal to the Burkes' eviction with the rent division of the OPA. The eviction was, according to the appeal, a "mockery" of Burke's wartime service with the Merchant Marines. The FPHA ruling of May 25, 1946, which precluded Merchant Marine eligibility for veterans' housing, was challenged as "unwarranted and arbitrary." They argued that the CHA had no right to seek the Burkes' eviction from Channel Heights, besides which the time consumed by Sidney's editorial duties at the *People's World* did not allow him the opportunity to seek another dwelling. On November 4, Ben C. Koepke of the OPA rent control division issued a certificate of eviction requiring the Burkes to move from Channel Heights within thirty days. This decision was immediately appealed by Moffatt and co-counsel McTernan. With the expiration of the thirty-day eviction notice on December 16, the Burkes refused to quit their apartment. In response, the CHA filed a complaint of unlawful retainer against the couple.[26]

The Burkes' legal attempts to retain their public housing domicile would be rendered moot when the couple was able to construct their own home in the Echo Park District. The Burke incident was the first occurrence of the Cold War that would bring negative notoriety to the judge on a citywide scale.[27]

Bringing the Police to Court

The unwarranted shooting of seventeen-year-old Augustín Salcido by LAPD officer William J. Keyes in March 1948 galvanized significant activism on the part of the city's left—led by the Civil Rights Congress—against police brutality. When Los Angeles courts refused to indict Keyes, Moffatt agreed to hold an indictment hearing in his Huntington Park courtroom. Under the California Constitution, it was legal to issue warrants and judgments from outside of a jurisdiction in which the crime was committed. On April 12, the preliminary hearing to determine if Keyes should be bound over to Superior Court to be tried on charges of manslaughter took place in Moffatt's court.[28]

At the opening of the two-hour hearing, Keyes's attorney Joseph Scott filed an affidavit that questioned the ability of Keyes to receive an objective hearing. "This defendant therefore alleges on information and belief," read the affidavit, "that certain communist-front organizations and certain well known communists were instrumental in securing the warrant of arrest in this action from the Honorable Stanley Moffatt, and that said Honorable Stanley Moffatt is a sponsor of one of said organizations." "This man doesn't believe he can get a fair trial before you," concluded Scott to Moffatt. Moffatt refused to disqualify himself as he had no knowledge of nor prejudice against the defendant and was certainly capable of conducting a fair preliminary hearing. His motion denied, Scott became openly hostile to the judge, opining that the proceedings were brought to Moffatt's court to "make you [Keyes] a sucker and a fall-guy for these people. . . . In that affidavit it states that back of this movement is a communist program that is behind this thing."[29]

FIGURE 3.4. Judge Moffatt hears arguments that police officer William Keyes is innocent in the murder of Augustín Salcido, 1948.
Los Angeles Daily News Negatives (Collection 1387), Library Special Collections, Charles E. Young Research Library, UCLA.

Scott objected that Leo Gallagher—a sponsor of the Civil Rights Congress, a former Communist Party candidate for California's Secretary of State, and, as Scott said, "an out-and-out Communist"—appeared as a friend of the court. "He has a perfect right to do so," Moffatt pointed out. "We also listen to Republicans in this court as well as Communists." A frustrated Scott abandoned his defense of Keyes and asked instead if the judge knew why the case had come into his court. "I do," proudly replied Moffatt, "because this court has been known to help the downtrodden people of the community. It is known as a people's court out here." Moffatt ruled that there was sufficient evidence to indicate that Keyes was guilty of manslaughter. With his bail set at two thousand dollars, Keyes was ordered to appear in Department 42 Los Angeles County Superior Court for arraignment on April 27. Salcido's death, concluded Moffatt, "seems to me a very outrageous killing without any justification whatever. . . . I don't like the spirit of Fascism that is sweeping America. It seems to me that the war hysteria has got everybody sort of crazy in this country, and the first thing they think about is to pull a gun and shoot somebody."[30]

On the morning of April 14, two days after the hearing, an editorial in the *Los Angeles Times* called for the "careful examination" of the California law that allowed any magistrate in the county to issue a warrant, regardless of jurisdiction, for a major crime. Though the complicity of Stanley Moffatt and Leo Gallagher with "Communist front" groups were "important elements" in this case, the paper took no position on Keyes's guilt or innocence. What was involved was a matter of local authority: "There is no reason to go elsewhere." Accused by the *People's World* of having "scrambled on the *Times* bandwagon," Los Angeles Councilman Lloyd G. Davies introduced a motion, seconded by Councilman Ed Davenport, instructing the city attorney to examine, as per that morning's *Times* editorial, the California law that had allowed Moffatt to issue a felony complaint against an LAPD officer for an offence committed outside Huntington Park. According to Davies, Moffatt "was solely concerned with using his court as the sounding board for certain opinions of certain groups." Davenport charged that Moffatt had received support from known communists and that this episode "is the greatest travesty on justice ever seen in California." The motion was adopted unanimously by the LA City Council.[31]

Some of the letters published by the *Times* in response to their April 14 editorial must have buoyed the spirits of the leftist activists embroiled in the Justice for Salcido campaign. "Justice Moffatt has long had a reputation for lawfully protecting the underdog," wrote Gwynne Mountain McCord. "His conscience and his ideals as well as his knowledge of the basic principles of American justice . . . have undoubtedly prompted his actions." Identifying himself as a Republican, "a Taft man—conservative enough to believe in justice," James D. Oakes stated, "I believe Justice Moffatt has taken a step necessary in the interests of justice which no Police Court or prosecuting authority would take. No Los Angeles policeman is ever held accountable for his acts." He maintained that "Scott's court conduct, as reported, was contemptible—Moffatt's and Gallagher's admirable." W.P.M. chastised the implications of the paper's editorial: "You seem to forget that a murderer should be brought to justice and that [this] . . . is the clear duty of our justices. Their own political persuasion or that of their associates seems to me to be beside the point."[32]

After the case was moved to Superior Court, Keyes was acquitted of manslaughter charges under what was regarded by some as questionable logic of the presiding judge. The Salcido case, occurring in the fateful year of 1948, would garnish Moffatt with even more negative coverage in the mainstream press than had the Burke incident of two years previous. Moffatt was by now a demonized left-wing partisan.[33]

The Democrats and the IPP

Moffatt had been elected to the Los Angeles County Central Democratic Committee (CDC) in 1934. Candidates for committeemen were able to file for election upon presentation of the nomination papers bearing at least ten sponsors' signatures. Seven committee members were elected for four-year terms from their respective assembly districts in Los Angeles County to form the CDC. The central committees throughout the state were involved with party finances as well as educational and legislative programs. They sought to assist party clubs and groups, to coordinate the activities of volunteer organizations, and to establish and coordinate various campaign committees. Dean Cresap wrote that the county central committees were the "nearest thing to a grassroots group in the official party organization in California."[34]

Moffatt's tenure within the CDC reveals an enthusiastic participant in Democratic Party politics. His role as a liaison between the EPIC clubs and the Democratic Party has already been mentioned. In 1944, Moffatt was reelected as vice-chairman of the Democratic County Central Committee over Joseph Aldman. Warning County Central Democratic Committee members against a split in the Democratic Party in the wake of his father's (President Roosevelt's) death, James Roosevelt would, in December 1945, urge the unification of the Southland Democrats. An enthusiastic Moffatt, according to the *Times*, "got to his feet on the rostrum and all but nominated or drafted Roosevelt 'for United States Senator.'"[35]

As the 1948 presidential elections approached, the California Democratic Party was deeply divided between conservatives, led by national committeeman Edwin Pauley, and the liberals marshaled by state party chairman James Roosevelt. A third faction, favoring the nomination of Henry A. Wallace, was championed among the Democrats in Los Angeles County by Stanley Moffatt. By February 1948, the ouster of Moffatt and "all of his Third Party Wallace followers" from the CDC, of which Moffatt was second vice-chairman, was being sought from within the party. The Democratic County Council, headed by W. C. Fields Jr., sought Moffatt's resignation as a Democratic committee member. The judge replied that he would not voluntarily surrender his party post, charging that those who were seeking his ouster were "Fascist minded."[36]

The following month, Moffatt abandoned the Democratic Party to register with the Independent Progressive Party (IPP). During the night of March 26, 1948, Moffatt was awakened by a knock on his door and discovered a hammer and sickle branded on his lawn with burning gasoline. An anonymous telephone caller warned the judge, "This is only the beginning." Understandably shaken, Moffatt asked for police protection against "a possibly unruly crowd" as he delivered a talk to the University of Southern California Students for Wallace, "For Henry Wallace and Against Universal Military Training." The twenty individuals who attended his lecture, however, posed no threat.[37]

Moffatt sought to represent the Eighteenth Congressional District in the 1948 elections. Comprising heavily industrialized southern Los Angeles and northern Long Beach, the Eighteenth was very similar to San Antonio Township, an area of working-class suburbs and industrial plants. Opposing him were Republican incumbent Willis W. Bradley and Democrat Clyde Doyle. Moffatt was urged to run by some local Congress of Industrial Organizations (CIO) unions, and his platform was prounion and supportive of Henry A. Wallace's peace plan. "I think Henry Wallace grows in stature with every speech," he enthused. "Everything he says I applaud, and want to shout from the housetops." Moffatt had sought to withdraw from the race in favor of Doyle pending a scheduled meeting in which he hoped that Doyle would adopt a more prolabor policy position. However, Doyle's campaign manager canceled the meeting, claiming the support of Moffatt or his followers was not needed. Apparently the campaign manager was not far from the mark. Doyle emerged victorious with 105,687 votes, compared to 92,721 for the Republican Bradley and only 8,232 for Moffatt.[38]

The Laughing Man

Moffatt's idiosyncratic ways eventually laid the groundwork for his political downfall and defeat in the 1950 election. Between mid-1949 and the end of 1951, the local press played up Judge Moffatt's distinctive behavior in its coverage of what it termed the "laughing man" case. On May 14, 1949, eating his lunch at the Red Wing Cafe at 2814 East Gage Avenue in Huntington Park (where he was a regular), Moffatt's luncheon was disturbed by the loud laughter of fellow patron John G. Frazier, a sixty-eight-year-old service station mechanic. After demanding that Frazier be quiet, Moffatt had Frazier arrested for disturbing the peace. "I'm going to make a test whether one diner can disturb others," Moffatt told the responding police. "This is the first time in my life," said Los Angeles district attorney William E. Simpson, "that I ever heard of anyone being arrested for laughing." Noted the *Examiner*, "The justice seemed taken aback by the public hilarity greeting the arrest of Frazier." Professing a healthy outlook toward hearty laughter, the judge told the *Times*, "What I had in mind was a rebuke, hardly anything more. But, after thinking it through I think I'll likely ask for a dismissal." The question posed by the press was, why all of the hubbub when Frazier was "merely" laughing? "It didn't sound like laughter to me," explained Moffatt. "It sounded like screaming. At the top of his voice. Like an Indian whooping on the warpath; something bloodcurdling like that." Frazier appeared before City Judge Charles G. Hedgecock of Huntington Park, who decided that he, rather than a jury, would decide the case. Represented by City Judge Harry Simon of Bell, described by the *Times* as "an old opponent of Moffatt in the political ring," Frazier pled not guilty to the charge of disturbing the peace.[39]

In an unusual trial with political overtones, the presiding judge took an active role in questioning, Frazier was not called to testify, and a supporting witness for Moffatt was refused the opportunity to testify. In June 1st testimony, Moffatt described the offending laugh: "It was a scream, like a coyote screaming or maybe the braying of a jackass. It almost pierced my eardrums." Both Simon as well as the prosecuting assistant district attorney asked Moffatt to demonstrate the offending laugh. "I've got too much respect for my throat," he answered Simon. The jurist continued his recount of the events: telling Frazier to stop his loud laughter, the judge identified himself as justice of the peace Stanley Moffatt. Replied Frazier, "Judge Moffatt don't spell anything to me." But both the owner of the Red Wing Café and the waitress who was working during the incident testified that though Frazier's laugh was certainly loud, it was not disturbing. "There was no malice in John's laughter," opined Judge Hedgecock. "Not guilty." "But after Judge Hedgecock rendered his verdict," observed the *Times*, "an extra hearty laugh sounded over the whooping and hollering of the audience. John Frazier was laughing last."[40]

In a suit filed on August 11, Frazier charged Moffatt with false arrest, saying Moffatt "acted with deliberate and premeditated malice," and without probable cause, and demanded $100,150 in damages—$50,000 as compensatory damages, $25,000 in punitive damages, and an additional $25,000 for injury to his good reputation. He also asked for $150 reimbursement for the attorney's fees that were spent in his acquittal. On August 26, 1949, Moffatt answered the charges brought against him in Superior Court. Moffatt said that the incident with Frazier had been seized upon by the judge's political enemies who desired Moffatt's defeat in his bid for reelection. In his answer to the lawsuit, the judge attributed his troubles to the fact that he is "a very independent and courageous judge and refuses to yield to pressure of certain newspapers who try to dictate to him as to the policies and judgments of his court." Moffatt saw himself as having "very progressive and liberal political views and has been repeatedly elected with the support of all branches of organized labor, rather than the financial big business interests." Moffatt held that his actions were legally justified as a magistrate has the power to order the police to act when a breach of the law is committed in the magistrate's presence. Using the episode of Moffatt's disturbed luncheon as a sounding board, the *Times* held that those, like Moffatt, who failed to uphold the "majesty of the law" in the lower courts would be confronted by "properly informed voters [who] have a remedy" to address such abuses. And during the following March, Harry A. Simon, the "laughing man's" lawyer, filed as a candidate for justice of the peace against Stanley Moffatt in San Antonio Township. Wrote the *Times*, "The man who defended the laughing man is going to give Justice of the Peace Stanley Moffatt a chance to laugh last—or not at all." In a three-way race in June, which also included Francis W. Bennett, Moffatt placed a narrow third.[41]

Frazier's suit was brought to trial on August 2, 1950, in the court of Superior Judge Samuel R. Blake. Frazier, again represented by Harry Simon, took the stand to give his account of the events during that fateful luncheon more than a year past. "For the enlightenment of the court and under the instructions from his lawyer," Frazier demonstrated his laugh. "He's laughing into a loudspeaker now," Simon reminded Blake. In his opening statement, Moffatt told the court that the laugh in question was more like a "blood-curdling war whoop" that had disturbed Moffatt's peace. Moffatt pointed out that the incident had caused him (Moffatt) a great deal of embarrassment and humiliation. "The newspapers made him the laughing boy hero," observed the justice of the peace, "and they made me appear like the worst of stinkers." Moffatt went on to assert that this episode had been instrumental in Moffatt's defeat in his reelection bid the previous June 6. As reported in the *Times*, Blake cut him short, commenting, "Politics had nothing to do with the case at hand." Blake held that Moffatt was not entitled to any judicial immunity: "Judicial immunity was never intended to extend to a judge eating his lunch in a public restaurant." The court found that Frazier's arrest was illegal as his laughter, loud as it may have been, did not constitute a breach of the peace. Blake ruled, on August 4, that Frazier was entitled to recover damages and expenses.[42]

On August 11, Blake announced his decision as to the amount of damages to be awarded to Frazier. Moffatt was directed to pay Frazier $3,000 compensatory damages, $1,000 exemplary damages, and $150 to cover attorney fees. "There is a limit to the persecution that one man can endure," the *Examiner* quoted Moffatt. "But I will try to bear up under it . . . until the war hysteria has died down. My Fascist enemies are trying to ruin me." To the *Times*, he vowed that he would appeal the decision "as far as the Supreme Court, if necessary."[43]

Moffatt appealed for a new trial in September, claiming that he had discovered new evidence and that the judgment for Frazier was both excessive and "given under the influence of passion and prejudice." His appeal was denied the following month. Heard by California's Second District Court of Appeals, the lower court ruling was reversed and the financial award was dropped on December 27, 1951. The court surveyed historical precedents from English common law to find "an unbroken line of authorities sustaining the principle that judicial officers are not liable for the erroneous exercise of judicial powers vested in them." The *People's World* noted that the case "was used as a weapon by reactionary opponents of the Huntington Park jurist in the election of 1950 in which the liberal judge was defeated." There was more than a little truth behind this observation. Moffatt's unsuccessful reelection bid for justice of the peace in the 1950 state primaries occurred during the height of the "laughing man" trial. His portrayal in the press was undoubtedly a large factor in his defeat.[44]

The Communist Registration Ordinance

Between his defeat in the June 1950 primary and the election of his successor in the November general elections, Moffatt became a central player in the legal struggle against communist registration. On August 22, 1950, the Los Angeles County Board of Supervisors adopted three interlocking ordinances, authored by Supervisor Leonard Roach, that prohibited communists from carrying weapons, handling explosives, or taking part in defense activities. Of most concern was Ordinance 5578, which required, under a maximum penalty of a five-hundred-dollar fine and six months' imprisonment for disobedience, that anyone who "is a member of any communist organization" residing, working, or regularly entering or traveling through any part of unincorporated Los Angeles County must register with the Sheriff's Department. It defined "communist organization" as "any organization which is organized, or which operates, primarily for the purpose of advancing the objectives of the world communism movement." "In Los Angeles County," the ordinance continued, "there are active, disciplined communist organizations presently functioning for the primary purpose of advancing the objectives of the world communism movement."[45]

Three arrests were made for violating the county's Communist Registration Ordinances. Arrested during the evening of September 7, Henry Steinberg, legislative director of the Communist Party in Los Angeles County, was jailed immediately and booked on order of Myer B. Marion, justice of the peace of Belvedere Township. Attorney Pauline Epstein secured a "midnight writ" from Moffatt to release Steinberg on five hundred dollars' bail (paid for by the Civil Rights Congress). According to the *Times*, Moffatt had Steinberg freed for an appearance into his court the following week under the mistaken belief that

Steinberg, of 4416 Comly Avenue, resided in San Antonio Township. A second arrest on September 14 was that of Gus Brown, a union official and labor organizer, who appeared in El Monte justice court. LaRue McCormick, a resident of Huntington Park, was arrested on September 25, 1950; she was brought before Moffatt immediately after she was booked and entered a not guilty plea. While the other two arrestees had their bail set at five hundred dollars, McCormick was freed on her own recognizance. Appearing before Moffatt again on October 2, with her attorney Ben Margolis, McCormick changed her plea from "not guilty" and sought, instead, a demurrer—a plea that challenged the constitutionality of the ordinance. Moffatt then imposed a token fifty-dollar bail.[46]

Somewhat "irked" (as the *Times* put it) by the decisions of Marion and Moffatt that held the Communist Registration Ordinances as invalid, the County Board of Supervisors called for a conference to debate means of strengthening them. Invited were County Counsel Harold W. Kennedy, District Attorney Simpson, County Sheriff Biscaluz, and top members of their staff. On November 24, Justice Eldred E. Wolfard overruled Brown's demurrer, upholding the county ordinance. The cases of McCormick and Steinberg had already been granted their demurrers and, as a result, were being appealed by Los Angeles County to the Appellate Department of Superior Court. On February 27, 1951, the court held, in *People v. McCormick*, that the ordinance was unconstitutional as it would essentially require a person who had registered to testify against himself. Moffatt's dismissal of the charges against LaRue McCormick was upheld. The unanimous decision determined that "the ordinance violates the principle written into the Bill of Rights of the Federal Constitution." The opinion concluded that "we find the ordinance to be without validity and, as a consequence, hold that the dismissals of the complaints based on it were proper."[47]

Postjudicial Politics

Following his rejection for a fourth term as justice of the peace, Moffatt acted exclusively as a private attorney. He also had several more forays into electoral politics. The former judge filed as a candidate for Municipal Court Office One, San Antonio Township, in March 1952. He later filed nomination papers for the June 5, 1956, primary election for a Democratic Party post in the Sixty-Ninth District (South Gate). Both of these attempts came to naught. He continued to be cited by CUAC, in 1951, 1955, and 1961, though, as the *Times* was quick to point out, the groups for which he was cited were more liberal than subversive.[48]

Along with several hundred other people, Moffatt wrote a letter to the Los Angeles City Housing Authority (CHA) asking for the reinstatement of Frank Wilkinson, who had been suspended from his position at the end of August 1952 for refusing to divulge the political organizations to which he belonged.

Mr. Wilkinson "is a man of great principle," claimed Moffatt in a letter to Howard Holtzendorff, executive director of the CHA,

> and he resents, as I do, this dragging in of the red herring at the last moment to stop the housing plan. . . . Why give aid and comfort to . . . those rascals on the City Council who have sold their souls for a mess of pottage to the Real Estate lobby? Please stand firm. This wave of hysteria is at its peak now and must recede soon and America will once again become the progressive country we have always loved.

Several days later Moffatt wrote to Wilkinson, who attended the same Unitarian Church as Moffatt, that "the crowd at the church Sunday were all with you 100% and greatly admire your courage." He enclosed a token of financial aid, apologizing that it was so small. "Keep up the fighting spirit," he continued. "We are bound to win as we are on the side of the great masses of the people all over the world."[49]

Stanley Moffatt died at Baldwin Hills Hospital on April 5, 1971, following a lengthy illness. Obituaries in the *Los Angeles Times* and the *San Francisco Chronicle* described him as a "controversial" and "colorful" justice of the peace. The papers mentioned his 1948 congressional bid and the famous laughing man lawsuit while neglecting to comment on the many other cases he heard on behalf of his diverse working-class constituents. Taken together, the range of issues he addressed and the resulting decisions defined his judicial career and presented his vision of a better world that "we are bound to win"—one that, with the decline of the anticommunist hysteria, would be more humane and progressive and that his interpretations of the law sought to play a role in realizing.[50]

A far more sympathetic and befitting eulogy was voiced by LaRue McCormick in her oral history: "He remained until the last of his days . . . a true civil libertarian, and a true liberal, and a man who steadfastly stood by his principles and beliefs in the face of the cold war, in the face of losing support for his job as the judge, and altogether he was a splendid, old-fashioned, American gentleman, the likes of which we don't see too often."[51]

NOTES

1. Sidney Burke, "Stanley Moffatt—'Judge with a Heart'," *People's World*, August 19, 1946, 1, 3; Stanley Moffatt, Ledgers, November 16, 1917–December 31, 1923, January 1, 1924–January 1, 1928, Fresno, Calif., Southern California Library for Social Studies and Research Pamphlet Collection.

2. Alice Catt Armstrong, ed., *Who's Who in Los Angeles County, 1949–51: Fourteen Hundred Illustrated Biographies of Leading Men and Women in Los Angeles County* (Los Angeles: Who's Who Historical Society, 1950), 261.

3. "Exciting Council Session," *Los Angeles Times*, July 28, 1929, C8, ProQuest Historical Newspapers (hereafter PQ); "Another Kiwanis Club Organized at South Gate," *Los*

Angeles Times, October 15, 1929, 14, PQ; "South Gate Recall Row Warms Up," *Los Angeles Times*, September 14, 1931, 12, PQ.

4. Becky M. Nicolaides, *My Blue Heaven: Life and Politics in the Working-Class Suburbs of Los Angeles, 1920–1965* (Chicago: University Of Chicago Press, 2002), 148.

5. "How to Mark Your Ballot Next Tuesday," *Los Angeles Times*, August 28, 1932, A1, PQ; "Committeeman Selected by Parties at Primary," *Los Angeles Times*, September 9, 1934, 20, PQ; Moffatt is quoted in Nicolaides, *My Blue Heaven*, 175.

6. "Posts Lost by Justices," *Los Angeles Times*, November 30, 1934, A1, PQ; "The Political Bandwagon," *Los Angeles Times*, July 27, 1936, A4, PQ; "County Office Oaths Taken," *Los Angeles Times*, December 2, 1938, 11, PQ.

7. California Commission on County Home Rule, "County Government in California, Final Report" (State of California, 1930), 61–63; John C. Bollens and Robert W. Binkley, *County Government Organization in California* (University of California, Berkeley, Bureau of Public Administration, October 1947), 20; Los Angeles County Bureau of Efficiency, "Survey of Judicial Townships in Los Angeles County" (n.d.), 1, 2, 11. The official boundaries of San Antonio Township can be found in ibid., 41–42. A more popular description of San Antonio Township can be found in Burke, "Stanley Moffatt," 1, 3. On the rationalization of lower courts, see Winston W. Crouch, XV, *Intergovernmental Relations, in Metropolitan Los Angeles: A Study in Integration* (Los Angeles: Haynes Foundation, 1954).

8. "Court Rules Marble Game Not Gambling," *Los Angeles Examiner*, December 9, 1939, clipping from the Examiner clipping file at the USC Regional History Center (hereafter RHC);"Justices on Carpet for Under-Fining," *Los Angeles Examiner*, December 12, 1940, RHC; "Traffic Ticket 'Racket' Hit," *Los Angeles Examiner*, March 26, 1946, RHC; "Mute with Fluent Fingers Acquitted," *Los Angeles Times*, April 21, 1940, 5, PQ; "Judge Assails Offenders' 'Chain Gang' in Court," *Los Angeles Times*, July 30, 1942, 9; "Vernon Chief Stars Jail Term," *Los Angeles Times*, December 19, 1945, 5, PQ; "Military Accused of Burning Child's Hands Wins Acquittal," *Los Angeles Times*, November 5, 1940, 12, PQ; "SPCA Seizes Rooster with Head Cut Off," *Los Angeles Times*, April 7, 1949, 17, PQ; "Feelings of Headless Rooster to Be Tested," *Los Angeles Times*, April 12, 1949, A1, PQ.

9. Conversation with Frank Wilkinson and Donna Wilkinson, January 31, 2007, in possession of the author. For more on Frank Wilkinson and the Red Scare in Los Angeles public housing program, see Don Parson, *Making a Better World: Public Housing, the Red Scare, and the Direction of Modern Los Angeles* (Minneapolis: University of Minnesota Press, 2005).

10. Moffatt to Kenny, May 6, 1945, in Kenny Papers, Bancroft Library, University of California, Berkeley, box 29, folder: Stanley Moffatt.

11. "Just How Fast Is Too Fast? It's Up to Court," *Los Angeles Examiner*, February 15, 1940; "Favoritism Charged by Judge in Handling of Speeding Cases," *Los Angeles Times*, February 22, 1940, A, PQ; "Do We Have Speed Laws?," *Los Angeles Times*, February 27, 1940, A4, PQ.

12. Moffatt to Council, Mayor Bowron, Chief of Police Horrall, July 26, 1943, Council File 15417 (1943); "War Work Speeders Offered Free Defense," *Los Angeles Times*, July 27, 1943, A3, PQ.

13. "Legal Fight on 'Dog Trot' Speed Limit Pledged," *Los Angeles Times*, August 5,

1943, A1, PQ; Walter Peterson (City Clerk) to Moffatt, August 23, 1943, Council File 15417 (1943); "Judge Plea Fails in Speeder Case," *Los Angeles Times*, September 9, 1943, A8, PQ; Moffatt to Kenny, May 6, 1945, in Kenny Papers, box 29, folder: Stanley Moffatt.

14. "Judge Scolds Unfair, Greedy Traffic Courts," *Los Angeles Times*, January 22, 1950, 9, PQ.

15. Burke, "Stanley Moffatt," 1, 3.

16. "Jury Dismissed in Suit over Strike Pay Delay," *Los Angeles Times*, March 1, 1946, A1, PQ; "End of Payroll Action Sought," *Los Angeles Times*, March 9, 1946, 3, PQ; "Two More Held on Jobless Insurance Chiseling Charges," *Los Angeles Times*, September 30, 1947, 7, PQ.

17. Larue McCormick, "Activist in the Radical Movement, 1930–1960; the International Labor Defense; the Communist Party," interviewed by Malca Chall, Regional Oral History Office, Bancroft Library, University of California, Berkeley, ca. 1980, 114.

18. "Pyramider Freed in Uproarious Trial," *Los Angeles Times*, February 1, 1949, A1, PQ; ""Cheers, Jeers, Kisses Enliven Pyramid Trial," *Los Angeles Examiner*, February 1, 1949, RHC; "Court's Procedure Challenged at 'Get Rich' Test Trial," *Los Angeles Examiner*, February 1, 1949, RHC; "Crackdown on Pyramids to Continue," *Los Angeles Times*, February 2, 1949, 1, PQ.

19. "Ouster of Pyramid Trial Judge Asked," *Los Angeles Times*, February 3, 1949, 2, PQ; "New Charges Face Pyramid Case Defendant," *Los Angeles Times*, February 18, 1949, 2, PQ.

20. "Hearing Delayed in First Crime Comics Ban Case," *Los Angeles Times*, April 24, 1949, A3, PQ; "Man Accused of Selling Crime Book to Minor Freed," *Los Angeles Times*, May 17, 1949, A3, PQ; "Comic Book Sale Upheld on Appeal," *Los Angeles Times*, December 28, 1949, 2, PQ.

21. "Moffatt Protest on Cut in His Territory Ignored," *Los Angeles Times*, January 18, 1950, A3, PQ; "Voter Loses Suit to Stop New Township," *Los Angeles Times*, March 11, 1950, A7, PQ.

22. "Councilman Ed Davenport Dies in Sleep," *Los Angeles Times*, June 25, 1953, 1.

23. Chester G. Hanson, "Gallagher Party Stirs Assembly," *Los Angeles Times*, May 25, 1941, 14, PQ; California Legislature, "Joint Fact-Finding Committee on Un-American Activities in California, Third Report" (Sacramento: California State Senate, 1947), 247; see, for example, Moffatt's questioning by the Tenney Committee, ibid., 247–50, and California Legislature, "Fourth Report of the Senate Fact-Finding Committee on Un-American Activities, Communist Front Organizations" (Sacramento: California Senate, 1948), 172.

24. "Justice Moffatt's Fitness Challenged in Rioting Case," *Los Angeles Times*, August 10, 1950, 18, PQ; "Sparks Fly in Anti-red Riot Beating Case Trial," *Los Angeles Times*, August 29, 1950, A3, PQ.

25. "Burkes Plan Court Fight on Eviction," *San Pedro News Pilot*, October 19, 1946, 1, 2; "Moffatt Will Fight for Burke," *People's World*, October 21, 1946, 1; Slade to "Dear Friends," October 21, 1946, Civil Rights Congress Collection, box 1, folder 9, Southern California Library for Social Science and Research; "Champions for the Communists," *Hollywood Citizen-News*, October 22, 1946, 14.

26. "Burke Argues Against Ouster from Public Housing Project," *Los Angeles Exam-*

iner, November 1, 1946, pt. 1, 7; "Burke Case Is Appealed to OPA," *People's World*, November 1, 1946, 3; "Sidney Burke May Be Forced Out of Channel Heights Project," *Hollywood Citizen-News*, November 5, 1946, 15; "Burkes to Be Evicted from Second Project," *Los Angeles Times*, November 5, 1946, pt. 1, 2; "Burke Eviction Taken to Court," *San Pedro Pilot News*, December 17, 1946, 4.

27. For an in-depth account of this episode, please see Don Parson, "The Burke Incident: Political Belief in Los Angeles' Public Housing during the Domestic Cold War," *Southern California Quarterly* 84, no. 1 (Spring 2002): 53–74.

28. See coverage by the press: "Charge Red Move in Arrest of Officer," *Los Angeles Daily News*, April 12, 1948, RHC; "Red Charges Fly in Tiff with Judge in Police Slaying Quiz," *Los Angeles Herald and Express*, April 12, 1948, RHC; "Judge Rows with Lawyer at Hearing," *Los Angeles Times*, April 13, 1948, pt. 1, 1, 2; "Moffatt Refuses to Step Down in Case," *Los Angeles Examiner*, April 13, 1948, RHC; "Cop Must Stand Trial for Killings," *People's World*, April 13, 1948, 1; "Communist, Red-Baiter Charges Fly between Lawyer, Judge in Court," *Hollywood Citizen-News*, April 13, 1948, RHC; "Officer Keyes Ordered Tried in Boy's Killing," *Los Angeles Times*, May 6, 1948, 4.

29. "Objections to the Qualifications of Honorable Stanley Moffatt, Justice of the Peace, to Sit on [or] Act in Any Further Proceedings Herein" [April 12, 1948], Council File 32796; "Reporter's Transcript," *People of the State of California v. William Keyes*, No. 29434, April 12, 1948, pp. 4–14, CRC Collection, box 3, folder 28.

30. "Reporter's Transcript," *People of the State of California v. William Keyes*, 62, 65–66.

31. "Case of Justice Stanley Moffatt," *Los Angeles Times*, April 14, 1948, pt. 2, 4; "Council Echoes L.A. Times, Joins Attack on Moffatt," *People's World*, April 15, 1948; "Moffatt Action Rouses Council," *Los Angeles Times*, April 15, 1948, pt. 1, 5; "Judge Moffatt Assailed by City Council," *Los Angeles Examiner*, April 15, 1948, RHC.

32. "Letters from Readers," *Los Angeles Times*, April 19, 1948, pt. 2, 4.

33. This case is explored in detail in Don Parson, "Injustice for Salcido: The Left Response to Police Brutality in Cold War Los Angeles," *Southern California Quarterly* 86, no. 2 (Summer 2004): 145–68.

34. Dean R. Cresap, *Party Politics in the Golden State* (Los Angeles: Haynes Foundation, 1954), chap. 2.

35. "Democrats Pick Vice-Chairmen," *Los Angeles Times*, July 28, 1944, pt. 1, PQ; The Watchman, "Col. Roosevelt Warns Against Bourbon Split," *Los Angeles Times*, December 12, 1945, 5, PQ.

36. "Wallace Hat Tossed in Ring," *Los Angeles Examiner*, June 7, 1947, RHC; "Moffatt Ouster Asked in Democratic Row," *Los Angeles Examiner*, February 26, 1948, RHC; "Pro-Wallace Man Charges 'Fascism,'" *Los Angeles Times*, February 27, 1948, 2, PQ.

37. "Moffatt Quits Democrats," *Los Angeles Examiner*, March 26, 1948, RHC; "Hammer, Sickle Brand Burned in Moffatt Lawn," *Los Angeles Examiner*, March 28, 1948, RHC; "Police Protect Judge Moffatt," *Los Angeles Examiner*, April 19, 1948, RHC.

38. "Judge Supports Strikers," *People's World*, October 22, 1948, 5; "CIO Backs Moffatt," *People's World*, October 18, 1948; "Wallace Trailed His Own Ticket," *Los Angeles Times*, December 11, 1948, 6, PQ; "Talk Slated on Red Law," *Los Angeles Times*, October 11, 1950, 10.

39. "Innocent Plea in Laugh Trial," *Los Angeles Examiner*, May 19, 1949, RHC; "Moffatt Laugh War Pressed," *Los Angeles Examiner*, May 28, 1949, RHC; "Judge Asks Police to Arrest Man Who Causes Laughter," *Los Angeles Examiner*, May, 17, 1949, 1, RHC; "Moffatt Hints He'll Forgive Laughing Man," *Los Angeles Examiner*, May 18, 1949, pt. 1, 7; "Judge Thinks He'll Laugh Off Disturbance," *Los Angeles Times*, May 18, 1949, 1, PQ; "Did Laughter Ruin Justices Lunch? Court Will Rule," *Los Angeles Times*, May 27, 1949, 2, PQ.

40. "Laugh Is on Justice Moffatt as 'Laughing Man' Goes Free," *Los Angeles Times*, June 3, 1949, 2, PQ.

41. "Moffatt Sued by Man He Jailed for Laughing," *Los Angeles Times*, August 12, 1949, A1, PQ; "Disturbed J. P. Pats Self in Laugh Trial," *Los Angeles Times*, August 27, 1949, A3, PQ; "How 'Inferior' Are These Courts?," *Los Angeles Times*, August 30, 1949, A4, PQ; "Laughing Man's Defender Will Oppose Moffatt," *Los Angeles Times*, March 30, 1950, 11, PQ.

42. "$100,150 Laughter Suit Doesn't Amuse Moffatt," *Los Angeles Times*, August 3, 1950, A1, PQ; "War Whoop No Plain Laugh, Says Moffatt," *Los Angeles Times*, August 4, 1950, 10, PQ; "'Laughing Man' in $125,150 Moffatt Suit Haw-Haws," *Los Angeles Examiner*, August 3, 1950, RHC; "Moffatt Refuses Bid to Be a Braying Judge," *Los Angeles Examiner*, August 4, 1950, RHC;"Mechanic Gets Final Chuckle over Moffatt," *Los Angeles Times*, August 5, 1950, 3.

43. "Laugh That Irked Judge Draws $4150," *Los Angeles Times*, August 12, 1950, 2, PQ; Harry Lang, "Judge Moffatt Must Pay $4150," *Los Angeles Examiner*, August 12, 1950.

44. "Moffatt Seeks New Trial in Laughing Case," *Los Angeles Times*, September 15, 1950, 10, PQ; "Justice Denied New Trial In Laughing Case," *Los Angeles Times*, October 18, 1950, 1, PQ; "High Tribune Upholds Judicial Immunity in Lawsuit," *Los Angeles Examiner*, December 28, 1951, RHC; *Frazier v. Moffatt*, 108 CA2d 379, 239 P.2ds 123 (1951); "Judge Moffatt Beats Suit," *People's World*, January 2, 1952; "Moffatt Out as Justice: Runs Third," *Los Angeles Examiner*, June 10, 1950, RHC.

45. "County Supervisors Pass Laws to Curb Communists," *Los Angeles Daily News*, August 23, 1950; "Registration Ordered for County's Reds," August 23, 1950, *Los Angeles Times* (clippings found in the CRC Collection); Leslie Claypool, "Anti-Red Ordinance Author Explains," *Los Angeles Daily News*, August 25, 1950, CRC.

46. "First Red Restriction Arrest in County Made," *Los Angeles Times*, September 8, 1950, 1, PQ; "Seized Reds Get Hearing for Failure to Register," *Los Angeles Times*, September 9, 1950, 6, PQ; "First Victims Spurs Fight Against LA County's 'Little Mundt' Law," *People's World*, September 11, 1950, 3; "County Books LA Housewife in Red Check," *Los Angeles Times*, September 26, 1950, A3, PQ; "Demurrer Sought by Woman in Red Law Arrest," *Los Angeles Times*, October 3, 1950, 28, PQ; "Four Attorneys Back Demurrer on Red Registry," *Los Angeles Times*, October 7, 1950, 5, PQ; McCormick oral history transcript, 114. In his oral history, Ben Margolis speaks about LaRue McCormick and the Communist Registration Ordinance but not Moffatt. See Ben Margolis, "Law and Social Conscience," interviewed by Michael S. Balter, Oral History Program, UCLA, ca. 1987, 311–14.

47. "County Red Law Upheld by Court," *Los Angeles Times*, November 25, 1950, 14, PQ; "County's Red Registry Law Held Illegal," *Los Angeles Times*, February 28, 1951, PQ; *People v. McCormick*, 102 Cal. App. 2d Supp. 954 (1951).

48. "Reps. Jackson, Poulson Bid for Renomination," *Los Angeles Times*, March 15, 1952, 2, PQ; "More Nomination Papers Filed for June 5 Primary," *Los Angeles Times*, March 28, 1956, 28, PQ.

49. Moffatt to Holtzendorff, September 1, 1952, copy in Wilkinson Papers, File: "Communications Rec'd After FW Suspension from Housing Authority," unprocessed material, Southern California Library for Social Studies and Research. The CHA had received about 700 letters in support of Wilkinson. They were all turned over to CUAC and still, to this date, have not been "declassified" and released to the public. Some copies, like that of Moffatt, are found in the Frank Wilkinson Papers. Moffatt to Wilkinson, September 8, 1952, Frank Wilkinson Papers.

50. "Ex-Justice of Peace Stanley Moffatt Dies," *Los Angeles Times*, April 7, 1971, pt. 2, 3; "Stanley Moffatt," *San Francisco Chronicle*, April 9, 1971, 33.

51. McCormick oral history transcripts, 115.

CHAPTER 4

Breeding Grounds of Communism

The Gwinn Amendment in Los Angeles' Public Housing

DON PARSON

In 1952 the U.S. Congress passed what would become known as the Gwinn Amendment. This rider on the annual appropriations bill forbade the occupation of public housing by a member of any group on the Attorney General's List of Subversive Organizations. "Seditious" tenants would be identified through the process of obtaining signed loyalty oaths from tenants, administered by local housing authorities.

The Gwinn Amendment was part of a national assault on the public housing program. It attempted to consolidate localized effects of Red Scare politics, which had already undermined housing programs in the cities, at the federal level. Since the beginning of the 1950s, Los Angeles' public housing program had been viciously red-baited, and Mayor Bowron would be electorally deposed in 1953, in part because of his support for public housing. While the statute was legally contested in a number of cities, Los Angeles became a focal point of this struggle. The U.S. Supreme Court's refusal in 1956 to hear Los Angeles' appeal of the lower court ruling overturning the Gwinn Amendment was one of the final nails to be driven into that legislation's coffin and helped prevent further erosion of civil liberties nationally.

The Historical Context: Public Housing, Subversion, and the Gwinn Amendment

Since its inception with the 1937 Housing Act, the U.S. public housing program had been derided by private housing interests—popularly known as "the real estate lobby"—as socialistic, communistic, or generally un-American. During the Cold War, the anticommunist assault on public housing intensified. The president of the National Association of Real Estate Boards argued, "There is no unsocialistic method by which you can socialize the ownership of 1,050,000 dwellings. . . . It [socialism] always moves in bit by bit." Trapped in Congress from 1945 to 1949, the legislation to extend the public housing program (which would become the Taft-Ellender-Wagner Bill) was blocked by, according to President Harry Truman, the opposition of "the real estate lobby, shortsighted and utterly selfish, [which] continues to cry 'socialism' in a last effort to smother the real facts and real issues which this bill is designed to meet." Following Truman's unexpected 1948 reelection, the Taft-Ellender-Wagner Bill finally garnered the needed votes in Congress to become the 1949 Housing Act. At this point the struggle against public housing shifted from the federal to the local level.[1]

After the popular victory of the Housing Act of 1949, public housing opponents coordinated a series of referenda at the municipal and state levels that allowed voters to reject the siting and/or scheduling of public housing projects previously approved by their respective local governments. "In their unrelenting fight against public housing," wrote Harry Conn in 1951, "real-estate operators are shifting much of their attention from Washington and putting their show on the road." By the end of 1952, the real estate lobby had emerged victorious in more than forty local referenda, including Los Angeles' Proposition B. By mid-1953, seventeen state legislatures had considered or had pending similar bills, although their success rate was less impressive. McCarthyism—the domestic counterpart to the international Cold War—was the calling card of these referenda battles. The Gwinn Amendment was, in many respects, an extension of the McCarthyism that had bedeviled the public housing program in the cities, attempting to shift the Red Scare from the local level and consolidate it on the federal level.[2]

Ralph Waldo Gwinn (1884–1962) served in the U.S. Congress as a Republican representative of New York State's suburban Twenty-Seventh Congressional District. He was elected to the Seventy-Ninth Congress and then reelected to six succeeding terms (1945–59). A conservative who strived to roll back the welfare state, Gwinn is remembered even today—more than fifty years after his death—with, depending on one's political perspective, either admiration or disdain. In 1952 the congressman introduced part of the proposed "Liberty Amendment" to the U.S. Constitution, which seeks to repeal income tax, promote individual liberty, and limit government; to date nine states have passed it. Organized labor remembers Gwinn as committed to reversing the power of labor unions with the Taft-Hartley Act. In 1947 Gwinn praised the "right to work" provision of the proposed legislation because it "recognizes and deals with the dangerous expansion of unionism."[3]

Gwinn had a marked antipathy toward public housing—he would call for a liquidation of the program with the proceeds being applied against the national debt—and particularly toward public housing tenants. In April 1948, the congressman testified to a House subcommittee investigating the public housing authorities in San Diego and Los Angeles, identifying the threat that public housing tenants posed to democracy. Weaned away from the self-reliance mandated by free enterprise in favor of "socialism or communism or devil statism," these tenants might view public housing "like a beacon of hope of what Government is going to 'give' them next year." Gwinn addressed the House on June 4 of that year, attacking the pending Taft-Ellender-Wagner Public Housing and Slum Clearance Bill (which would become the 1949 Housing Act) on moral, economic, and constitutional grounds. "When government goes into housing," pontificated the congressman, "freedom must go out the door." Especially dangerous and subversive were public housing tenants: "At the core of these projects are the Socialists and Communists nicely bedded down with low rents . . . while they agitate, organize, and lead the other tenants in the agitation for more plunder and corruption of government."[4]

Four years later, on March 20, 1952, Gwinn found a way to remedy his concerns by offering a proviso to the Independent Offices Appropriation Act: "Provided further, That no part of any appropriation contained in this section shall be used to pay annual contributions on any housing unit of a project assisted by the United States Housing Act of 1937, as amended, which is occupied by a person who is a member of an organization designated as subversive by the Attorney General." The Attorney General's List of Subversive Organizations (AGLOSO) had been formalized in 1947 as only one part of President Truman's attempt to determine the "loyalty" of federal employees, but it quickly became the official, nationally recognized black list used by all levels of government, educational institutions, private organizations, businesses, and others. Despite the lack of transparency about criteria for being placed on the list and the inability to contest the decision, by the time Ralph Gwinn wrote his amendment, two years before Joseph McCarthy took center stage, the use of AGLOSO to root out "subversion" was ubiquitous. (This list appears in appendix A.)[5]

Gwinn spoke of the need for such legislation due to the high proportion of communists who gravitated to "the disastrous American experiment in socialized housing," building cells and subverting the other tenants. The congressman summarized his amendment: "It requires the [local housing] authority to evict Communists if the authority wants to collect subsidies from the general taxpayer." With neither dissent nor discussion, the House agreed to the amendment.[6]

On April 22, in an extension of previous remarks titled "Public Housing Breeds Communists," Gwinn complained in Congress of the confessed inability of the Public Housing Administration (PHA) to screen their tenants in order to keep communists from living in the public housing projects and, according to a recent newspaper story, the opposition of the PHA to his proposed amendment. "The facts are," stated Gwinn, "that many of the public-housing projects are breeding places for Communists, all supported by the general taxpayer and managed by Government housing authorities. . . . Communists find the assembly halls and associations of tenants in these projects made to order for their agitation." As "part of the job and cost of all police-state business," he went on, his amendment would "stop subversive groups from living at public expense." Should public housing authorities insist on housing communist tenants without discrimination, concluded Gwinn, "that raises a fatal question as to the whole idea of public housing."[7]

Indeed, the PHA was wary of the Gwinn Amendment. "Federal housing officials almost fell out of their swivel chairs when the amendment zoomed through the House," wrote the *Los Angeles Daily News*, and they called off the planned sale of housing bonds worth more than $167 million. With doubt cast on the reliability of government subsidy, the public housing bond market was frozen. Though not at odds with the idea of the Gwinn Amendments proposal to remove subversives from their housing, the PHA protested that it would be impossible to administer. Further, the legislation would probably be extended to encompass all federal housing programs including FHA and VA loans for homebuyers. "Otherwise," commented Joseph P. McMurray, staff director of the Senate Banking Committee, "Congress would be discriminating against poor commies and letting the better-heeled comrades cash in on the taxpayer."[8]

On July 5, 1952, the appropriations act that contained the Gwinn Amendment was signed into law (Public Law 455). In its entirety, the rider read,

> Provided further, That no housing unit constructed under the United States Housing Act of 1937, as amended, shall be occupied by a person who is a member of an organization designated as subversive by the Attorney General: Provided further, That the foregoing prohibition shall be enforced by the local housing authority, and that such prohibitions shall not impair or affect the powers or obligations of the Public Housing Administration with respect to the making of loans and manual contributions under the United States Housing Act of 1937, as amended.[9]

Despite any surprise on the part of housing officials, loyalty oaths were already endemic to the political landscape. Twenty-four states and the District of Columbia had instituted loyalty oaths for all public employees, including teachers, by 1950, and the number was soaring (almost double by 1956). After a bruising struggle the University of California dismissed thirty-one professors in August 1950 for refusing to sign a version of the state's loyalty oath specifically revised to deny involvement with AGLOSO organizations. In December, CBS, following in the footsteps of NBC, demanded its twenty-five hundred employees sign an oath similar to one federal employees signed. As the Gwinn Amendment was being debated, the California legislature was proposing a loyalty oath for barbers, dry cleaners, undertakers, lawyers, and other businesses they regulated— and an Ohio act requiring oaths of those receiving unemployment insurance was "defended on the ground of 'Why feed the hand that bites us?'"[10]

Los Angeles

Loyalty oaths for public housing tenants in Los Angeles had first been proposed in 1946 in response to the brouhaha surrounding what the popular press and the City Council would term "the Burke incident." Sidney and Libby Burke had lived in and were evicted from Rodger Young Village and Channel Heights public housing projects for being acknowledged members of the Communist Party. A resolution by Councilman Ed J. Davenport stated that the Burke incident "has heightened the conviction . . . that projects are targets of Communistic propaganda and fertile fields for cultivating support by the subversive groups who would change the American way of life to that of the Communism of Russia." Nicola Giulii, president of the city's housing commission, had proposed adding the following paragraph to the dwelling application of the Los Angeles City Housing Authority (CHA):

> Do you advocate or have you ever advocated, or are you now or have you ever been a member of any organization that advocates the overthrow of the government of the United States by force or violence? _ Yes _No
> If so, give complete details.

In a subsequent legal opinion, however, City Attorney Ray Chesebro indicated that loyalty oaths were probably not a constitutional means to qualify for public housing occupancy.[11]

In August 1949, with unanimous City Council approval, Los Angeles entered into a contract with the federal government to construct ten thousand units of public housing under the 1949 Housing Act. Continually plagued by red-baiting and anticommunist attacks, the council reversed its position two years later and attempted to rescind the contract but was prevented by the courts from doing so. The matter was nevertheless submitted to a popular referendum—1952's Proposition B—where voters overwhelmingly rejected the public housing program.[12]

The generalized anticommunism that had been directed at the principle of public housing took on the form of personalized attack when Frank Wilkinson, public relations officer for the CHA, refused to divulge which organizations, "political or otherwise," he had belonged to since 1932 while testifying in a lawsuit regarding condemnation proceedings for one of the contested housing projects in 1952. Out of the resulting political bedlam, the California Un-American Activities Committee (CUAC) was called in to investigate communist infiltration in the CHA.[13]

"I have become convinced," Councilmember John Holland told the council at the close of the CUAC hearings, "that the public housing scheme is a Communist product and that its operations here have been following the Communist pattern." In its final report on these hearings, CUAC concluded that all of the

FIGURE 4.1. Mayor Fletcher Bowron signing the contract to build
ten thousand units of public housing, with Housing Commissioner
Nicola Giulii (left) and Deputy City Attorney Neal (right), 1949.
Housing Authority of the City of Los Angeles Photograph Collection,
Southern California Library, Los Angeles.

alleged communists in the CHA—Frank Wilkinson, Sidney Green, Elizabeth
Smith, Jack Naiditch, and Adina Williamson—had been identified and duly
dismissed. While the committee noted that "five Communists out of a total of
450 employees in the Los Angeles City Housing Authority is obviously not a
very heavy incidence of infiltration," the danger of communism was not to be
underestimated as public housing was a breeding ground for subversives:

> The housing authority is a natural target for Communist infiltration because the
> people who are forced to live in public housing units are more apt to be socially
> maladjusted and dissatisfied and therefore more susceptible to the blandishment of
> clever Communist recruiting specialists than the average person who has a home
> of his own. Furthermore, the element of congestion and the high incidence of ra-
> cial minority groups combine to make the field even more fertile.[14]

The specter of communism would lead to another congressional investigation by the Special Subcommittee of the Committee on Government Operations. These hearings took place in Los Angeles just prior to the municipal

FIGURE 4.2. Members of the Los Angeles City Council urge voters to halt
the city's public housing program and vote no on Proposition B, 1952.
Los Angeles Times *Photographic Archives (Collection 1429), Library Special Collections,
Charles E. Young Research Library,* UCLA.

elections in 1953 in which the pro-public-housing mayor, Fletcher Bowron,
would be voted out of office.[15]

Into this caustic anticommunist milieu of the domestic Cold War, the Gwinn
Amendment was introduced in Los Angeles. Left organizations, such as the
Civil Rights Congress (CRC), viewed the 1952 passage of the Gwinn Amendment
with alarm. Founded in 1946 as a national organization that was supported by a
network of local chapters in thirty-three cities, the CRC provided, throughout its
ten-year existence, legal advocacy for unions, minorities, and democratic organizations on a broad range of civil rights grievances. This included such issues as
police brutality as well as racial and political discrimination in employment and
housing. The CRC found itself, due to its close ties to the Communist Party, on
AGLOSO. The "Communist front" label, however, tended to obscure and isolate
the CRC's work building bridges among diverse communities in pursuit of social
justice. "The attack on CRC as a 'Communist front,'" writes Gerald Horne, "was
meant to destabilize a 'popular front' of communists and non-communists."[16]

"It is easy to see which way this thing is going," the Los Angeles CRC chapter wrote to public housing tenants in city and county-owned housing projects
on the foreboding implications of the Gwinn Amendment. "Tomorrow a new

group is added to [the attorney general's] list. If you have ever been a member of such an organization, out you go. . . . The regulation will make the project a haven for stoolpigeons." The CRC noted that workers as well as the "Mexican and Negro people" would be among those most affected by the Gwinn Amendment and, on September 25, 1952, offered to defend anyone facing eviction for their refusal to sign a loyalty oath in connection with the new legislation. The virulent attack upon the city's public housing program, in particular the CUAC accusations against the CHA, was seen by the Communist Party as a precursor to a witch hunt against public housing tenants themselves.[17]

On January 5, 1953, the CHA began to mail out loyalty oath forms (appendix B) to the 4,818 families—comprising about 23,000 individuals—living in the city's thirteen permanent public housing projects (see appendix C). The accompanying letter sent to those living in the Estrada Courts project asked residents there to study, without delay, the attorney general's list, which was posted in the project's management office, and schedule an appointment for signing the oath. Tenants were instructed to sign the oath by February 1 or face eviction. Meeting at Estrada Courts on January 21, loyalty-oath opponents from a number of projects—thirty-six tenants—constituted themselves as the Residents Committee Against Loyalty Oaths and elected Sidney Moore Jr. as their temporary chairman (see appendix D). The committee mimeographed a leaflet that outlined the danger loyalty oaths posed to public housing tenants and called for those tenants to challenge the enactment of the Gwinn Amendment. "The Communists here have started an organization to try to get the people not to sign," said Howard Holtzendorff, executive director of the CHA. "I understand they have passed out circulars claiming the requirement is a 'violation of civil rights' and is 'unconstitutional.'"[18]

Sidney Moore Jr. and his wife Adele were a young biracial couple (Sidney was African American and Adele was Jewish) who had lived in Estrada Courts since December 1950. Sidney was an American Federation of Labor (AFL) apprentice electrician, while Adele had been active in community organizing in Estrada Courts, helping to initiate the residents council there. Adele recalls that several of the dissident families used to meet at the Estrada Courts Recreation Center. The meetings were small, as most of the public housing tenants did not feel that the Gwinn Amendment posed much of a problem for them. "They had many other problems, like feeding their families and paying the rent. Some were on welfare and jobs were hard to find." Assured of a larger apartment upon the birth of their second child, the Moores were told by Robert Sefren, Estrada Courts manager, that they could move into their new quarters as soon as they signed the loyalty oath. Failure to sign the oath would result in an eviction notice. "We are deeply shocked by your suddenly cancelling an apartment for Mr. and Mrs. Moore," fellow tenants Louise Huling, Mary Mendoza, and A. Gutierrez angrily wrote to Sefren. "They packed and thoroughly cleaned the house all weekend preparing themselves to be moved. Then you suddenly cancelled their transfer. We urge you to give Mr. and Mrs. Moore the apartment promised them. If Mr. and Mrs. Moore can receive such treatment, then none of us in Public Housing are safe."[19]

By early 1953, in an apparently amiable transfer of advocacy from the CRC, the Southern California Chapter of the American Civil Liberties Union (ACLU) began to represent the Residents Committee in their legal struggle against the Gwinn Amendment. While the CRC was undergoing internal strain, financial difficulties, and diminishing effectiveness due to its subversive label, legal challenges to the Gwinn Amendment nationally were being handled directly by ACLU counsel or with ACLU participation as a friend of the court. These challenges included those made in Denver, Seattle, Milwaukee, Washington, D.C., New York, Chicago, Philadelphia, Newark, New Jersey, Buffalo, New York, Richmond, California, San Antonio, Texas, and Baltimore, Maryland.[20]

The ACLU questioned the Gwinn Amendment's underlying principle "that the state may withhold privileges from those who do not give the state unquestioned loyalty." Accepting this, the door would be open to requiring loyalty oaths for all government subsidized services—e.g., municipal busses, public streets and sidewalks, public libraries, municipal water and power, etc, etc.— "all of which would not in any way make the state more secure."[21]

On January 26, the Residents Committee announced that the ACLU had filed a brief in Superior Court on the committee's behalf. The suit sought a restraining order against the CHA to prevent evictions and challenged the Gwinn Amendment as a violation of the First, Fifth, and Fourteenth Amendments. The committee urged individuals and organizations to communicate to Mayor Bowron, the City Council, and public officials that Holtzendorff should withdraw the loyalty oath forms and to join the committee at a March 6 meeting with Holtzendorff to make this request in person. They also suggested that all candidates for public office be questioned as to their stand on loyalty oaths. In a series of meetings over the weekend of February 19 and 20, tenants of both the city and county housing authorities merged their respective programs of resistance in a joint action committee.[22]

Representing the Residents Committee for the ACLU, attorneys A. L. Wirin, Fred Okrand, Loren Miller, and Edward Carter Maddox threatened an injunction against the CHA should evictions proceed. The February 1 deadline for tenants to either sign the loyalty oath or face eviction proceedings passed with no action being taken by the CHA. On February 14, the ACLU filed a suit in the Superior Court of Los Angeles County—*David Hankerson v. Housing Authority of the City of Los Angeles*—securing an order for the CHA to "show cause" for carrying out the evictions stipulated by the Gwinn Amendment. The imposition of the loyalty oath by the CHA, maintained ACLU attorney Fred Okrand, made no allowance for scienter—specific intent to engage in criminal conduct—on the part of tenants. The case challenging the oath mandated by the Gwinn Amendment was analogous to the recently decided U.S. Supreme Court case of *Wieman v. Updegraff*, where the loyalty oath for public employees in Oklahoma—which likewise utilized membership in an organization on the attorney general's subversive list as a criterion of loyalty—was struck down as a denial of due process. Other legal precedents raised serious questions as to whether the oath violated the constitutional guarantees of due process as well as freedoms of speech, association, and assembly.[23]

On February 27—just a few hours prior to the scheduled hearing of the ACLU lawsuit—the CHA issued a stipulation, signed by Edward C. Maddox for the ACLU and Stanley Furman for the CHA. They agreed to halt all eviction proceedings against or otherwise inconvenience the non-signers of the oath pending the outcome of similar cases in other states' high courts that dealt with the constitutionality of the Gwinn Amendment. Though opposed by Holtzendorff, the stipulation was entered into on the instruction of the PHA with the purpose of avoiding the expense of a lawsuit so similar to others being decided across the country.[24]

The appropriateness of this decision was subsequently questioned by the House Special Subcommittee on Government Operations when they convened in Los Angeles in May. As the Gwinn Amendment had not been enforced by evicting the families who refused to sign loyalty oaths, the CHA, by signing the stipulation, was accused of allowing communist tenants to continue having their rent paid by the loyal citizenry while they occupied public housing units that might be utilized by the non-subversive needy. In the seminal municipal elections later that month, this was cannon fodder for the myriad anti-public-housing attacks on the incumbent pro-public-housing mayor, Fletcher Bowron.[25]

The Residents Committee began the long legal march from lower to higher courts, beginning in Los Angeles Municipal Court and eventually appealing directly to the U.S. Supreme Court. ACLU counsel A. L. Wirin and Fred Okrand of the law firm of Wirin, Rissman, and Okrand took five cases—those of Sam and Helen Konick (who resided in Estrada Courts), Sidney and Adele Moore Jr. (of Estrada Courts), Jim and Ramona Cordova (of Aliso Village), Louise P. Huling (of Estrada Courts), and Eleanor Wycoff (of Aliso Village)—to the Municipal Court of Los Angeles County in April 1954. In June, Judge Lucius Green struck down the ACLU arguments about the unconstitutionality of the Gwinn Amendment and issued a summary judgment in favor of the CHA, upholding the agency's eviction proceedings.[26]

On August 19, 1954, this ruling was appealed by the Cordovas, the Moores, the Konicks, and Wycoff (Huling had dropped her suit) to the Appellate Department of the Superior Court of Los Angeles County. CHA lawyer James J. Arnditto contended that the CHA was not required to give a reason to cancel tenancy and that such a reason would be, in fact, immaterial as, like that of a private landlord, either party was allowed to terminate the lease on ten-day notice. ACLU attorneys Wirin and Okrand argued that the refusal to sign the stipulated loyalty oath was the only reason for eviction and that the Gwinn Amendment was unconstitutional on a number of grounds.[27]

Citing *Joint Anti-Fascist Refugee Committee v. McGrath*, counsel observed that the amendment violated due process as no notice or hearing was given to the organizations on the attorney general's list. The designations of certain groups as subversive are, as Justice Douglas said in that decision, "weapons which can be made as sharp or as blunt as the occasion requires" and as they are "subject to grave abuse, they have no place in our system of law." The denial of housing mandated by the Gwinn Amendment was based solely on guilt by association. The attorneys also maintained that the statute violated due process because of the statute's vagueness and lack of legislative standard, because there was no notice or opportunity for the tenants to be heard, and because it had no reasonable relationship to the public welfare. In the absence of any "clear and present danger," the Gwinn Amendment violated the freedom of speech and association guarantees of the First and Fourteenth Amendments. "A tenant has to step lightly indeed," observed the lawyers, "lest he suddenly find his family on the street because he innocently joined an organization which the Attorney General later designates as subversive." Further, the Gwinn Amendment functioned as a bill of attainder, that is, legislation that imposes punishment on named groups or individuals without a trial, in violation of Article I, Section 9, Clause 3 of the U.S. Constitution. In addition the Gwinn Amendment, as applied, was unconstitutional because association was condemned, the element of scienter was missing, and the CHA exceeded the authority given by the Gwinn Amendment. The legislation allowed for the eviction only of members of organizations on the attorney general's list—not for those who failed to sign a certificate.[28]

The Appellate Department of the Superior Court of Los Angeles County was "mindful of the grave threats" posed by subversives to the constitutional government of the United States and reluctant to strike down any governmental actions that might deal with such threats. In spite of these concerns, on January 19, 1955, Judge Julius Patrosso wrote in the unanimous opinion (with Judges Hartley Shaw and Edward Bishop concurring) that "we are not at liberty to disregard settled rules of law and the limitations inherent in our constitutional form of government, observance of which in our view compels a reversal of the judgment." Dismissing the CHA's primary argument, the justices held that, unlike a private landlord, housing authorities could not discriminate in leasing or in the termination of a lease. Loyalty oaths could not, ruled the court, be imposed as a condition of residence in public housing, citing the 1954 Gwinn Amendment case in the Illinois Supreme Court (*Chicago Housing Authority v. Blackman*). The purpose of a housing authority is to eradicate slums and provide low-income housing—not to exclude otherwise qualified persons from occupying public housing facilities solely on the basis of belonging to an organization designated as subversive by the attorney general. "Nor is it apparent," added the court, "that the laudable purpose of combating the efforts of subversives is advanced by compelling them to live in slums or substandard housing accommodations." The judgment was reversed and the case remanded to Municipal Court for retrial to determine if the refusal to sign a loyalty oath was indeed the sole cause of their eviction.[29]

In Los Angeles' Municipal Court, Judge Vernon W. Hunt considered the three consolidated cases of Jim and Ramona Cordova, Eleanor Wycoff, and Sidney and Adele Moore Jr., which had been remanded by the Appellate Department. In his July 18, 1955, opinion, the judge ruled that the determination of the higher court—that the CHA cannot demand the signing of a loyalty oath as a condition for the occupancy of public housing—was conclusive and binding. Other points raised by the CHA were secondary to the stipulation of fact that had halted evictions until decisions were reached in similar cases nationally and had been agreed upon by both the CHA and its tenant/challengers. The CHA announced that, if necessary, the ruling would be appealed to the U.S. Supreme Court.[30]

The Death of the Gwinn Amendment

The Gwinn Amendment was again introduced as a rider to the appropriations act of July 31, 1953 (Public Law 176), and duly codified. Its wording remained the same as the 1952 rider. The amendment was not, however, included in subsequent legislation. The fact that it was a part of an annual appropriations bill gave rise to questioning the amendment's permanent status. Efforts to give the Gwinn Amendment a more secure legal foothold were not successful. In the words of the *Journal of Housing*, the amendment was "conspicuous by its absence" from the Housing Act of 1954. It had been included in the House version of the act but was eliminated by the Senate when the provision was not agreed to in conference. Despite its ambiguous status, the PHA held that the original proviso of 1952 was still in effect.[31]

Beginning in 1953 rulings in several of the ACLU cases challenging loyalty oaths in public housing were issued, figuring prominently in the Gwinn Amendment's ultimate downfall. In March, an attempt by the International Workers Order, representing New York tenants in Federal Court, failed to have the U.S. Supreme Court make an early ruling on the constitutionality of loyalty oaths in public housing. *Peters v. New York City Housing Authority* reached that state's high court in 1954; the judiciary did not rule on the constitutionality of the act but remanded the case back to the trial court to determine if the tenants involved were indeed covered by the statute. In November 1954, the Illinois Supreme Court declared the Gwinn Amendment unconstitutional in *Chicago Housing Authority v. Blackman*, ruling that Illinois public housing tenants could not be evicted for failure to sign a loyalty oath. The Wisconsin Supreme Court found likewise, in the June 1955 case *Lawson v. Housing Authority of the City of Milwaukee*, that suppression of the First Amendment far outweighed any threatened evil posed by subversives living in public housing. The contest of tenant John Rudder and the National Capital Housing Authority worked its way up to the U.S. Court of Appeals for Washington, D.C.—the nation's highest court to rule on the Gwinn Amendment—which in July 1955 found the legislation's requirements to be arbitrary and a violation of due process. The regulations were "running into serious legal trouble," wrote the *New York Times*. "Simply put, courts in general across the country do not like the Federal legislation.[32]

On November 7, 1955, the U.S. Supreme Court refused to review the Wisconsin Supreme Court's *Lawson* decision, setting off within the PHA a "new furor of speculation on the law's constitutionality," according to the *Journal of Housing*. The PHA's assistant general counsel, Lawrence C. Davern, issued an interpretation that the Gwinn Amendment was still the law of the land except in Wisconsin. In December 1955, decisions by the State Supreme Court of New Jersey and New York's Appellate Division against the Gwinn Amendment made its ineffectiveness clear. The conclusion to this string of legal defeats came when Los Angeles' CHA appealed *Cordova* to the U.S. Supreme Court. On February 27, 1956, the High Court refused to hear the case, allowing the lower court rulings to stand.[33]

On July 30, 1956, the PHA issued a directive to its regional offices as well as local housing authorities, declaring that it would no longer enforce loyalty oath provisions. The Department of Justice announced likewise on August 2. The Gwinn Amendment, pronounced the *Journal of Housing*, "is dead." Though the PHA disallowed the loyalty oath procedure, it was assumed that local housing authorities would "exercise administrative authority to prevent occupancy of any low-rent housing project by any person who is subversive."[34]

◻ ◻ ◻

The Gwinn Amendment was one component of the wave of repressive legislation that swept the country in the early 1950s. The origin of that amendment lay in conservative opposition to the public housing program, which the Gwinn Amendment then broadened to combat public housing tenants as well. The Red Scare that inundated Los Angeles and other cities during the 1950s would worm its way up to the federal level and threaten civil liberties nationally.

The public housing conflict in Los Angeles—distinguished by an ubiquitous McCarthyism—was one of the hottest battles of the domestic Cold War. This episode, in particular the 1953 mayoral election in which the ten-thousand-unit public housing contract was a central issue, was a focal point for public housing opponents throughout the nation. The success of local challenges in halting public housing sent a signal to the U.S. Congress, which drastically curtailed the contentious public housing program for the remainder of the decade.[35]

The legal arguments in opposition to the Gwinn Amendment presented by the ACLU in Los Angeles were similar to those of ACLU test cases in other cities. In the Supreme Court's refusal to hear the case, the Los Angeles case appears as the straw that broke the camel's back. The PHA would eventually, in calmer times, refuse to administer the loyalty oath, and the Gwinn Amendment, though never repealed, would eventually be omitted from the U.S. Codes. The ACLU victory in the Gwinn Amendment cases did not contribute to reviving the moribund housing program but did serve as a legal precedent against further erosion of civil liberties.

Appendix A

THE ATTORNEY GENERAL'S LIST OF SUBVERSIVE ORGANIZATIONS

Consolidated List of Organizations Designated by the Attorney General of the United States as Within Executive Order No. 10450 (18 F.R. 2489) and in Accordance With Regulations Promulgated by Him Under Date of April 29, 1953 (18 F.R. 2619)

In 1947, President Harry Truman instructed Attorney General Tom Clark to develop a list of subversive organizations. Arguably conceived as a precautionary and defensive precedent, the Attorney General's list would be used during the domestic Cold War to deprive many Americans of employment and even public housing. The listed organizations included those of both the left and right, but the focus was on the Communist Party and its "fronts."

Abraham Lincoln Brigade

Abraham Lincoln School, Chicago, Ill.

Action Committee To Free Spain Now

Alabama Peoples Educational Association

American Association for Reconstruction In Yugoslavia, Inc.

American Branch of the Federation of Greek Maritime Unions

American Christian Nationalist Party

American Committee for European Workers Relief

American Committee for Protection of Foreign Born

American Committee for the Settlement of Jews in Birobidjan, Inc.

American Committee for Spanish Freedom

American Committee to Survey Labor Conditions in Europe

American Committee for Yugoslav Relief, Inc.

American Council for a Democratic Greece, formerly known as the Greek American Council

American Council on Soviet Relations

American Croatian Congress

American Jewish Labor Council

American League Against War and Fascism

American League for Peace and Democracy

American Nationalist Party

American National Labor Party

American National Socialist League

American National Socialist Party

American Patriots, Inc.

American Peace Mobilization

American Poles for Peace

American Polish Labor Council

American Rescue Ship Mission (a
Project of the United American
Spanish Aid Committee)

American-Russian Fraternal Society

American Russian Institute, New York,
also known as the American-Russian
Institute for Cultural Relations with
the Soviet Union

American Russian Institute,
Philadelphia

American Russian Institute (of San
Francisco)

American Russian Institute of Southern
California, Los Angeles

American Slav Congress

American Youth Congress

American Youth for Democracy

Armenian Progressive League of
America

Associated Klans of America

Association of Georgia Klans

Association of German Nationals
(Reichsdeutsche Vereinigung)

Ausland-Organization der
NSDAP, Overseas Branch of
Nazi Party

Baltimore Forum

Black Dragon Society

Boston School for Marxist Studies,
Boston, Mass.

Bridges-Robertson-Schmidt Defense
Committee

Bulgarian American People s League of
the United States of America

California Emergency Defense
Committee

California Labor School, Inc., 216
Market Street, San Francisco, Calif.

Carpatho-Russian Peoples Society

Central Council of American Women
of Croatian Descent, also known
as Central Council of American
Croatian Women, National Council of
Croatian Women

Central Japanese Association (Beikoku
Chuo Nipponjin Kai)

Central Japanese Association of
Southern California

Central Organization of the German-
American National Alliance
(Deutsche-Amerikanische
Einheitsfront)

Cervantes Fraternal Society

Chopin Cultural Center

Citizens Committee To Free Earl
Browder

Citizens Committee for Harry Bridges

Citizens Committee of the Upper West
Side (New York City)

Citizens Protective League

Civil Rights Congress and its affiliated
organizations

Civil Rights Congress for Texas

Columbians

Comite Coordinador Pro Republica
Espanola

Committee To Aid the Fighting South

Committee for Constitutional and
Political Freedom Committee to
Defend Marie Richardson

Committee for the Defense of the
Pittsburgh Six

Committee for a Democratic Far
Eastern Policy

Committee for Nationalist Action

Committee for Peace and Brotherhood
Festival in Philadelphia

Committee for the Protection of the Bill
of Rights

Committee to Uphold the Bill of
Rights

Committee for World Youth Friendship
and Cultural Exchange

Commonwealth College, Mena, Ark.

Communist Party, U.S.A., its
subdivisions, subsidiaries, and
affiliates

Communist Political Association,
its subdivisions, subsidiaries, and
affiliates

Congress of American Revolutionary
Writers

Congress of American Women

Connecticut State Youth Conference

Council on African Affairs

Council of Greek Americans

Council for Jobs, Relief and Housing

Council for Pan-American Democracy

Croatian Benevolent Fraternity

Dai Nippon Butoku Kai (Military
Virtue Society of Japan or
Military Art)

Daily Worker Press Club

Dante Alighieri Society (between 1935
and 1940)

Dennis Defense Committee

Detroit Youth Assembly

Emergency Conference To Save Spanish
Refugees (founding body of the North
American Spanish Aid Committee)

Federation of Italian War Veterans
in the U.S.A., Inc. (Associazione
Nazionale Combattenti Italiani,
Fedetazionede Gli Stati Uniti
d'America)

Finnish-American Mutual Aid Society

Florida Press and Educational League

Frederick Douglass Educational Center

Friends of the New Germany (Freunds
des Neuen Deutschlands)

Friends of the Soviet Union

Garibaldi American Fraternal Society

George Washington Carver School,
New York City German-American
Bund (Amerikadeutscher Volksbund)

German-American Republican League

German-Americans of Chicago

German-American Vocational
League (Deutsche-Amerikanische
Betufsgemeinschaft)

Greek American Committee for
National Unity

Harlem Trade Union Council

Hawaii Civil Liberties Committee

Heimuska Kai, also known as Nokubei
Heieki Gimusha Kai, Zaibel Nihonjin,
Heiyaku Gimusha Kai, and Zaibei
Heimusha Kai (Japanese Residing
in America Military Conscripts
Association)

Hellenic-American Brotherhood

Hinode Kai (Imperial Japanese
Reservists)

Hinomaru Kai (Rising Sun Flag Society,
a group of Japanese war veterans)

Hokubei Zaigo Shake Dan (North
American Reserve Officers
Association)

Hollywood Writers Mobilization for
Defense

Hungarian-American Council for
Democracy

Hungarian Brotherhood

Independent Socialist League

Industrial Workers of the World

International Labor Defense

International Workers Order, its
subdivisions, subsidiaries, and
affiliates

Japanese Association of America

Japanese Overseas Central Society
(Kaigai Dobo Chuo Kai)

Japanese Overseas Convention, Tokyo,
Japan, 1940

Japanese Protective Association
(Recruiting Organization)

Jefferson School of Social Science, New
York City

Jewish Cultural Society

Jewish Peoples Committee

Jewish Peoples Fraternal Order

Jikyokulinkai (The Committee for the
Crisis)

Joint Anti-Fascist Refugee Committee

Joint Council of Progressive Italian-
Americans, Inc.

Joseph Weydemeyer School of Social Science, St. Louis, Mo.

Kibei Semen Kai (Association of United States Citizens of Japanese Ancestry who have returned to America after studying in Japan)

Knights of the White Camelia

Ku Klux Klan

Kyffhaeuser, also known as Kyffhaeuser League (Kyffhaeuser Bund), Kyffhaeuser Fellowship (Kyffhaeuser Kameradschaft)

Kyffhaeuser War Relief (Kyffhaeuser Kreigshilfswerk)

Labor Council for Negro Rights

Labor Research Association, Inc.

Labor Youth League

League of American Writers

Lictor Society (Italian Black Shirts)

Macedonian-American People's League

Mario Morgantini Circle

Maritime Labor Committee to Defend Al Lannon

Maurice Braverman Defense Committee

Michigan Civil Rights Federation

Michigan School of Social Science

Nanca Teikoku Gunyudan (Imperial Military or Southern California War Veterans)

National Blue Star Mothers of America (Not to be confused with the Blue Star Mothers of America organized in February 1942)

National Committee for the Defense of Political Prisoners

National Committee for Freedom of the Press

National Committee To Win the Peace

National Conference on American Policy in China and the Far East (a Conference called by the Committee for a Democratic Far Eastern Policy)

National Council of Americans of Croatian Descent

National Council of American Soviet Friendship

National Federation for Constitutional Liberties

National Labor Conference for Peace

National Negro Congress

Nationalist Action League

Nationalist Party of Puerto Rico

Nature Friends of America (since 1935)

Negro Labor Victory Committee

New Committee for Publications

Nichibei Kogyo Kaisha (The Great Fujii Theatre)

North American Committee To Aid Spanish Democracy

North American Spanish Aid Committee

North Philadelphia Forum

Northwest Japanese Association

Ohio School of Social Sciences

Oklahoma Committee To Defend Political Prisoners

Oklahoma League for Political Education

Original Southern Klans, Incorporated

Pacific Northwest Labor School, Seattle, Wash.

Partido del Pueblo of Panama (operating in the Canal Zone)

Peace Information Center

Peace Movement of Ethiopia

People's Drama, Inc.

Peoples Educational Association (Incorporated under name Los Angeles Educational Association, Inc.), also known as Peoples Educational Center, Peoples University, Peoples School, Peoples Educational and Press Association of Texas

People's Institute of Applied Religion

People's Radio Foundation, Inc.

Philadelphia Labor Committee for Negro Rights

Philadelphia School of Social Science

and Art Photo League (New York City)

Political Prisoners' Welfare Committee

Polonia Society of the IWO

Progressive German-Americans, also known as Progressive Proletarian Party of America

Protestant War Veterans of the United States, Inc.

Provisional Committee of Citizens for Peace, Southwest Area

Puertorriquenos Unidos (Puerto Ricans United)

Quad City Committee for Peace

Revolutionary Workers League

Romanian-American Fraternal Society

Russian American Society, Inc.

Sakura Kai (Patriotic Society, or Cherry Association composed of veterans of Russo-Japanese War)

Samuel Adams School, Boston, Mass.

Santa Barbara Peace Forum

Schappes Defense Committee

Schneiderman-Darcy Defense Committee

School of Jewish Studies, New York City

Seattle Labor School, Seattle, Wash.

Serbian-American Fraternal Society

Serbian Vidovdan Council

Shinto Temples

Silver Shirt Legion of America

Slovak Workers Society

Slovenian-American National Council

Socialist Workers Party, including American Committee for European Workers Relief

Socialist Youth League

Sokoku Kai (Fatherland Society)

Southern Negro Youth Congress

SuikoSha (Reserve Officers Association, Los Angeles)

Tom Paine School of Social Science, Philadelphia, Pa.

Tom Paine School of Westchester, N.Y.

Tri-State Negro Trade Union Council

Ukrainian-American Fraternal Union

Union of American Croatians

Union of New York Veterans

United American Spanish Aid Committee

United Committee of Jewish Societies and Landsmanschaft Federations, also known as Coordination Committee of Jewish Landsmanschaften and Fraternal Organizations

United Committee of South Slavic Americans

United Harlem Tenants and Consumers Organization

United May Day Committee

United Negro and Allied Veterans of America

Veterans of the Abraham Lincoln Brigade

Veterans Against Discrimination of Civil Rights

Virginia League of Peoples Education

Voice of Freedom Committee

Walt Whitman School of Social Science

Washington Bookshop Association

Washington Committee to Defend the Bill of Rights

Washington Committee for Democratic Action

Washington Commonwealth Federation

Wisconsin Conference on Social Legislation

Workers Alliance (since April 1936)

Workers Party, including Socialist Youth League

Yiddisher Kultur Farband

Young Communist League

Yugoslav-American Cooperative Home, Inc.

Appendix B

THE LOYALTY OATH ADMINISTERED BY THE LOS ANGELES CHA IN 1953
Certificate of the Non-Membership in Subversive Organizations

I hereby certify that I am not a member of any of the organizations listed in the document entitled CONSOLIDATED LIST, DATED NOVEMBER 10, 1952, OF ORGANIZATIONS DESIGNATED BY THE ATTORNEY GENERAL OF THE UNITED STATES AS WITHIN EXECUTIVE ORDER NO. 9835," said document as reproduced on page 2, 3 and 4 of, and being a part of, this Certificate, and that, to the best of my knowledge, information, and belief, no person who is to occupy the housing accommodations in connection with which this Certificate is furnished (that is, the accommodations for which I am making, or have made, application) is a member of such organization. I hereby further certify that I have carefully read, or have had read to me, the document referred to in the preceding sentence.

Source: ACLU Collection, box 929, folder: ACLU—HOUSING AUTHORITY ETC. V. CORDOVA No. 171371.

Appendix C

LOS ANGELES CHA PUBLIC HOUSING PROJECTS SUBJECT TO THE GWINN AMENDMENT

Not subject to the Gwinn Amendment's loyalty oath requirements were the CHA-managed veterans projects or temporary public war housing projects. The tenants of thirteen projects—the ten projects constructed under the 1937 Housing Act as well as three permanent public war housing projects—were required to publicly profess their loyalty. These projects were:

Aliso Village	Channel Heights	Avalon Gardens
Estrada Courts	Dana Strand Village	Hacienda Village
Pico Gardens	Pueblo del Rio	Ramona Gardens
Rose Hill Courts	Rancho San Pedro	Normont Terrace
William Mead Homes		

Source: "23,000 L.A. Tenants Told to Sign 'Loyalty' Oath," *People's World*, January 21, 1953, 8.

Appendix D

THE RESIDENTS COMMITTEE AGAINST LOYALTY OATHS IN HOUSING

The thirty-six tenants on whose behalf a "show cause" order was filed against the Los Angeles CHA in February 1953 were:

David Hankerson, M. C. Anderson, Geneva Borkins, Velma Clark, Jim C. Cordova, Ramona Cordova, Aldythe Gaman, Garrison Gaman, Edith Gerowitz, Ralph Gerowitz, Herman Halmowitz, Mrs. Herman Halmowitz, Shelin Hall, Helen Hanks, Milton Hanks, Dudley H. Hay, Eleanor Hay, Louise Huling, Ken Jones, Nina L. Jones,

Helen Konick, Sam Konick, Bertha Marshall, Walter A. Meadows, Adele Moore, Sidney Moore Jr., Clarence McGee, Pearlie McGee, Ruby Nelson, Charles Shanks, Vercy Singleton, Christa B. Stokes, James Washington, Mrs. James Washington, Eleanor Wycoff, James C. York.

Source: "Loyalty Oath Ouster Halted," *Los Angeles Examiner*, February 17, 1953.

NOTES

1. Don Parson, "The Decline of Public Housing and the Politics of the Red Scare: The Significance of the Los Angeles Public Housing War," *Journal of Urban History* 33 (March 2007): 400–17; Associated Press, "Real Estate Men Answer Truman Blast," *Washington Post*, June 19, 1949, M1; Truman letter in Nathaniel S. Keith, *Politics and the Housing Crisis since 1930* (New York: Universe Books, 1973), 97.

2. Harry Conn, "Housing: A Vanishing Vision," *New Republic* 125 (July 30, 1951): 12–13; "Public Housing 'Battle' Hits in Washington, the States, Local Communities," *Journal of Housing* 9 (March 1952): 79–80, 94.

3. Press Release—Paul introduces Liberty Amendment to Constitution, April 8, 1998, http://www.house.gov/paul/press/press98/pr042898liberty.htm; Pennsylvania AFL-CIO, "The Right to Work," http://www.paaflcio.org/rightto.htm.

4. U.S. Congress, *Congressional Record: Proceedings and Debates of the Congress*, vol. 99, pt. 3, 83rd Cong., 1st sess., April 9–April 30, 1953, Government Printing Office, 3602; U.S. Congress, Committee on Expenditures in the Executive Departments, *Investigation of Public Housing Authority at San Diego and Los Angeles*, hearings, 80th Cong., 2nd sess., April 15, 16, 21, 1948, Government Printing Office), 52–63; Ralph W. Gwinn, "Public Housing—Disastrous Here and Abroad," speech (Washington, D.C.: Government Printing Office, June 4, 1948), 4, 5.

5. Robert Justin Goldstein, *American Blacklist: The Attorney General's List of Subversive Organizations* (Lawrence: University of Kansas Press, 2008), 62–63, 74.

6. U.S. Congress, *Congressional Record: Proceedings and Debates of the Congress*, vol. 98, pt. 2, 82nd Cong., 2nd sess., February 26–March 24, 1952, Government Printing Office, 2648–49.

7. "Public Housing Breeds Communists," extension of remarks of Hon. Ralph W. Gwinn, April 22, 1952, in U.S. Congress, *Congressional Record: Proceedings and Debates of the Congress*, vol. 98, pt. 9, 82nd Cong., 2nd sess., February 26–March 24, 1952, Government Printing Office, A2498.

8. "FBI may have to put public housing tenants to Red test," *Los Angeles Daily News*, April 21, 1952, 9.

9. Gwinn Amendment, 82nd Cong., 2nd Sess., chap. 578, *U.S. Statutes at Large* 66 (July 5, 1952): 403.

10. "Loyalty Oaths," The First Amendment and Higher Education, Wikispaces, May 27, 2011, https://firstamendmentandhighered.wikispaces.com/Loyalty+Oaths ;SteveFinacom; "Summary of Loyalty Oath Events" (Loyalty Oath Controversy, University of California, 1949–51), www.lib.berkeley.edu/uchistory/archives_exhibits /loyaltyoath/timelinesummary.html; Jack Gould, "Demanding Loyalty Oaths from Its 2,500 Regular Employees," *New York Times*, December 21, 1950, 1; Nanette Dembitz, "Swearing to One's Loyalty," *Antioch Review*, June 1, 1952, 2, PQ.

11. Don Parson, "The Burke Incident: Political Belief in Los Angeles' Public Housing during the Domestic Cold War," *Southern California Quarterly* 84, no. 1 (Spring 2002): 53–74; Resolution by Ed J. Davenport, October 30, 1946, in Council File 25551, City Archives; Nicola Giulii to City Council, October 24, 1946 (3 pp.) and attached memorandum to Veterans Advisory Committee, October 23, 1946 (6 pp.), Council File 25298; Ray L. Chesebro, "Opinion re Authority of the Housing Authority of the City of Los Angeles . . . Tenant Selection," November 4, 1946, in Council File 25551.

12. I have discussed, in detail, the Los Angeles public housing war elsewhere. Please see Don Parson, "Los Angeles' Headline-Happy Public Housing War," *Southern California Quarterly* 65, no. 3 (Fall 1983): 251–85; Don Parson, *Making a Better World: Public Housing, the Red Scare, and the Direction of Modern Los Angeles* (Minneapolis: University of Minnesota Press, 2005).

13. Transcript of *Housing Authority of the City of Los Angeles v. Mosier M. Meyer, et. al.*, Los Angeles County Superior Court No. 584912 (1952), August 29, 1952, Frank Wilkinson Papers, unprocessed material; California Legislature, "Seventh Report of the Senate Fact-Finding Committee on Un-American Activities," 1953, California State Senate, 78–79.

14. "Housing Seen as Red Plan," *Los Angeles Herald and Express*, October 30, 1952, A-4; California Legislature, "Seventh Report of the Senate Fact-Finding Committee," 132.

15. U.S. Congress, Special Subcommittee of the Committee on Government Operations, *Hearings on Investigation of Public Housing Activities in Los Angeles*, 83rd Cong., 1st Sess., May 13, 18, 19, 20, 21, 27, 1953, Government Printing Office.

16. Congress on Civil Rights press release, April 3, 1946, American Civil Liberties Union of Southern California (hereafter ACLU) Collection, box 40, folder 5, Special Collections, UCLA; Gerald Horne, *Communist Front? The Civil Rights Congress, 1946–1956* (London: Associated University Presses, 1988), 25, 45.

17. CRC, "You Should Know . . . about the New Public Housing Regulation," n.d., Civil Rights Congress, Los Angeles Chapter Collection, 1946–56 (hereafter CRC Collection), box 14, folder 9, Southern California Library for Social Studies and Research; "CRC Alerts Tenants against 'loyalty' Oaths," *People's World*, September 26, 1952, 2, 6; "Project Tenants Target as LA Witch-Hunt Expands," *People's World*, October 1, 1952, 3.

18. CHA to Sidney and Adele Moore Jr., January 13, 1953, CRC Collection, box 14, folder 9; "23,000 L.A. Tenants Told to Sign 'Loyalty' Oath," *People's World*, January 21, 1953, 8; Art White, "Public Housing Tenants Given Loyalty Oath; 1% Spurn Pledge," *Los Angeles Mirror*, January 22, 1953, 51; "LA Tenants Launch 'Loyalty' Oath Fight," *People's World*, January 22, 1953, 3; Residents Committee Against Loyalty Oaths, "Residents of Public Housing: CAUTION!," n.d., CRC Collection, box 14, folder 9; "Tenants Told to Sign Oath or Be Ousted," *Los Angeles Examiner*, January 23, 1953.

19. CHA Resident Lease Agreement, Sidney S. Moore Jr., and Adele Moore, December 4, 1950, CRC Collection, box 14, folder 9; "Sought Housing Reforms, Hit by 'loyalty' Oath Club," *People's World*, January 23, 1953, 6; "Gwinn Oath Case," n.d., ACLU Collection, box 7, folder 1; Adele Moore to Don Parson, May 29, 2005, in possession of Don Parson; Louise Huling et al. to Sefren, n.d., CRC Collection, box 14, folder 9. Sidney's father, Sidney Moore Sr., had been a field representative of the CIO United Public Workers and, at the end of 1947, was appointed chairman of the CIO's Political Action

Committee in the 14th congressional district. He was the Independent Progressive Party candidate for Congress in that district in 1948, but had withdrawn in favor of the successful Democratic incumbent Helen Gahagan Douglas. Los Angeles CIO Council Press Release, November 1947, Philip Connelly Collection, box 3, folder 7, Special Collections, UCLA; Dorothy Healey and Maurice Isserman, *Dorothy Healey Remembers: A Life in the American Communist Party* (New York: Oxford University Press, 1990), 111.

20. "ACLU to File Suit to Halt Tenant Oath," *People's World*, February 6, 1953; Morris Miller, "The Gwinn Amendment—Series of Conflicting Court Decisions on Its Enforceability Summarized," *Journal of Housing* 12 (February 1955): 53, 56, 66, 70; Memo from Herbert Monte Levy to Affiliates, "Re: Gwinn Amendment Test Cases," October 14, 1955, ACLU Collection, box 6, folder 11; many of the files of the ACLU Gwinn Amendment test cases can be found in the Arthur Garfield Hayes Papers and the American Civil Liberties Union Washington, D.C. Office Records, both in the Seeley G. Mudd Manuscript Library at Princeton University; see also the HHFA files located in the National Archives at College Park, Md.

21. "Municipal Court Ruling on Housing Authority Loyalty Oath Requirement," *San Francisco Recorder*, May 2, 1955, ACLU Collection, box 930, folder: ACLU—housing authority etc. v. Wycoff.

22. Residents Committee Against Loyalty Oath in Housing, "Is Your Home Safe?," n.d., CRC Collection, box 14, folder 9; "'Ultimatum' Charged in Tenant Oath Fight," *People's World*, January 27, 1953; "LA Tenants Merge Fight Against Oath," *People's World*, February 25, 1953, 3.

23. "Housing Chief Stalls Showdown on Oath," *People's World*, February 9, 1953; "L.A. Housing Tenants Seek Injunction on Signing Oath," *Los Angeles Examiner*, February 14, 1953; "ACLU Suit Lists Illegalities in Housing Oath," *People's World*, February 17, 1953, 3, 6; "Loyalty Oath Ouster Halted," *Los Angeles Examiner*, February 17, 1953; Fred Okrand, "Memorandum re Requirement of the Los Angeles City Housing Authority . . . ," n.d., ACLU Collection, box 7, folder 1; *Wieman v. Updegraff*, 344 U.S. 183 (1952).

24. News Release, ACLU, February 27, [1953], ACLU Collection, box 7, folder 1; "'Loyalty' Evictions Halted in LA," *People's World*, March 2, 1953, 3; "Housing Oath Cases Taken Off Calendar," *Los Angeles Examiner*, March 14, 1953.

25. *Hearings on Investigation of Public Housing Activities in Los Angeles*, 241–43, 356–57; Parson, *Making a Better World*.

26. Fred Okrand, "Forty Years Defending the Constitution," interviewed by Michael Balter (Oral History Program, University of California, Los Angeles, 1984), 316–17; Fred Okrand to Don Parson, January 1, 2001, in possession of the author; *Housing Authority v. Cordova*, Municipal Court of Los Angeles Judicial District County of Los Angeles No. 171371 (1954); *Housing Authority v. Konick*, Municipal Court of Los Angeles Judicial District County of Los Angeles No. 171372 (1954); *Housing Authority v. Huling*, Municipal Court of Los Angeles Judicial District County of Los Angeles No. 171373 (1954); *Housing Authority v. Wycoff*, Municipal Court of Los Angeles Judicial District County of Los Angeles No. 171374 (1954); *Housing Authority v. Moore*, Municipal Court of Los Angeles Judicial District County of Los Angeles No. 173307 (1954); "Housing 'Loyalty' Goes to Court," *People's World*, April 16, 1954, 6.

27. "Loyalty Oath Case Argued," *Los Angeles Examiner*, August 20, 1954; "LA Court

Weighs Oath Evictions," *People's World*, August 23, 1954, 3; "L.A. Tenants Test Loyalty Proviso," *Open Forum*, August 1954, ACLU Collection, box 7, folder 1.

28. *Joint Anti-Fascist Refugee Committee v. McGrath*, 341 U.S. 123 (1951); "Consolidated Brief for Appellants," *Housing Authority v. Cordova*, August 2, 1954, ACLU Collection, box 930, folder: Gwinn Special No. 2; "Applicant's Reply Brief to Respondent's Supplemental Brief," *Housing Authority v. Cordova*, n.d.

29. *Housing Authority v. Cordova*, 130 C.A.2d Supp. 883; 279 P.2d 215 (1955); *Chicago Housing Authority v. Blackman*, 122 N.E.2d 522 (1954); "Oath Held No Basis for Eviction," *Los Angeles Examiner*, January 21, 1955, sec. 1, 11; "Appeals Court Voids 'Loyalty' Oath Evictions," *People's World*, January 24, 1955, 3, 6.

30. *Housing Authority v. Cordova*, Los Angeles Municipal Court No. 171371, *Housing Authority v. Wycoff*, Los Angeles Municipal Court No. 171374, *Housing Authority v. Moore*, Los Angeles Municipal Court No. 173307, Stipulation of Facts, n.d., ACLU Collection, box 929, Folder "ACLU—(Gwinn) Housing Authority v Cordova." Hunt's opinion is reprinted in "Can't Ask for Non-Membership Affidavit as Rental Condition," *Los Angeles Daily Journal*, n.d., box 925, folder: "Gwinn Amendment (supplemental)," ACLU Collection; "Housing Oath Loses in Test," *Los Angeles Examiner*, June 21, 1955.

31. "Gwinn Amendment," in Public Law 176, July 31, 1953, 67 Stat. 307; codified at 42 USC 1411c; "Housing Act of 1954," *Journal of Housing* 11 (August–September 1954): 262.

32. "Effort Take Gwinn Case to Supreme Court Balked," *Journal of Housing* 10 (April 1953): 116; like the CRC, the IWO was on the Attorney General's list. The IWO also leant its support to the struggle against the Gwinn Amendment in Los Angeles—"IWO to Seek Ban on LA Tenant Oath," *People's World*, February 6, 1953, 3, 6; *Peters v. New York City Housing Authority*, 128 N.Y.S.2d 712 (1954); *Peters v. New York City Housing Authority*, 307 N.Y. 519, 121 N.E.2d 529 (1954); *Chicago Housing Authority v. Blackman*, 122 N.E.2d 522 (1954); *Lawson v. Housing Authority of the City of Milwaukee*, 70 N.W.2d 605 (1955); *Rudder v. United States*, 226 F.2d 51 (1955); ACLU Weekly Bulletin 1686, "Legal Campaign to Invalidate Gwinn Amendment Scores Success," February 21, 1955, ACLU Collection, box 7, folder 1; Alvin Shuster, "Courts Balk U.S. on Housing Oaths," *New York Times*, August 7, 1955, 9.

33. *Housing Authority of the City of Milwaukee et al. v. Lawson et ux.*, certiorari denied, 350 U.S. No. 354 (November 7, 1955); "U.S. Supreme Court Refuses to Review Gwinn Decision," *Journal of Housing* 12 (December 1955): 428; *Kutcher v. Housing Authority of the City of Newark*, 20 N.J. 181, 119 A.2d 1 (1955); *Peters v. New York City Housing Authority*, 147 N.Y.S.2d 859 (1955); "New York and New Jersey High Courts Declare Gwinn Amendment Ineffective," *Journal of Housing* 13 (January 1956): 21; *Housing Authority of the City of Los Angeles v. Cordova, et al.*, certiorari denied, 350 U.S. No. 628 (February 27, 1956); "Top Court Backs Aliso Village Tenants on 'Loyalty' Oaths," *People's World*, February 28, 1956, 8.

34. "Gwinn Amendment Is Dead," *Journal of Housing* 13 (August–September 1956): 279; "Staff Counsel Information Report No. 3, Re: Gwinn Amendment," October 23, 1956, ACLU Collection, box 6, folder 11.

35. Don Parson, "The Decline of Public Housing and the Politics of the Red Scare: The Significance of the Los Angeles Public Housing War," *Journal of Urban History* 33, no. 3 (March 2007): 400–417.

CHAPTER 5

Housing Is a Labor Process

Housing Policy and Housework

DON PARSON

Housing policy in the United States had, by the 1960s, resulted in a spatial mosaic of suburbs and ghettos that divided the cityscape by gender and race. Staunchly supported by organized labor, such a policy found the junior members of the labor-liberal coalition—women and non-Anglo "minorities"—spatially sequestered in the inner city or behind suburban kitchen counters. Elsewhere I have analyzed this "housing question" from the viewpoint of organized labor, yet women's struggles around housing issues present a very different outlook from that of the domination of national housing policy by the unions. In contrast to organized labor, which saw housing policy as primarily an economic stimulus that would expand waged employment for its membership, many women tended to view housing policy in terms of the politics of housework. In this chapter I would like to trace the politics of housework as it has affected housing policy. I intend to delineate some broader, historical trends from this perspective, which might serve as a foundation for further, specific research.[1]

The "material feminists," as Dolores Hayden labeled them, and the Progressives called for a socialized and rationalized housework that was incorporated into the public housing program from its inception in 1937 until the advent of the Cold War. These demands were seemingly abandoned with the exodus of the families of union workers to the suburbs during the postwar period. In the suburbs, women's struggles around housework took the form not of socializing, rationalizing, or sharing this "socially necessary labor," but rather of refusing it and rejecting the role of housewife.[2]

By the early 1970s the Wages for Housework Campaign in the United States, Britain, and Italy was developing a very sophisticated analysis of contemporary capitalism as a social factory—where both waged and unwaged labor were subject to exploitation, regimentation, and alienation—from the perspective of women and, in particular, from the viewpoint of the housewife. As Sylvia Federici, a member of the campaign, later observed, "Like other feminists before us we discovered that the kitchen is our slaveship, our plantation, and if

FIGURE 5.1. *A Woman's Home Is Not Her Castle*, detail from a pamphlet by New York Wages for Housework Committee. *Courtesy of MayDay Rooms, https://maydayrooms.omeka.net/items/show/99.*

FIGURE 5.2. Fuck Housework—Women's Liberation, Shirley J. Boccaccio / Virtue Hathaway, 1971, offset. *Courtesy of the Center for the Study of Political Graphics. This poster is available on eBay by searching for F**k Housework.*

we want to liberate ourselves we first have to break with our identification with housework." In her introduction to *The Power of Women and the Subversion of the Community*, Selma James made explicit the theoretical point of departure of such an analysis:

> The community therefore is not an area of freedom and leisure auxiliary to the factory, where by chance there happen to be women who are degraded as the personal servants of men. The community is the other half of capitalist organization, the other area of hidden capitalist exploitation, the other, hidden, source of surplus labor. It becomes increasingly regimented like a factory, what Mariarosa [Dalla Costa] calls a social factory. . . . And this social factory has at its pivot the woman producing labor power as a commodity, and her struggle not to.[3]

Domestic Revolutions, Settlement Houses, and Progressive Legislation

In the years between the Civil War and World War I there was an explosion of experimentation, both theoretical and practical, with different ways to reduce, share, or democratize the amount and the nature of the housework performed by women. Such experiments frequently involved the removal from or de-emphasis of the kitchen in the home so as to eliminate, in the words of Melusina Fay Pierce, the "stomach as a family tie." Feminist philosopher Charlotte Perkins popularized the idea of cooperative kitchens, laundries, and day care for children. Kitchen-less apartment-hotels that were built in New York and utopian communities, like Llano del Rio in the desert outside Los Angeles, incorporated these principles into their design. In the early 1900s home economist Christine Frederick applied Taylorism to the kitchen in an attempt to rationalize housework, make it more efficient, and reduce the amount of time involved in its performance.[4]

Many of these principles and goals were adopted and promoted by the settlement house movement, which flourished from the 1890s until World War I. Settlements were colonies of college-educated, middle-class, and primarily female social workers who worked and lived in the slums with the goal of disseminating methods of neighborhood and personal improvement. Settlement workers were, as Roy Lubove observed, "humanitarian efficiency experts anxious to organize the social environment in such a way that every individual could attain his [or her] maximum physical, mental and cultural development." There was a certain amount of noblesse oblige in their approach, but there was an emphasis placed on what they could learn in the slums and not solely on what they could teach. Politically many of the settlement workers were progressives in the vein of Jane Addams or committed socialists like Florence Kelly.[5]

FIGURE 5.3. Architect Alice Constance Austin showing her model for kitchenless Llano del Rio homes to colonists, ca. 1916.
Paul Kagan Utopian Communities Collection, Yale Collection of Western Americana, Beinecke Rare Book and Manuscript Library, Yale University.

However, to the detriment of the attempts of the material feminists to reconstruct housing in light of the recognized drudgery of housework, settlement workers placed priorities on the elimination of slums over that of the elimination of kitchens. And, as the majority of the slums of the time were inhabited by immigrants, housing policy became integrated with "Americanization"—helping the immigrant adapt to the inequalities of the housing market of industrial capitalism and eliminating the most flagrant problems. Mary McDowell, a settlement worker helping to draft protective labor legislation for working women, seemingly reinforced the social role of the housewife: "It is of vital importance that [immigrant women] be given the chance to be decently self-supporting under conditions which shall not unfit them for wifehood and motherhood, and the care of the home." Perhaps the most comprehensive statement of this strategy appeared on the eve of the Great Depression, written by a worker in the Department of Americanization and Homemaking of Covina (California) City Elementary Schools. In *Americanization through Homemaking*, Pearl Idelia Ellis reinforced racial stereotypes and advocated the implementation of a barrage of home economics courses for Mexican girls to prepare them for the role of housewife, thereby establishing the house as the locus of assimilation and Americanization for Mexican immigrants in Southern California.[6]

Progressive reformers, such as Lawrence Veiller and Jacob Riis, sought to implement restrictive legislation and did not incorporate positive proposals for less complicated and more collaborative performance of housework. That is to say, housing policy dealt with the enforcement of building and safety codes, fireproofing, ventilation, and the evaluation of tenements—and not with co-operative cooking, laundry, or child care. Thus, the legacy of the material feminists and their call for the reduction of housework was reduced in scope so that it was subordinated to, rather than added to, progressive housing policy. The feminist impact on progressive legislation should not be underestimated, however. Veiller worked very closely with, for instance, Florence Kelly in drafting housing legislation in New York. The Housing Commission of the City of Los Angeles became, in 1907, the first city agency in the United States to hire a female housing inspector—Johanna von Wagner, a settlement house worker. Mary Veeder, a member of the Housing Commission, was also a worker at the College Settlement House in Los Angeles.[7]

This subordination of the politics of housework to the Americanization of the slums left open the possibility of a conservative manipulation of the theoretical legacy of the material feminists. A "rationalized" housework could now be

A COOKING CLASS OF MEXICAN GIRLS

FIGURE 5.4. Cooking, sewing, budgeting, mothering, and decorating the home were the expectations for the "foreign girl."
Pearl Idelia Ellis, Americanization through Homemaking *(Los Angeles: Wetzel, 1929).*

intensified to become a material cornerstone of the modern, American household. Ruth Schwartz Cowan has shown how the industrialization of household technology led, in the 1920s, to an expansion of the job description of the housewife—the planning and execution of household tasks were combined so that the housewife became a "Jane of all trades." The red-baiting and political conservatism of the period following World War I severely limited the scope and impact of the reforms and experimentation advocated by material feminists. Still, many of these concerns were consolidated (though not popularized) by women's professional organizations: "Social feminists worked up an agenda for reform in the Progressive Era and in the 1920s which required the emergency climate of the New Deal for passage."[8]

Public Housing and the New Deal

Public housing was the arena in which the politics of housework was to forcefully reemerge from its lull during the 1920s. A glance at the leadership of the public housing movement demonstrates the connection with earlier feminist concerns: Mary Simkhovich had been a settlement house worker, Helen Alfred was a socialist associated with the settlement house movement, and Catherine Bauer came out of the intellectual circle of the Regional Planning Association of America, which had close contacts with, again, the settlement houses. Edith Elmer Wood was forbidden by her parents in the 1890s to become a settlement resident (her mother identified settlement houses with anarchism). Initially working closely with Lawrence Veiller, Wood abandoned the restrictive housing legislation of the earlier Progressives to become one of the leading housing theorists and activists of the 1930s.[9]

The legislative efforts to formulate a public housing program and its fruition in the 1937 Wagner Act have been thoroughly dealt with elsewhere. Here I want to emphasize that the Wagner Act was heavily weighted to accommodate the employment demands of organized labor and the restrictions advocated by the real estate lobby. Still, the impact of housework and household drudgery became a prominent component of the design and implementation of public housing projects. Indeed

> the American housewife has at last been called in as a government consultant. Representatives of the country's greatest industry, housekeeping, have lately met in a conference in Washington to advise with the United States Housing Authority in its work of creating 160,000 new homes for low-income families. . . . These USHA homes will be efficient modern workshops for the housewife.[10]

These reforms were not legislated from Washington as much as they were realized in the everyday life of the public housing projects during World War II.

For example, the 1942 consolidated report of the City Housing Authority of Los Angeles was titled "Homes for Heroes," referring not to male warriors fighting overseas but to production workers, women and men, on the home front. The home and the work performed by housewives were seen as indispensable to the war effort and integral to the struggle against fascism.[11]

The politics of everyday life during the war in the Channel Heights Public Housing Project, located near the defense industries in the Los Angeles Harbor area, was later chronicled by Henry Kraus in conjunction with his wife Dorothy. Upon their arrival in 1942, Kraus recalled that, with the exception of a shared washing machine (a rare commodity during the war), there was very little community organization around the issues of housework. As the war progressed, however, it was the housewives of the project, burdened by the double duty of domestic chores as well as the role of "Rosie the Riveter" production worker, who organized around issues of laundry, housework, and child care. Kraus wrote that such organization "flowed out of the very spirit of social cooperation that for us constituted the essence of the New Deal."[12]

During the war, many women began to look ahead and question the nature and form of postwar housing policy, especially in light of their wartime experience with housework. Pricilla Robertson and Hawley Jones asked if the "Hitlerian routine" of housewives "being mere servants for their husbands and children" would continue. "Will it be the same old routine in a new shell?" Drawing on the experimentation in public housing, the authors concluded that most beneficial for "the individual housekeeper are the projects which involve some attempt at commercial or cooperative organization on a community basis."[13]

FAREWELL TO ROSIE THE RIVETER   DEVELOPMENT OF S[

FIGURE 5.5. After the war women were indeed pulled back into "the same old routine in a new shell." "Farewell to Rosie the Riveter," detail from the *Great Wall of Los Angeles*, Judy F. Baca, © 1976. *Photo courtesy of SPARC Archives, SPARCinLA.org.*

The Social Factory and Suburbanization

In 1940, Edith Elmer Wood wrote that houses were "like factories. Their output is children—the citizens of tomorrow. The full time workers are the mothers and homemakers." This was a succinct expression of housing as one element of a social factory, where the labor of housewives was recognized as essential to societal reproduction. In 1947 Kate Bretnall was examining the growth of suburbia, arguing that "it takes two of you to make a family and a home. Your housework, and the care you give your children that belong to both of you, are quite as important as his paycheck. So why shouldn't both of you be paid?" The acceptance of housewives as workers in a social factory served to pose two interrelated corollaries. First, though integral to the material (re)production of society, the labor of housewives was, unlike that of their husbands, unwaged. Second, tactics of labor militancy in the factory could be disseminated to housewives in the social factory—the strike, the slow-down, the sick-out, work to rule, and so forth.[14]

Within the social factory there was a tendency to subordinate the housing needs and demands of (female and not formally organized) housewives to the more powerful (male and organized) labor unions. Many of the struggles to rationalize, socialize, and share housework that had been expressed in the public housing projects of the 1930s and 1940s were eclipsed by the growth of the suburbs where each individual house had its own private laundry room and kitchen that spatially mitigated against socialization and cooperation. As Adele Chatfield-Taylor recounted, "When America went to the suburbs, the women's movement went to pieces." The suburbs may have been, according to David Riesman, "a tacit revolt against industrialism," but such a revolt was male-dominated and ignored the extent to which unwaged housework provided the basis for the suburban retreat. Indeed, Edith Stern concluded that "if the male upon whom her [the housewife's] scale of living depends prospers, about all she can look forward to is a larger house—and more work." As such, housework could now, in the words of Betty Friedan, "expand to fill the time available," allowing the home to become a "comfortable concentration camp."[15]

During the 1950s, the principles of industrial sociology were applied to housework and to housewives in the suburban house. An industrial engineer wrote, "Your Wife Has an Easy Racket!" in which the results of a scientific survey were reported to prove that "if she wasn't stubborn, tied down by tradition, a poor organizer, and just plain lazy, [the housewife] could be free most of the day." One efficiency expert asked "Should Your Wife Be Fired?," illustrating his thesis with the claim that "even mopping floors can be fun if you prove to yourself that you have licked the job by finding an easier way to do it than you have already used in the past."[16]

The scope and intensity of housework as well as the management of household appliances and consumerism intensified in the move to suburbia. "Are Housewives Necessary?" asked Eve Merriam in a 1959 issue of *The Nation*: "She is the lucky little lady on whom we can unload our products. . . . Where planned obsolescence is the only thing planned in our economy, we need the myth of the necessary housewife to help us plan it better." Indeed, the unwaged labor of housewives was seen not only as the fulcrum of the consumer economy but as the mainstay of a successful suburban housing market as well: the *Los Angeles Times* warned housewives not to neglect housework as "government, business and industry leaders aren't happy with this situation [of women abandoning housework], because they know lack of home upkeep brings home deterioration and this leads to an inevitable deadend—slums." In terms of ideology, the work ethic of the American housewife would provide a barrier to dangerous, communistic philosophies. In his 1952 presidential campaign, Adlai Stevenson addressed the women of Smith College: "You may be hitched to one of those creatures we call 'Western man' and I think your part of the job is to keep him Western. . . . [This involves] home work—you can do it in the living room with a baby in your lap, or in the kitchen with a can opener in your hands."[17]

Not surprisingly, housework and the suburban home of the Cold War period became a focus of women's protest. In 1956, the Housing and Home Finance Agency (HHFA) hosted the Women's Congress on Housing in order "to obtain the ideas of American housewives on home planning and design." Much of the discussion centered around the seeming anomaly in which labor-saving devices did not ease the burden of housework as much as they served to make more housework possible. Suburban houses were, according to a delegate, "a disgrace to the American standard of living—ugly outside and inefficient inside."[18]

It was exactly these realities that would provide a basis for the organizing efforts of the Wages for Housework Campaign—to eliminate the drudgery of housework called for the elimination of the houseworker. Mariarosa Dalla Costa and Selma James saw this as "rejecting our role as housewives and the home as our ghetto of existence." The scope and intensity of unwaged housework were seen not only as the material basis for a male-dominated suburban built environment, but as the management of the consumerism of the national economy, which intensified waged work as well:

> Electric appliances in the home are lovely things to have, but for the workers who make them, to make many is to spend time and to exhaust yourself. That every wage has to buy all of them is tough, and presumes that every wife must run all these appliances alone; but now on a more mechanized level. Lucky worker, lucky wife![19]

Housewives were thus central to the postwar economic expansion—"the necessary housewife" was not only a stimulant to consumer demand but a means to stimulate the productivity of the waged worker whose labor was utilized in the manufacture of consumer goods, all of which resulted in more work for the housewife.

The decline of the patriarchal nuclear family—the social foundation of the suburban household—was apparent by the end of the Cold War. Between 1960 and 1970 there was a 14.6 percent increase in the number of family households, accompanied by a 51.3 percent increase in the number of non-family households. I am not trying to establish a direct link between these figures and the "housewives' revolt," but they are suggestive. The rejection of the role of the housewife not only contributed to the disarray of the suburban housing market but was a foundation of contemporary feminism as well. As Sylvia Federici observed of the 1960s, "Women who ten years earlier may perhaps have been subdued suburban housewives . . . from [the] vantage point from our position at the bottom declared that we had to shake the entire social system off its foundations."[20]

Conclusions

The politics of housework surveyed here indicates a major change of direction in the attitudes and opinions of housewives during the Cold War. Drawing on the concept of the social factory in the 1930s and 1940s, women sought to rationalize and reduce the amount and nature of housework that they, as housewives, had to perform. The fruition of this strategy could be seen in the public housing projects of World War II that were designed for more efficient and cooperative living. In contrast, the 1950s were marked by the beginnings of the refusal of housework and rejection of the expanding role of housewife. During the turbulent 1960s, housewives, along with those on the assembly line and throughout the social factory, rejected the role of subservient worker, contributing to the idea that housing is not only shelter but a labor process as well.

NOTES

1. Don Parson, "Organized Labor and the Housing Question: Public Housing, Suburbanization and Urban Renewal," *Society and Space: Environment and Planning D* 2 (1984): 75–86.

2. This was the intention of my doctoral dissertation, where I tried to apply this theoretical basis to the case of housing in Los Angeles. See Don Parson, "Urban Politics during the Cold War: Public Housing, Urban Renewal, and Suburbanization in Los Angeles" (PhD diss., University of California, Los Angeles, 1985).

3. Sylvia Federici, "Putting Feminism Back on Its Feet," in *The 60s without Apology*, ed. S. Sayers et al. (Minneapolis: University of Minnesota Press, 1984), 339; Mariarosa

Dalla Costa and Selma James, *The Power of Women and the Subversion of the Community* (Bristol: Falling Wall Press, 1972), 11.

4. Dolores Hayden, *The Grand Domestic Revolution* (Cambridge, Mass.: MIT Press, 1981); David Handlin, *The American Home: Architecture and Society, 1815–1915* (Boston: Little, Brown, 1979), chap. 6; Leslie Kanes Weisman, *Discrimination by Design: A Feminist Critique of the Man-Made Environment* (Urbana: University of Illinois Press, 1992), 86–99.

5. Roy Lubove, *The Progressives and the Slums* (Pittsburgh: University of Pennsylvania Press, 1962); Allen Davis, *Spearheads for Reform: The Social Settlements and the Progressive Movement, 1890–1914* (New York: Oxford University Press, 1967).

6. Davis, *Spearheads for Reform*, 135; Pearl Idelia Ellis, *Americanization through Homemaking* (Los Angeles: Wetzel, 1929).

7. "Report to the Housing Commission of the City of Los Angeles," February 26, 1906, to June 30, 1908.

8. Ruth Schwartz Cowan, "The 'Industrial Revolution' in the Home: Household Technology and Social Change in the 20th Century," *Technology and Culture* 17 (1976): 1–23; J. Stanley Lemons, *The Woman Citizen: Social Feminism in the 1920s* (Urbana: University of Illinois Press, 1973).

9. Eugenie Ladner Birch, "Edith Elmer Wood and the Genesis of Liberal Housing Thought, 1910–1942" (PhD diss., Columbia University, 1976); "Woman-Made America: The Case of Early Public Housing Policy," *Journal of the American Institute of Planners* 44 (1978); Susan Cole, "Catherine Bauer and the Public Housing Movement, 1926–1937" (PhD diss., George Washington University, 1975).

10. Timothy McDonnell, *The Wagner Housing Act* (Chicago: Loyola University Press, 1957); Parson, "Urban Politics during the Cold War"; "American Women Become Government Consultants in Home Planning," *Architect and Engineer* 137 (May 1939): 66.

11. "Homes for Heroes, the 4th Annual Report of the Housing Authority of the City of Los Angeles" (1942), 12; Henry Kraus, *In the City Was a Garden: A Housing Project Chronicle* (New York: Renaissance Press, 1951), 141.

12. Kraus, *In the City Was a Garden*, 141.

13. Pricilla Robertson and Hawley Jones, "Housekeeping After the War," *Harper's Bazaar* 188 (April 1944): 430–37.

14. Edith Elmer Wood, "That 'One Third of a Nation,'" *Survey Graphic* 29, no. 2 (1940): 83; Kate Bretnall, "Should Housewives Be Paid a Salary?," *American Home* 37, no. 2 (February 1947): 62.

15. Parson, "Urban Politics during the Cold War"; Adele Chatfield-Taylor, "Hitting Home," *Architectural Forum* 138 (1973): 58–61; David Riesman, "The Suburban Sadness," in *The Suburban Community*, ed. W. Dobriner (New York: Putnam, 1958), 375–408; Edith Stern, "Women Are Household Slaves," *American Mercury* 68, no. 2 (1949): 58; Betty Friedan, *The Feminine Mystique* (New York: Norton, 1963).

16. R Knowlton, "Your Wife Has an Easy Racket!," *American Magazine* 152, no. 11 (1951): 24; G. Varga, "Should Your Wife Be Fired?," *American Magazine* 147 (1949): 145.

17. Eve Merriam, "Are Housewives Necessary," *The Nation* 188 (1959): 98; *Los Angeles Times*, May 4, 1956; as quoted in Paul Carter, *Another Part of the Fifties* (New York: Columbia University Press, 1983), 86–87.

18. "Angry Housewives on Housing," *Life* 40, no. 23 (June 4, 1956): 66–70.

19. Dalla Costa and James, *Power of Women*, 36, 40.

20. U.S. Department of Commerce, Bureau of the Census, *Statistical Abstract of the United States* (Washington, D.C.: Government Printing Office, 1981), 42; Federici, "Putting Feminism Back on Its Feet," 344.

PART 2

Hunting Elmer Fudd
DON PARSON'S JOURNEY
THROUGH LOS ANGELES

Introduction

JUDY BRANFMAN

> So here's the moral without a doubt,
> If you want to be free, you've got to sing out.
>
> —Talking Un-American Blues, Irwin Silber and Betty Sanders, 1952

Don Parson rails against injustice through the carefully chosen stories he tells and the memorable characters who animate them. Focusing mainly on housing-related episodes in this book, he takes us on an exploration of back-alley housing courts, public housing design, loyalty and loyalty oaths, resistance to the housework factory, and more in early to mid-twentieth-century Los Angeles. Today, in the early twenty-first century, with the neoliberal-induced tragedy of homelessness, the renewed repression against immigrants and activists, and the courtroom as a site of confrontation, Don's writing has strong resonance. In part 2 of *Public Los Angeles*, four friends and scholars write about Don and the significance of his work, and the reach of his work into the present.

I met Don in 1993 at one of his favorite research haunts, the Southern California Library for Social Studies and Research (SCL), itself a story of resistance. The library got its precarious start as secret caches of radical literature headed for the incinerator but salvaged by activist Emil Freed from friends terrified that possessing them could contribute to the possibility of public branding as "communists" and forced testimony before the House Un-American Activities Committee (HUAC). Freed's rescue mission, an act of brave defiance against the suppression of LA's vibrant radical community, amassed hundreds of boxes of "dangerous" books and documents he hid in garages across LA in the 1950s. His collection quickly outgrew available space and was moved into and out of two storefront libraries he opened before he managed to acquire an industrial building on Vermont Avenue in South LA in 1973. Here the archive has multiplied its holdings several times over and become a valuable resource and gathering place for scholars and the larger community, including many whose writings help shape this book.

Mutual friends had been telling me about Don and his exceptional library, and encouraging me to go meet him, so I had a good idea who the guy was wheeling around SCL with the help of a friend. It was during one of SCL's annual celebrations honoring several generations of remarkable LA activists and intellectuals. Among them were people central to events Don had written or would soon write about, including Alice McGrath and Frank Wilkinson. Both Alice, secretary for the Sleepy Lagoon Defense Committee in the 1940s, and Frank, the "infamous" assistant director of the Los Angeles Housing Authority in the early 1950s who was later instrumental in dismantling HUAC and features prominently in Don's book *Making a Better World* (and less prominently in chapter 3), became Don's close friends.

Ultimately sharing SCL's mission of rescuing LA's activist history, Don spent many days delving deeply into their archives. It was a long haul from his home in Thousand Oaks, roughly fifty miles away. Growing up in almost rural Ventura County in the 1950s and 1960s, he witnessed the dramatic transformation of his environment and LA in general, fueling his aversion to the never-ending narrative of unfettered "market-rate" development as an inherent good for Los Angeles—and setting him on his search for historic visions for a better city.

Meeting Don at SCL set the stage for our friendship and my joining his team of researcher-friends as things got increasingly difficult for him. Interestingly, our concerns and work intersected in unexpected ways. Through my research for Don on the Gwinn Amendment in LA (see chapter 4) I discovered that his work overlapped with my own family's activist past. They were from Boyle Heights, and my parents had organized on the Eastside while living in Estrada Courts during the persistent postwar housing shortage. From Don I learned that period coincided with the adoption of the federal Gwinn Amendment—what must have been just one more chilling episode for my family during the McCarthy era—and that after my parents moved away, their neighbors and longtime friends became plaintiffs in the successful legal challenge to LA's public housing loyalty oath. I had never heard about it, and it's unlikely any of the activist parents who were involved passed that experience down since they generally avoided using the word "communist" around curious kids largely unaware of the potential threat to their families. In light of the historical gaps imposed by that profound fear, Don's detailed attention to the Red Scare's many forms expands our understanding of the complex ways it penetrated society and impacted individual lives—and provided a model for repressive tactics in the ensuing decades. At the same time Don has broadened our knowledge of the dedicated organizing—by housewives and tenants, lawyers and politicians, social workers and ministers, and radical organizations, among others—that challenged the injustices he writes about in this book.

In several chapters (chapters 2, 3, 4), Don describes how his characters and the organizations they belong to are demonized endlessly as "communists" and "reds"—and in fact many of them were or had been communists. Others were "fellow travelers" or friends, but all were maligned for their prounion, economic justice, and antiracist beliefs, eternal problems for the city's ruling class. J. Edgar Hoover and the FBI brought their files full of "evidence," gathered partly by the Los Angeles Police Department throughout the 1920s, 1930s, and 1940s, to the task of ending LA's public housing program by attempting to discredit housing leaders as subversives. Don's work updates the history and cost of Los Angeles' deep antiradical roots, dating back at least to the late nineteenth century when the *Los Angeles Times* and Chamber of Commerce, with loyal backing from LA's police, escalated their attacks on labor supporters and tried to make LA an open shop town.

I have at times wondered about Don's apparently uncritical respect for some of his fascinating but idiosyncratic characters; surely justice of the peace Stanley Moffatt deserved a rebuke for suing "the laughing man" (see chapter 3). But I suspect that Don's veneration comes from a deep admiration for their courage and risk taking during an era of powerful intimidation and repression. In some ways his characters' courage mirrors Don's own in the face of many decades of increasing disability. His passion, drive, and humor—and commitment to these stories and characters—gave him a life far beyond the limited "expectations" of the medical establishment, which has been entirely to our benefit.

◻ ◻ ◻

In response to our request for essays for this volume, Tom Sitton, Sue Ruddick, and Steven Flusty offered to share their thoughts about Don and his work; all three entered Don's extensive network at different points over the years. Tom Sitton and Don's complementary research interests led to a valuable exchange of ideas and materials that found their way into each other's work; as Don's illness progressed, Sitton continued to provide Don with documents and information he found as he pursued his own research. Sitton underscores the importance of Don's writing about LA's Cold War–era urban politics as the city's elite once again exploited the Red Scare to marginalize progressives, a repeating theme in our history, and sees Don's latest work as arriving at the perfect time, urging us to consider what alternatives might be possible today.

UCLA's Graduate School in Architecture and Urban Planning provided a dynamic base for both Sue Ruddick and Don in the early 1980s, and Ruddick was instrumental in the earliest moments of getting this book project launched. In "History Repeating . . ." she reminds us of the importance of understanding history and proposes that Don has written a "history of the present," allowing us to see our contemporary struggles set against a past that grappled with similar issues: the refusal to build affordable housing, harsh racial and economic disparities, and misinformation parading as truth. Mobilizing her own 1980s ethnographies of homeless youth in Los Angeles, Ruddick celebrates Don's contribution to helping us "understand the longer durée" with its offerings of both despair and hope.

Steven Flusty was introduced to Don and his legendary, home-based research library by Mike Davis (other friends reported similarly memorable pilgrimages). Flusty was living Thousand Oaks–adjacent in the San Fernando Valley, which practically made them neighbors and certainly logical investigative partners. In "Of Bunnies and Barricades" we are taken on a circuitous journey through LA as these two urban historians weave on-the-ground research with analysis of Disney's most famous comic characters. Flusty's own writing frames a commentary written jointly with Don, as well as a book review Don wrote in 1993 exploring public space as theme park. Flusty's ingenious story of their adventures highlights Don's wit, his disdain for LA's development barons, and his strategy of not "telegraphing one's punch lines," much in evidence in the preceding chapters. Flusty's exploits with Don also point to the likely trajectory Don's work would have taken had his health allowed, as both an urban historian and a cutting-edge critic and commentator on contemporary issues.

Our "new" America sheds light on Don's stories in a particularly striking way. Many Americans have felt overwhelmed and anxious since the 2016 presidential election, a mood strongly reminiscent of a time Don often writes about, 1950s McCarthy-era Los Angeles. Living in these times reminds us how easy it is to turn away from both injustice and those standing up for justice and helps us grasp the importance of Don's admiration for the courageous people he writes about. Don's unwritten but clear message couldn't be more relevant: have courage, dig deep, question authority, work together, and have fun!

CHAPTER 6

"Making a Better World"

My Intersections with Don Parson

TOM SITTON

At around the turn of the millennium, my book manuscript concerning Los Angeles mayor Fletcher Bowron's administration from 1938 to 1953 had been accepted for publication. There was one major problem: it had to be cut down considerably in size to meet the needs of the publisher. Like most writers, I was crushed by this directive but soon found several solutions to that dilemma. One major change allowed me to remove a large portion of the material on public housing in the 1930s and 1940s, for which I had spent many hours researching. That might sound like a surprising conclusion since that was the central political issue leading to Mayor Bowron's defeat in his final reelection bid.

It made sense, however, because I knew Don Parson's book manuscript on Los Angeles public housing was well on its way to completion and would cover a lot of the same territory as I had in a much more detailed manner within the context of Cold War Los Angeles. (In fact, his book was published in the same year as mine on Mayor Bowron.) At that time Don and I were sharing our research on the topic, so I knew where he was going with it. Luckily, that allowed me to refer readers to Don's book for additional discussion of housing so I could devote more space to the many other challenges facing the city and its government in that period. Thanks again, Don.

Donald Craig Parson, the full name that he rarely used, completed his master's program in urban planning at UCLA in 1979 with his thesis "Regional Planning, Housing Policy and Community Action in Northern Ireland." He then began work on his doctorate in the same department under the direction of the notable urban theorist Ed Soja and a remarkable dissertation committee including urban planner Margaret Fitzsimmons, sociologist Clarence Lo, and historians Dolores Hayden and Kathryn Kish Sklar. His dissertation, "Urban Politics during the Cold War: Public Housing, Urban Renewal, and Suburbanization in Los Angeles," was filed in 1985 when he received his PhD.

Over the next two decades he continued to publish articles and eventually began revising his dissertation into his book, *Making a Better World: Public*

Housing, the Red Scare, and the Direction of Modern Los Angeles (2005). It was in these years that his physical affliction gradually took its toll on his mobility and communication, although not on his sharp mind.

I became acquainted with Don's work in the 1980s with the publication of some of his journal articles both before and after the completion of his dissertation. I first met him about 1999, and we found that there was an obvious intersection in our research interests. I was especially impressed with his provocative and well-researched dissertation and publications that demonstrated an incredible knowledge of public housing in Los Angeles and the United States overall, of municipal governance, and of many other issues relating to Los Angeles in the twentieth century (particularly in the early Cold War era), and the serious thought he devoted to various political theories.

Since our first meeting I and many other of his friends were able to help him with some of his research at locations that were physically inaccessible to him over the last two decades. I am also proud of the fact that he asked me to read early drafts of some of the essays in this book.

Don's published articles and his book are abundantly detailed and smartly interpretive, revealing his wide array of interests in analyzing public housing, urban politics, architecture, race relations, gender issues, and the various dimensions of the pursuit of social justice. In several of his articles he is particularly adept in viewing these issues through the experiences of individual characters: the removal of Sidney Burke, editor of a newspaper affiliated with the Communist Party, and his spouse, Libby, and their children from city housing projects after the 1930s and 1940s popular front collapsed at the end of World War II; the transition of moderate Los Angeles City Council member Ed Davenport to his leadership of the far right wing of that body by the early 1950s; and the killing of Augustín Salcido, a Latino teenager, by an LAPD officer who was defended by the city's conservative establishment. In all of them Don provides a rich contextual overview of the changing city in terms of its political direction and the seemingly unchanged attitudes in such areas as race relations.

Don's *Making a Better World* is now the bible for historians of Los Angeles when it comes to public housing and its role in municipal politics. He begins this tome by setting a Keynesian conceptual framework for U.S. politics as it evolved in the 1930s as a response to the political and economic effects of the Great Depression. The rise of the left in this decade and its coalition with organized labor, ethnic minorities, and others became the "social foundation of the planned economy of the welfare state."[1] A major goal of this movement was improving the everyday lives of the nation's less affluent citizens, and public housing emerged as a key element as housing reformers set out to create a "better world" reflecting a "social democratic aesthetic of a planned civic culture."[2] This concept of "community modernism" was accepted in the popular front era of the late 1930s and World War II, when public housing became a solution to urban problems in many U.S. cities and received substantial subsidies from the federal government.

Los Angeles was no exception. This city of single-family residences and apartment buildings embraced public housing in the 1930s, when private industry could not meet the needs of low-cost housing for the present and increasing population, and in the 1940s, when housing became a crisis with the influx of families of those returning from service in the armed forces. Both the city and the county erected housing projects for the poor and working poor, nearly all of them segregated by race and ethnicity, but certainly better than the crude alternatives. In 1949 Mayor Fletcher Bowron and the City Council unanimously approved a plan to build ten thousand federally subsidized housing units, testimony to the accepted need for this solution to house those who could not afford any other option.

In two years the "community modernism" in Los Angeles would change drastically with the demise of the popular front and emergence of McCarthyism. Real estate and financial interests, conservative politicians, and others led the charge against public housing as both radical and unnecessary, and housing reformers were tainted as socialists or communists. "Corporate modernism" became the overarching concept, as organized labor and growth-minded liberals joined the campaign for "inner-city redevelopment for commercial purposes on a monumental scale."[3] In 1953 Mayor Bowron was defeated in his bid for reelection based on this issue, and his successor negotiated with the federal government to complete less than half of those ten thousand units. For Don Parson and many other Los Angeles historians, the defeat of Bowron and public housing was the end of an era in Los Angeles.

For a number of years Don worked diligently on other articles that display this same expertise, and it is to our benefit that, despite his challenges, those essays are printed here with the help of his friends. They demonstrate his interest in Progressive-era planning in addressing slums and urban problems that serves as the foundation for later challenges, in architecture and landscape architecture history related to certain building types, in the changing role of women in their households after World War II, and in the national drive to keep leftists out of public housing viewed through the campaign of an influential U.S. congressman. In the most character-driven essay in this group, Don chronicles the private crusade of a justice of the peace in opposing the Red Scare witch hunt for those on the left by striking down a Los Angeles County ordinance requiring the registration of resident communists as well as upholding the equality of a citizen of color victimized by an LAPD officer.

In my estimation, Don's most important contribution to Los Angeles history is his interpretation of Cold War urban politics as it changed the city after World War II, when the entrepreneurial elite composed of major regional businesses and professions and their national allies crusaded for a private enterprise approach to planning for the metropolis. The elite did so by taking advantage of the nationwide Red Scare to marginalize public housing advocates, social justice adherents, other liberals, and the left in order to continue the segregation of racial minorities and protect white property values. The elite's growth machine embraced union labor (particularly the construction trades), political moderates who feared the wrath of conservative voters, and citizens alarmed by charges of communist activism and government control over private property. Ideological conflicts among municipal officials were encouraged, as the City Council, which unanimously supported the public housing contract in 1949, became increasingly stratified and ultimately opposed it. The business elite supported limited local government meddling in the local economy, but only when it suited their needs.

The result was a loss for many: Los Angeles' progressive housing advocates who had campaigned for the California Community Redevelopment Act of 1945 as a method to eradicate slums and replace them with modern and affordable structures for the working poor; many veterans and their families who arrived in the city and could not afford a decent home at a reasonable price; low-income residents on Bunker Hill who lost their homes at the sites of proposed public housing units that were replaced in the 1950s by redevelopment projects built by private developers who instead provided offices and dwellings for more affluent citizens; and the inhabitants of Chavez Ravine who were forced to give up their homes for a baseball stadium for the Los Angeles Dodgers. As in other major American cities, public housing came to be seen as the crowded and deteriorating domicile of poor citizens of color.

In the stories presented above and all of his other work, Don created a masterful context for developments within Los Angeles, as well as in the broader overall story in the United States. His discussion of Cold War Los Angeles politics based on political theory, both general and specific to his subjects, informs us as to how and why Los Angeles was an important site within the United States for public housing and other concerns in this era. His command of secondary sources, which have approached the subject with different views and through various single issues, contributes to his overall narrative of Los Angeles political history. And the timing of this book seems perfect for our situation today, when housing is again a major issue in Los Angeles, the capital of homelessness. Don's analysis of public housing in the last century can provide a perspective on how we treat those families and individuals with limited means needing decent habitation.

Don Parson certainly was the reigning expert on the history of the public housing movement in Los Angeles as he chronicled and interpreted how it was regarded positively by many residents during its rise in the late 1930s and early 1940s and its decline beginning in the early 1950s, a victim of more powerful forces in the metropolis. His scholarship exhibited in published articles and his book, as well as the essays in this volume, demonstrates his interest in related issues and continues to reinforce his interpretive framework for the study of Cold War politics and the social milieu at the local level within the larger context of developments on the national scene. The corpus of all of this work certainly marks Don Parson as one of the major historians of Los Angeles political history in the twentieth century.

NOTES

1. Don Parson, *Making a Better World: Public Housing, the Red Scare, and the Direction of Modern Los Angeles* (Minneapolis: University of Minnesota Press, 2005), 3.

2. Ibid., 7.

3. Ibid., 9.

CHAPTER 7

History Repeating . . .

SUE RUDDICK

There are many ways one might engage Don Parson's work—he presents a richly detailed and lovingly crafted history of the Los Angeles region, drawing on an expansive range of sources, part history, part biography of the personalities and politicians involved in shaping the region. Although Parson writes more in the genre of historical-geographical case study, we might read his work obliquely as a kind of history of the present. It is as much a history of the accounts and recountings of the story of the region, the persistent social imaginaries, as it is a historical geography of the region. If we set Parson's historical account against the trends that emerged in the deepening of the neoliberal project in Los Angeles in the later period, we get the feeling, not unlike the narrative lyrics of jazz singer Shirley Bassey, that "History [is] Repeating." I read Parson's account of the housing issues in the region from the 1900s to the 1950s against my own work on homelessness in the subsequent period from 1970 through 1990.[1]

What strikes me most in reading Parson's work, then, is that certain tropes and processes that seemed to characterize the liberal era (early 1900s) and the postwar years reemerge (if they were at all dormant) in the neoliberal period. In his first chapter, "A Mecca for the Unfortunate," Parson charts the history of housing dereliction and reform, but it is as much about the ways the story of Los Angeles was told and retold through the decades. He draws on the early 1900s writings on housing conditions by social reformers such as Bartlett, Stoddart, and Riis, short stories by Amanda Mathews from the same period, later novels by George Santos and Sandro Neblo, and the observations of W. E. B. Du Bois.

There was however a marked shift through the "transformation of academic paradigms from moral outrage [in the 1910s and 1920s] to dispassionate urban sociology." This shift to sociological approaches and a management ethos characterized both housing reform (reminiscent of the Chicago School) and later the management of the housewife who, in the 1950s, was increasingly entreated to embrace her limited role as a cornerstone to the expansion of postwar suburbs. In the field of public housing in the late 1930s and 1940s, the City Housing Authority initiated a series of public housing projects emblematic of what Parson terms the "ethos of community modernism," oriented in design and philosophy to the raising of children. As Parson notes in his accounts of the careful attention paid to public housing design in this period—often crafted by well-known local architects—including play spaces for children, communal gardens, and leading-edge design (an approach that has all but fallen from favor in the current period with limited exceptions, such as the projects in Vienna), public housing was more than mere shelter. It was a family matter. In the 1950s, this family matter rooted itself in the growth of the suburbs' attention on the role of the housewife, who was encouraged, with the expansion of the suburbs, to embrace her role as unpaid laborer with a sense of mission.

The 1970s through 1990s marked an undoing of many aspects of the social contract at home and in the workplace, through the disengagement of federal involvement in public housing to the increasing precarity of work culminating in Los Angeles' somewhat infamous reputation as the homeless capital of the nation. But many of the themes Parson surfaces have persisted.

> In the early 1900s, Los Angeles presented itself to the world as a city of sunshine, orange groves, and single-family bungalows. (Parson 29)

The trope of a sunshine city, a perpetual paradise, a marketing image that obscured the reality of housing conditions equal in their abject dereliction to those of New York City, emerged in the early 1900s. If this image of Los Angeles as paradise and playground, masking social miseries, a "reality at odds with popular imagery," was characteristic of the liberal era in the early 1900s, before organized state intervention, it was a trope that served well—if only for a time—in the neoliberalization of the region in the 1970s as work became more precarious and social housing contracts crumbled.

Well after the social contract for public housing disintegrated, as job loss in South Central Los Angeles intensified housing precarity and casual laborers began to concentrate in Skid Row, this doubled image of mecca and "mecca for the unfortunate" persisted. It persisted not only in the dubious "toilet wars" that emerged in the 1980s, as politicians fought policy makers who wished to install public toilets in Los Angeles' Skid Row, on the grounds that the availability of public toilets downtown would act as a magnet to homeless people across the country, but also in early attempts to deal with homeless youth who began to congregate in the region, as their tendencies to gather—not in Skid Row but on the beaches of the city and in Hollywood—gave credence to the idea that they were simply derelict youth avoiding the responsibilities of home and school, rather than young people fleeing abuse. For young people fleeing abusive family life, Los Angeles was indeed something of a mecca—as they congregated in Santa Monica, Venice Beach, and Hollywood, avoiding the sites typically associated with the homeless day laborers and older men. But this contributed to the popular notion that runaways were juvenile delinquents seeking sun and fun rather than abused young people escaping domestic violence, and early policy reflected this as young people were repeatedly returned home, only to run away again.

Running concurrently with this century-long construct was the social imagery surrounding early practices of progressive reformers. In the 1900s, this took the form of the Settlement House, part of a reform ethos that coexisted in a curious disconnect with the more effusive images of the sunshine city. This reform ethos resurfaced in the 1970s in Hollywood, eventually fusing by the 1990s into a patchwork of nongovernmental and religious organizations in Hollywood dealing with homeless youth, a constellation of drop-in centers, temporary shelters, and limited experiments in longer term care.

> The *Los Angeles Times* warned housewives not to neglect housework as "government, business and industry leaders aren't happy with this situation [of women abandoning housework], because they know lack of home upkeep brings home deterioration and this leads to an inevitable deadend—slums." (Parson 153)

From midcentury on, however, the trope of idyllic suburban family life was resurrected, in the romanticizing of the region's suburbs and their happy nuclear families as the social bulwark of Western society. From the 1950s through the 1970s this trope was mobilized to frame social policy addressing homeless youth in the region, as many young people running away from abusive family contexts were either returned home or sent to live in a network of suburban families in the Los Angeles region.

> The geography of race and class would circumscribe and inform the development of housing reform in Los Angeles. (Parson 29)

Finally, enduring class structures and racialized divides that shaped division between neighborhoods through the twentieth century reverberated in state and nongovernmental responses to those no longer housed—in the swelling numbers of both the unemployed and dispossessed African Americans contained within downtown's Skid Row and the "sorting" of homeless people across the city. Undoubtedly this was a result of both existing social networks and repressive policing practices, whereby black and Hispanic homeless congregated in increasing numbers on LA's Eastside, while young, white homeless people—able to "pass" as housed—congregated in West LA, along the beaches, and in tourist and recreation areas.

I think the strength of Don Parson's work is that it helps to shape our understanding of the longue durée, to set the stage of contemporary struggles in the twenty-first century against a past—as Skid Row itself is dismantled with the gentrification of downtown, as homelessness intensifies, as racialized and class divisions become more pronounced. A history not understood is doomed to repetition. What Parson offers us is both a reason for despair and a reason for hope.

NOTE

1. Susan Ruddick, *Young and Homeless in Hollywood* (London: Routledge, 1995).

CHAPTER 8

Of Bunnies and Barricades

STEVEN FLUSTY, WITH DON PARSON

There is a story I want to relate. It is the story of an unemployed Southern Californian, although not one troubled by that unemployment as, in the world of this tale, there is no employment. Rather, work is happily no more, and like everybody else the protagonist of this story spends his time doing only what he and his fellows have agreed is necessary, desirable, and enjoyable, which for our protagonist, living nomadically as he and all others do, camped out at present on the shore of the Pacific Ocean, includes a great deal of fishing and surfing. But neither our protagonist nor his fellows are, in fact, *he* or *his*, nor are they *she* or *hers*, as sex and gender in this world have through great struggle become optional, flexible, and diversely inventive. Thus, our protagonist is neither a he nor a she but what I like to call an o (from the Turkish gender-neutral pronoun, although the Magyar *ö* or Finnish *hän* would do equally well), and what's more o is only optionally and temporarily human—species in this story's world has become mutable as well, and o is preparing to deepen o's connection to the sea by transitioning into a dolphin.

As much as I want to relate this tale, though, I am unable. It has been many years since I last encountered it, and search as I may after multiple displacements and relocations I cannot find the pages of it anywhere. Its details and subtleties have faded with time, and I have no business reinventing them as it is, in fact, not my story at all. Rather, it is Don Parson's (as opposed to Don Parsons' for, as Don is ever careful to enumerate, there is only one of him), the first writing he ever shared upon our initial meeting in the earliest years of the 1990s. I regret the story now exists only as a précis in my memory, for it perfectly embodies Don's utopian imagination in both its unfettered creativity and its heartfelt utopianism. And I use the term "embodies" pointedly, as the shoreside zero-work utopia of Don's imagination is a bodily one, deeply manifesting space, the specificities of place, and the body that strives to escape its own limitations, while deeply experiencing and reforging both place and space around itself. And really, is it any surprise a mind like Don's would chafe at the ever-narrowing limits imposed by the body?

But as I haven't the story to fully and properly relate, I will tell instead of something I do have. It is neither an exceptional thing nor a particularly fresh one, a T-shirt now entering its twenty-fifth year of life, but as a material culturist I do tend to fall back on such quotidian things for my own storytelling. It is a black T-shirt emblazoned with a cherry red and day-glo orange reproduction of a 1920 Dmitri Moor Soviet propaganda poster, a Red Army trooper in peasant *kosovorotka* smock and pointed felt *budenovska* helmet, with two significant divergences from its artistic source. Rather than reading "**ТЫ** ЗАПИСАЛСЯ ДОБРОВОЛЬЦЕМ?," Russian for "HAVE **YOU** VOLUNTEERED?," the shirt proclaims, in faux Constructivist Cyrillic, "MARXISM FOR THE PEOPLE." More crucially, though, the face of the soldier pointing accusingly off the shirt front has been augmented with the spectacles, bulbous nose, and bushy eyebrows and moustache of Groucho Marx. But least evidently, and most significantly for this telling, is that Don provided me both this shirt and its source: one of the many enduring literary contributions Don made to my own research canon was the mail-order catalog for the shirt's manufacturer and "Outfitters of Popular Culture," the comedic novelty purveyor Archie McPhee.

Don always exhibited that truest hallmark of the deep thinker, a principled commitment to ideological irreverence. In Don's personal lexicon, by way of example, historical materialism is shortened to "histomat," which then becomes the place to which he asserts one takes one's dialectical dirty laundry for a good purging. Our mutual forays into such "diabolical immaterialism," as radical planner Richard Milgrom once termed it, began with our first meeting. As a harbinger of the aforesaid shirt, we found ourselves debating the problematics of particular Marxist variants. Don, for his part, asserted a fondness for Groucho-ist thought, prizing its dialogical demolition of opponents' verbal rectitudes and underpinning logical assumptions, whereas I complained that Groucho-ism was both overly textualized and unrehabilitatably hostile to feminist thought, preferring instead the incisively materialist Harpo-ite techniques of silently performative critique.[1]

Another place where Don and I found ourselves in unfailing agreement was in the all-important cultural- and political-economic arena of cartoons. Mickey Mouse, we concluded after prolonged discussion in the vein of Ariel Dorfman and Armand Mattelart's *How to Read Donald Duck*, is not so much a rodent as a capitalist running dog, a milquetoast submissive urging squeaking compliance with the inherent abuses of the status quo. Against this, consider Bugs Bunny—the perfect synthesis of Groucho-ist and Harpo-ite schools, the working-class Brooklyn-accented trickster habitually skewering the oppressor with everything from wisecracks to explosive-laden cigars and gift boxes, and with cross-dressing thrown in to boot! This analysis had to be applicable to our present condition, we were certain, and the uprisings of LA's summer of 1992 presented us with just the site of application; in September we published a joint report from Los Angeles:

Preconscious Popular Opposition to Global Post-Fuddism: Counter-Accumulative Tendencies in Los Angeles' T.V. Dinner Society

STEVEN FLUSTY AND DON PARSON

There is a specter haunting Los Angeles, hovering omnipresent above the hypertribalized territories of the region, continuously sucking up yummy capital from the pay-points and work places of each race and class partitioned community like a hyperactive couch potato ravenously inhaling his T.V. dinner.[2]

What better analogy describes the current sociospatial condition of the supranational appropriation of resource from the segregated stomping grounds of the underpaid and unpaid labor of the wannabe nonworking class, who cry out from the inner cities of LA, Hollywood and the San Fernando Valley, "We want stuff, not work!"

The couch potato is none other than a complacent, flatulent and globalized Elmer Fudd, who gags on his McMulticultural LA Tossed Salad Lite as he sits in his high-rise chrome, glass and pseudo-marble living room on Bunker Hill, in Century City, in Beverly Hills, Warner Center and Simi Valley, and flips in terror from channel to channel, unable to evade the panicky aerial images of millions of Bugs Bunnies pilfering the precious commodified carrots rooted in the pwiwate pwopewty of chain wetail outlets spread throughout the low wage/tax exempt Fwee Entewpwise Zones constituting Elmer's back garden. Porky, invested in with black riot gear and an LAPD badge so as to relieve Elmer of the dirty job of rabbit hunting, cowers behind a barricade of otherwise useless RTD busses as Bugs sullenly cracks, "Be vewy vewy quiet, I'm hunting Elmers."

What are the implications for critical urban theory? That, we assume, is what our research is intended to determine. In the meanwhile, we find some small satisfaction in having begun to recognize the emergence of nascent Bugsist tendencies in popular opposition to the monolithic flaccid-accumulative forces of global post-Fuddism. As Bugs himself has said, "Don't think it hasn't been fun, because it hasn't."

"Cartoons are good," as Jean-Martin Charcot would have observed had he too been an Angeleno, "but they don't prevent live-action from existing." Don was always well aware of this, focused as he was on the ever-present reactions that have trampled the built realization of utopian imaginings across Southern California over the course of the past half century plus. This awareness was aided and abetted by my own obsession with the intensifying militarization of urban space against any and all forms of putative deviance, a complementarity responsible for our inaugural meeting. But how, then, to apprehend that perversion of the carnivalesque that is capital's oppressive hybridization of the cartoon and the concrete, the irruption of animated aesthetics and (il)logics into material spaces to strictly delimit potentials for live flesh and blood action? This was the question that confronted us when, shortly after the publication of our paean to our favorite wadical wabbit, a candy-colored simulacrum of the city suddenly bloomed like an antique triffid atop a high plateau on Hollywood's farthest edge. Jon Jerde's Universal CityWalk opened in May 1993. Clearly, Don and I had no choice but to mount an expedition.

The expedition was fraught with peril, largely because Don made the grave mistake of allowing me to drive his car. The car was like nothing I had encountered before, adapted to Don's unique neuromuscular requisites by means of an ingenious system of levers, rods, and bunny pegs that enabled the driver to simultaneously operate the accelerator and brakes with complex movements of the right hand along both horizontal and vertical axes while steering with only the left, a task that is no doubt child's play if one is as experienced with it as Don and does not suffer from the sensorimotor impairments attendant upon my dyslexia.

And so we proceeded in fits, starts, and near misses across the length of the San Fernando Valley, with me stubbornly resistant until quite belatedly to the fact the car could also be operated in the conventional manner. Yet despite these perils, we did at last scale the heights to the self-proclaimed "capital of fun," where we set about alternately exploring its precincts and seeking out places to rest our backsides while taking notes. This last was no mean feat, as the place strictly enforced a sitting-only-on-designated-seating policy while providing precious few actual seats, and here Don was at a distinct advantage. Being both the founder and sole official member of Gimp Nation, as he called it, Don riffed repeatedly on his own foresight in having arrived ensconced in his own free-wheeling self-propelled seating. And so, having attained the summit and with our quest at an end, I set to the task of filing our expedition report with the academy via *L.A. Architect*:

City Lite

STEVEN FLUSTY

CityWalk architect Jon Jerde stood before his audience, spouting a viscous stream of urbanistic koans. We'd heard this spiel before, but usually it was better ordered. This time it seemed as though someone had run his notes through a blunted Cuisinart; ". . . because the theme of Los Angeles is it has no theme. Los Angeles is comprised of a languageless language; it is a thing without edges and it's hard to love a thing without edges because you can't get your arms around it . . ." The "Cityroof," he continued, demonstrating a well-

honed capacity for cute corporate catch phrases, "serves as Citywalk's organizing element, a height limitation increasing towards the site's center that will form development
on the hill into a kind of arch or dome. . . ."[3] As my mind rebelled at the doublethink of
a "themeless theme" contained within an overarching formal device, Mr. Jerde pressed
on, oblivious to the mounting absurdities of his presentation: "We've been getting lots of
weird press about building a fake LA. and privatizing public spaces," he griped, "but that's
not what this is about. . . ." There was a sudden shower of sparks and the architect fell
silent, a bundle of color coded wires protruding from his back and a little pile of scorched
microchips spilling onto the floor.

Spungin and Gilmore, the President of MCA Development and the leasing director respectively, hurried onstage, lifted the architect onto a dolly and wheeled him away while
apologizing for Matsushita's inexperience in the field of audioanimatronics. Apparently,
neither Mr. Spungin nor Mr. Gilmore had a direct hand in programming the architect's understanding of "what this is about," as both proceeded to leave no urban fear unexagger-
ated in order to hawk their admittedly artificial, proprietary LA. Mr. Spungin said of Venice
Beach that "there's someone on every corner with a 'Work for Food' sign. . . . It's not fun
anymore," while Mr. Gilmore chimed in of Melrose Avenue that, "I don't need the excitement of dodging bullets." He went on to demonstrate his appreciation of LA's rich cultural
resources by adding, "I don't need to go to a Third World country."[4] This attitude was
no doubt synergistic with the segregationist assumptions implicit in Jerde's response to
observations that his earlier Citicorp Plaza design seemed limited to a primarily "yuppie"
clientele. "I do not think that the place can attract any other clientele but the downtown
white-collar employee. Hispanics would not come; they want to shop in Hispanic environments; Orientals want to shop in Oriental environments. Little Tokyo is for the Japanese,
Chinatown for the Chinese. In many ways you do not want to mix people too much. It is
clearly self-segregating, but not necessarily with negative results."[5]

After a few more slogans to the effect of "planned compositional accidents," "creating
a sense of comfort and awe," and Mr. Wemple's revealing reference to the project as
"the object," we stepped out onto the Walk, and directly into a pile of well . . . Godzilla, it
would seem, had been busily grazing her way across the landmarks of the LA basin when,
overcome by a chunk of Frederick's of Hollywood caught in the back of her throat, she
retched a stream of half-digested facades into Universal City's lap. This was it?! For all the
hype and counterhype, the thrusts of "a whole city built in a brief instant" and the parries
of "fortified playground for the privileged," all we get is this overpriced, inaccessible,
tarted-up tourist trap of a shopping mall?!

Huddled up against a vast parking lot, this "city" is a chasm of 36' thick storefronts
doglegging through a circular plaza. The actual promenade is an emphatically lousy place
to be, devoid of shade or substantial vegetation beyond the relentlessly hackneyed pin-
headed palm trees, punctuated by a precious few out-of-the-way stemwalls of concrete
and tile forlornly impersonating seating. The plaza itself, serving as a planographic hinge
piece in a burlesque formal gesture one would expect from a first-year architectural stu-

dent, looks as if someone has ripped downtown's 7th Street Marketplace out by the roots and pitched it atop this hill as scrap.

Mr. Spungin and Mr. Gilmore did get what they wanted, as the place is unarguably free of those spoil-sport poor people, bears no resemblance whatsoever to Sarajevo's Sniper Alley, and is wholly lacking in saris, chilied mangos, powdered ginseng, Teen Angels magazine and such other "Third World" trappings as increasingly make the real LA a place worth toughing it out. And CityWalk will stay this way, with video cameras soon to feed 100% coverage to a Sheriff's substation, shared with private security who patrol the premises in numbers ranging from 4 to 20. These draconian measures are no doubt just part of the fun of simulating LA right down to its emergent paranoia, as it is unlikely there will ever be undesirables able to afford, let alone comprehend, the parking policy. It reads like the rules of an Avalon Hill war game; a 5½" x 8½" sheet riddled with variable fees for general, valet and short term parking and a validation process seemingly developed in consultation with Scrooge McDuck. A lot to wade through for the privilege of consuming all the same books, clothes and food available at most regional shopping centers, but at prices as much as 50% higher; a $6 green salad at a snack bar, a $30 stuffed brontosaurus available at any Imaginarium for about $20.[6] If this is the new privatized social space of the elite, the rest of us can relax. We're not missing anything. Because a mall is no more a city than a window dresser is an urban designer.

First published in *L.A. Architect*, September 1993, pp. 8–9.

Throughout our time together, Don and I developed a propensity for intoning a particular pair of slogans. One, cribbed from the Szegerely musical ensemble 3 Mustaphas 3, was "Forward in all directions!," and the other, pilfered from the waiting room of every dentist's office we'd ever visited, was the motto of the periodical *Children's Highlights*: "Fun with a purpose." It should be evident how these commands jointly influenced the trajectory of our investigations.

What is less evident, however, is how the output driven by these urgings was received. Consider, by way of example, the effects of my report on our expedition. Upon its appearance in print, I was immediately banned from the pages of the publishing periodical, and the editor was thenceforth subjected to such strenuous oversight that she left and went on to a successful alternative career in public broadcasting. Perhaps we should have been no less attentive to another slogan, first introduced to me by my doctoral studies supervisor: "The academy is not a place that appreciates creativity."

But when I say "we" in this instance, I in fact mean "I," as Don always excelled at something with which I have time and again proven entirely hopeless—the capacity to first perfectly synthesize the critically comedic with the historically tragic, and then to let his commitment to enacting a greater justice determine how that synthesis will most effectively be put across to any given audience.

But do not take my word for it. Behold these particularly relevant segments of a seamless fugue (with variations!), a book review on the problematics of urban militarization and sociospatial justice, complete with our field excursions and explorations of the cartoonish, all rolled into one unassailably respectable package.

EEK! A MICKEY MOUSE!
The Post-Fuddist Recomposition of Urban Space

DON PARSON

The idea that city spaces can be organized as a multitude of theme parks—where the spectacle of urban life can be orchestrated in order to conjure up a complete, albeit counterfeit, everyday experience—is the thread uniting the eight essays that constitute Michael Sorkin's *Variations on a Theme Park*. Shopping malls, Silicon Valley, Orange County, pedestrian streets, real estate markets, the architecture of "fortress Los Angeles," and the use of the prototypical theme park—Disneyland itself—as a semiotic signpost from which to read postmodern urbanity, are the variations explored in this volume.

The emergent urban form that results from the agglomeration of theme parks is seen as embodying three types: an "ageographical city," where the telephone and the modem have rendered "fixed" urban geographies of central places, suburbs and public spaces obsolete; the surveillance and control of those who cannot or will not be incorporated as members of the army of uniform mass culture into a militarized urbanism; and the city of simulations—the creation of idealized urban spaces, the building of the themescape. The result is, as Michael Sorkin observes in the Introduction, a "happy regulated vision of pleasure . . . [which is] stripping troubled urbanity of its sting, of the presence of the poor, of crime, of dirt, of work" (p. xv).[7]

The implications as to the direction and future of public space in the city unite the essays in this volume: in the ageographical city public space becomes intangible; it is monitored, reformulated and subject to surveillance in Fortress Los Angeles; and it is divided, filtered and sanitized in the simulated city. Unfortunately, the aversion of most of the theme park's exponents described here to comprehend the recomposition of urban space in political terms leaves us only with the ability to lament the demise of public space.

Mickey Mouse v. Bugs Bunny

While the essays in *Variations on a Theme Park* are organized around a radical analysis, the conceptualization of capitalism as class struggle, with a working class—comprising waged and unwaged labor, and containing a myriad of racial and sexual hierarchies—that has the capacity to act for itself, is missing. The idea of a theme park is founded on the presumed passivity of an unquestioning working class bedazzled, befuddled, and struck mute and speechless by the society of the spectacle. Within the unidimensional fantasy of a non-contentious capitalism, a historical and geographical amnesia affects the stroller on the Main Street of Disneyland:

> Instead of an acknowledgement of colonialism there is simply a journey through exotic, primitive places; instead of genocide there is the triumphal conquest of the American West; instead of poverty and unemployment there is Main Street, USA, the small-town paradise of American popular culture: the answer to Metropolis.[8]

The limitations of such an analysis might be illustrated by the following example: as Mike Davis has correctly asserted, the Olmstedian vision of the use of public space cutting across class boundaries has been abandoned in Los Angeles in favor of militarized spatial control, but he gives no clues as to what antecedents—except perhaps a devious and omniscient capital which maliciously destroys every vestige of working-class pleasure— might have presaged "fortress Los Angeles." I would argue that it is exactly because the working class is not a passive and inert element in the mode of production but one that provides the political definition of capitalism that we see a recomposition of space from the Olmstedian vision to the theme park.

Thus, in the early decades of the century in Los Angeles, when the working class there abused their Olmstedian privileges to actively use public space for the purposes of political agitation, the *Los Angeles Times* complained of a "serious and continuous misuse" of Central Park (renamed Pershing Square in 1918) whereby "crowds of idlers have gathered there . . . for the 'discussion' of all sorts of questions. . . . They have no moral right to appropriate public property for such use."[9] The City Council subsequently passed draconian legislation that, despite the First Amendment, prohibited the right to verbal expression in public space which, in turn, engendered a free speech fight by the International Workers of the World—so much for the Olmstedian vision![10]

To be sure, urban space organized as a theme park is a powerful analogy that can portend a frightening future. In Harlan Ellison's *A Boy and His Dog*, some of the survivors of the nuclear holocaust have abandoned the subsequent social and environmental problems on the earth's crust to construct their own Mainstreet USA beneath the planet's surface, not in the memory of the way things were but the way they were wished to have been. In a similar vein, I have written elsewhere of the attempts to restructure Olvera Street and the Plaza of Los Angeles into a "multi-ethnic Disneyland"[11]—complete with subservient Mexican peons in the re-creation of a fantasy past—as part of a "homogenous layer of processed and depoliticized histories . . . on which the postmodern city is built."[12]

Undiscussed in Variations on a Theme Park is the development by MCA Development Co. of CityWalk shopping district, which will be located adjacent to the Universal Studio entertainment complex in Los Angeles. With candy wrappers imbedded in the sidewalk (to look as if they have been casually discarded), a mixture of Art Deco, streamline modern and "California Vernacular" architecture, and an ersatz Venice Beach, no gangs, no rowdy or unruly crowds, and no unemployed people with "will work for food" signs, CityWalk will be, according to the president of MCA, an "idealized reality" of urban life. As the *Los Angeles Times* observes:

> Tired of feeling guilty about the homeless? Weary of fighting traffic or worrying about crime? When CityWalk opens this fall, its creators promise a poverty-free pedestrian promenade with plenty of parking and a sheriffs substation on the premises.[13] (Wallace, 1992)

Kevin Starr, a professor of urban planning at the University of Southern California, sees CityWalk as introducing a spatial "level of social control" to substitute for the authentic urban experience of Los Angeles. Further, he sees an analogy between Ray Bradbury's *Martian Chronicles* and CityWalk. In the novel, the first astronauts from Earth encounter an idealized mid-western town on Mars. Too late, the expedition discovers that the Martians have utilized the subconscious needs, desires and memories of the Earthlings to create a comfortable built environment in order to lull the astronauts into a false sense of complacency and to ultimately destroy them.[14]

It is precisely this sort of speculation or, rather, its translation into political terms that is missing from the essays in *Variations on a Theme Park*. To be fair, Michael Sorkin states in the introduction that "This book is not an attempt to theorize the new city but to describe it" (p. xv), yet, especially in Sorkin's "See you in Disneyland," one has no reference to causal agents (if any) that may have propagated the realities of a Disneyfied urbanity. One can only sanctimoniously bleat "Eek!" in feigned disgust or mock fright when the emerging urban themescapes are described.

Starting out as a sort of gospel according to Mickey—the World Fair begat Disneyland, which begat Disneyworld, which begat a myriad of urban Disneyzones ('Eek!')—Sorkin's finale portrays the emerging cityscape in an obtuse Latinization of English, viz.: "This consumption of the city as spectacle . . . recapitulates the more global possibilities of both the multinational corridor created by air travel and the simultaneous electronics everywhere of television" (p. 218). I'm not quite sure how to interpret this, but the best response is probably "Eek!"

Most descriptions within this volume leave the impression that the city of simulations is the extension and distortion of elements imbedded within a capitalism with no oppositional movements or tendencies. The theme park's simulations do not acknowledge the presence, nor even the possibility, of a working class for itself. To return to the Sim City analogy (an analogy of an analogy?): in Sim City there are no revolutions, no demonstrations, no political parties, no anarchism, no worker absenteeism, no strikes, no cooperatives and no refusal. Neither Sim City nor the City of Simulations can incorporate the unprogrammable, self-activism of the working class.

I feel that the use of Mickey Mouse as a metaphor for the composition of urban space is thus a bit one dimensional—it describes spatial transformation only from the perspective of capital while ignoring the flipside of the capitalist totality—the working class. Were I to use cartoon figures to symbolize capitalism (and I must confess, I often do just that), I would choose the dynamic of Bugs Bunny and his skirmishes with Elmer Fudd as a metaphor for class conflict over that of the rather insipid Mickey ("a clean mouse" as described by Walt Disney himself). Bugs is the working-class trickster whose vocation is pilfering carrots from the garden of the bourgeois Elmer Fudd—an avid bunny hunter (that is, he disciplines the working class) whose favourite admonishment is "Be vewy, vewy quiet! I'm hunting wabbits. . . ." As Rosemont points out:

> If the Bunny/Fudd choreography reflects a particular historic moment in the class struggle—a period of class "symmetry" in which the workers here and there win a few of their demands, only to be chased back into their holes in the ground—nonetheless the mythic content of this drama exceeds its original formal limitations. The very appearance on the stage of history of a character such as Bugs Bunny is proof that some day the Fudds will be vanquished—that some day all the carrots in the world will be ours.[15]

In a sense, the recomposition of urban space of Los Angeles with the commodity riots of 1992 might be more precisely described as "post-Fuddist" rather than symbolized by the petit-bourgeois rodent Mickey. Despite the best efforts of the authors in *Variations on a Theme Park* to convince us that public space in the American city is either already dead or not long for this world, to be replaced by a pseudo-public spectacle, the riots in Los Angeles presented us with a "spectacular anti-spectacle" where the streets, with apologies to Le Corbusier, were very much alive. Rather than a Mickey squeaking the joys of commodities to a passive, strolling public on Main Street USA, Bugs was directly appropriating commodified carrots while mocking the former Fudd-Bunny symmetry: "Be vewy, vewy quiet, I'm hunting Elmers. . . ."

This is an abridged version of a text that first appeared as a review of *Variations on a Theme Park: The New American City and the End of Public Space*, ed. Michael Sorkin (New York: Noonday Press, 1992), in *Science and Culture* 4, no. 2 (1993). Thanks to Steve Flusty for his witty and perverse comments on earlier drafts of this review.

One of Don's precepts, a precept I myself have taken to heart (and one shared, and expressed to me decades ago, by the editor of this very volume), is the importance of not telegraphing one's punch lines. Within the context of academia, there is little less fun than slogging through a treatise that evidently felt compelled to tell how it would end at its very beginning. It is my hope that in the telling of this story I have honored that precept in practice, only now arriving at the real crux of the matter. Don Parson is the most uproarious of serious scholars I have ever encountered, and, in the words of Mel Blanc's own epitaph: "That's all folks."

NOTES

1. Despite these differences of opinion with regard to Comrades Groucho and Harpo, we proceeded to heartily derisive laughter at the intolerant pomposities of some of the Angeleno left's more insufferable (and, ultimately, ineffectual) Staliny-flavored personality cults.

2. First published in *INURA Bulletin* 4 (September 1992), Zurich, Switzerland. Elmer

Fudd is a person from the Bugs Bunny comics; LAPD stands for Los Angeles Police Department; RTD is the acronym for the former Rapid Transit District of Southern California, now restructured and renamed into the Los Angeles County Metropolitan Transportation Authority commonly known as MTA.

3. Quotes from presentation to the University of Southern California Architectural Guild CityWalk Preview.

4. Amy Wallace, "Like It's So L.A.! Not Really!," *Los Angeles Times*, February 29, 1992.

5. Anastasia Loukaitou-Sideris, "Private Production of Public Open Space: the Downtown Los Angeles Experience" (PhD diss., University of Southern California, 1988).

6. In 1993 dollars, adjusted for inflation, the current value of the two commodities would be approximately $187 and $3,620, respectively, the 1999 acquisition by Toys "R" Us notwithstanding.

7. Page numbers here and below refer to Sorkin's *Variations on a Theme Park*.

8. Elizabeth Wilson, *The Sphinx and the City: Urban Life, the Control of Disorder, and Women* (Berkeley: University of California Press, 1992).

9. "To Abate a Nuisance," *Los Angeles Times*, March 19, 1901.

10. The wording of the legislation was, "It shall be unlawful for any person to discuss, expound, advocate or oppose the principles or creed of any political party, partisan body, or organization, or religious denomination or sect, or the doctrines of any economic or social system in any public speech, lecture, or discourse, made or delivered in any public park in the city of Los Angeles."

11. Don Parson, "Many Histories: Postmodern Politics in Los Angeles," *Science as Culture* 12 (1991): 418.

12. Ibid., 424.

13. Amy Wallace, "Like It's So L.A.! Not really," *Los Angeles Times*, February 29, 1992.

14. Ibid.

15. Franklin Rosemont, "Bugs Bunny," in *Surrealism and Its Popular Accomplices*, ed. Franklin Rosemont (San Francisco: City Lights, 1980), 55.

PART 3

Alternative Futures

DON PARSON REVISITED

Introduction

ROGER KEIL AND JUDY BRANFMAN

In the following chapters in this final part of the book, we have interven-
tions by some powerful voices in the debate on housing, policy, and politics in Southern California. These contributions have all been published in
different contexts before, but they gain new significance in light of Parson's
historical work. While the authors don't engage directly with Parson, they
implicitly take up the themes he introduces through his scholarship. These
chapters are, in this sense, to be read as a contextualization and a more or
less explicit appreciation of Parson's oeuvre and an acknowledgment of his
scholarship.

The cycle begins with Greg Goldin's essay "Ben Margolis and Gregory Ain: A Meeting of Radical Minds," highlighting the road midcentury
architectural design has traveled, from the early experimentation with
social planning Parson terms "Community Modernism" to commodification.
Few admirers or purchasers of midcentury housing today see it as the
embodiment of a set of social ideals. But these homes, whether public
housing or private, were meant not to be a retreat from society but rather
an extension of the social commitment to bettering oneself and engaging
with the community and larger world. And while public housing has been
racialized and criminalized, and in some cases disappeared, private homes
have become valuable trophies, constituting proof that one stands apart
from the hoi polloi. This reality couldn't be further from what the modernists and their early clients, many of them dedicated social justice activists
who inhabit various settings in Parson's work, conceived of as their mission
in design or life.

Dana Cuff, in her essay "Power Lines," using the iconic example of
the redevelopment of Chavez Ravine involving the erasure and displacement of a Chicano community to build a baseball stadium, discusses the
significance of lines and boundaries in the "horizontal city" of Los Angeles.
Cuff's work directly intersects with Parson's interest in the ephemeral
but real histories of social spaces in the expanses of Los Angeles, their

concrete extinction in the face of real estate projects that superseded them over time. In a similar spirit, Jennifer Wolch and Dana Cuff excavate some of the layers of historical geography in their interview with Mike Davis, the following chapter in this book. Central to this conversation is, in fact, the "economic logic of real estate and land development" that has been so central to Parson's work, especially where it is to do with housing. Davis also points to the continued dialectics of center and periphery, working-class and middle-class spaces in the Los Angeles region. This has been one of the core interests in Parson's work. For Davis, this has often been the key to understanding the region in its contradictory dynamics. While (white) privilege has long been understood to be located in the hills and along the coasts of the Southland, it has now claimed pockets of hipster urbanity in the core and the inner suburbs while poverty and diversity have been pushed to the periphery (see also his prescient 1994 column for the *Los Angeles Times*).[1]

The following chapter by the late Jackie Leavitt on public housing in Southern California, especially Normont and Nickerson Gardens, takes up Parson's historical narrative in three important ways. First, Leavitt writes about street-level everyday life in the projects and brings the modernist blueprints of the architects and reformers to real life; second, she talks about public housing as sites of the negotiation of race and gender and, at least in some cases, places of female and black hegemony; and third, she points to public housing as a terrain of (progressive) politics.

In the next chapter, by Don Parson's late PhD supervisor and renowned geographer Edward Soja, we leave the street-level ethnography and dust of the archives for the ordering heights of spatial theory. In this remarkably dense and elegant piece, Soja outlines the contours of a conceptual framework with which to understand the relationships of space, justice, and the city. It is here where Los Angeles is marked as a site of multiple interconnections: of agency, of theory, of struggle. That space has to do with justice (and isn't just a second-order dimension following social stratification) is clearly argued here.

The cycle of essays in this section is concluded by Laura Pulido's work on the antiracist and anticapitalist movements that were generated in Los Angeles among the region's burgeoning communities of color. Exemplified in the rise of the Los Angeles chapter of the Black Panther Party, the Centro de Accion Social Autonomo (CASA), and East Wind, the African American, Chicano, and Japanese American communities of the Southland displayed distinct but overlapping cultures of political organizing. Pulido's narrative is a key to and a continuation of Parson's own writings of a different future for Los Angeles and the social and political movements beyond the political mainstream that supported its possibilities.

NOTE

1. Mike Davis, "The Suburban Nightmare: While Older Suburbs Experience Many Problems of the Inner City, 'Edge Cities' Now Offer a New Escape," *Los Angeles Times*, October 23, 1994, http://articles.latimes.com/1994-10-23/opinion /op-53893_1_edge-cities.

CHAPTER 9

Ben Margolis and Gregory Ain

A Meeting of Radical Minds

GREG GOLDIN

If walls could speak. That's what came to mind when I noticed a short newspaper item announcing that the former home of Ben Margolis, an attorney who advocated on behalf of downtrodden workers, besieged Reds, and persecuted labor activists, was for sale. The hillside Los Feliz house, designed by Gregory Ain in the early 1950s, with a twenty-first-century addition by Pierre Koenig, is being offered for just under two million.

The house Ain built Margolis is likely to sell even in the current slow market: midcentury modern architecture is in demand at the moment. But it's unlikely the buyer will understand the meeting of minds that went into its creation.

Margolis is perhaps best known for his defense of the Hollywood 10, a group of mostly screenwriters called before the House Committee on Un-American Activities because of their ties to leftist groups. The "unfriendly" witnesses refused to answer questions about their political beliefs and associations, and were convicted of contempt of Congress. But they were gambling that the Supreme Court would overturn their convictions on grounds that the committee had violated their 1st Amendment rights. They bet wrong. Margolis lost when the Supreme Court, which got the case shortly after two of its most liberal members had died, refused to hear the appeal.

Margolis was successful, though, in the appeal he handled on behalf of twenty-two Mexican American defendants in the 1942 Sleepy Lagoon murder case. The judge had refused to let the men talk to their lawyers during trial, which Margolis used to get their convictions reversed, thereby establishing the right to unimpaired access to counsel for defendants during a criminal trial.

A decade later, Margolis convinced a conservative Supreme Court that bail set for the self-avowed communists he was then defending was unreasonably high. He kept the great 1930s longshoreman Harry Bridges from being deported to his native Australia, and he prevented modern architect David Hyun from being sent back to South Korea. Later in his career, he guided litigation that forced banks to assume some financial responsibility for the slumlords to whom they'd lent millions.

Margolis was, in short, a trenchant advocate for the underdog. Before his own appearance before the House Committee on Un-American Activities, he inveighed that he would "fry in hell before they get any information out of me about my clients." He meant it.

All of which brings us to why Ain was the natural architect for Margolis to turn to when he decided to build a house.

As much a radical as Margolis, Ain believed that modern architecture could and should deliver affordable housing (a dire need in postwar years) that amplified, rather than confined, its residents. Throughout the 1940s, he sketched plans to "refine and dignify the low-cost house." Most of the housing he planned was never built because banks were uncomfortable with the kind of collective ownership he was proposing.

Fortunately, some of the homes he planned were built, including the Avenel Cooperative Housing Project, a group of ten nearly identical three-bedroom units stagger-stepped along a slope in Silver Lake. Commissioned by ten leftists—at least four were blacklisted or questioned by the House Committee on Un-American Activities—the design for the project, which was built in 1947, has been hailed as "a model for effective use of limited space for low-cost urban housing." Using movable walls and sliding patio doors, he coaxed fluid, flexible, and shared space out of tiny footprints.

In his best work, Ain was able to liberate even the smallest room with a suffusion of light and easy access to the outdoors. He made public spaces the axis on which the whole house turned, stripping away the pretenses and formality of a conventional lifestyle. Ain, like his fellow Modernists, naively believed that his designs could transform *homo rapacious*—acquisitive, selfish, disengaged— into an active steward of the commonweal.

As with many of the people Margolis represented, Ain's radical views cost him professionally. Margolis hired the architect during the height of the national witch hunt for communists and other undesirables as an act of loyalty and friendship at a time when not everyone was willing to hire an architect with radical ideas.

But without radical ideas—and without patrons like Margolis—there would be no Modernist houses to collect as status symbols today, even as reliquary objects from a forgotten crusade.

NOTE

This article originally appeared in the *Los Angeles Times*, August 18, 2011, http://articles.latimes.com/2011/aug/18/opinion/la-oe-goldin-margolis-ain-architectur20110818.

CHAPTER 10

Power Lines

Boundaries of Erasure and Expansion in Los Angeles

DANA CUFF

The aerial photograph (figure 10.1) shows Chavez Ravine in the late 1940s, an area just north of downtown Los Angeles surrounded by the region's ubiquitous sprawl. The white line drawn over the photograph commands a disproportionate and unmistakable power: inside that line, all will be demolished; outside that line is safe. An abstraction with real and violent implications, it has not only spatial but also temporal meaning. Soon, this newly defined territory will be scraped clean to make way for something else, something big, we know not what. The boundary line is inscribed by the same hand as the textual references to reality: the roads, cardinal directions, and, by implication, the "project" named Elysian Park Heights.[1] If the text appears to inhabit a layer above the image, the boundary appears within the picture plane yet hovering slightly above the ground, as a kind of site plan to define inside from out, ours versus yours, one space of activity from another, what *could be* from what is present—all forms of spatial speculation. Although it may appear as though Chavez Ravine is on the city's outskirts, instead it was already by the 1940s inhabited by a long-standing community as well as ringed by even more densely populated residential fabric just beyond a band of parkland. The line creates a new and singular "here," as in "here is where we intend to build," where residents had not recognized their common fate. Encircled by a virtual net, two schools, over eleven hundred houses, markets, a church, some roads, a valley—all are swept into one predicament by the line.

A history of the line in Los Angeles provides a context for Chavez Ravine's predicament, locating the abstraction in the city and placing it within the realm of political and spatial action. Compared to other cities, the line carries undue authority in Los Angeles, a horizontal city that is more plan than section, more extension than compression, more periphery than interior. From the dash-dot-dot-dash encircling property to the boundary-filled areas that were red-lined, graphic tools of spatial politics were anything but abstract in the development of Los Angeles. From surveys that constructed boundaries around "slums" for

FIGURE 10.1. What appears to be a simple boundary around the Chavez Ravine public housing site is actually a violent line demarcating the zone of total destruction where households will be displaced, structures demolished, and hillsides flattened.
Housing Authority of the City of Los Angeles. Courtesy of Dana Cuff.

demolition to the recent and relatively arbitrary naming of districts as a means to attract development, the making of Los Angeles can be told through the narrative history of the line. Encircling some terrain within the larger landscape, boundaries defined inside from outside, blight from merely substandard, industrial from residential land uses, preservation-worthy from demolition-ready, and East LA and South LA from the rest of the city. Los Angeles was historically susceptible to power lines due to the vast postwar growth in the region and the dominant imaginary of a plastic city. In the twentieth century, layers of connections and divides shaped LA's built environment particularly in the contested space of "downtown." This contestation has been one of erasure, protest, and violence, masked in the rhetoric of revitalization and civic betterment. The 1939 survey of neighborhood conditions (figure 10.2) is one of many data maps created to study residential "blight" around downtown so that it could be razed to advance the commercial core's possibility. All the neighborhoods, council districts, community plan areas, cities, and census tracts delineate, in more and less fixed manners, a topography of power in Los Angeles particularly in and around downtown. Indeed, a forceful effort was needed to generate a downtown.

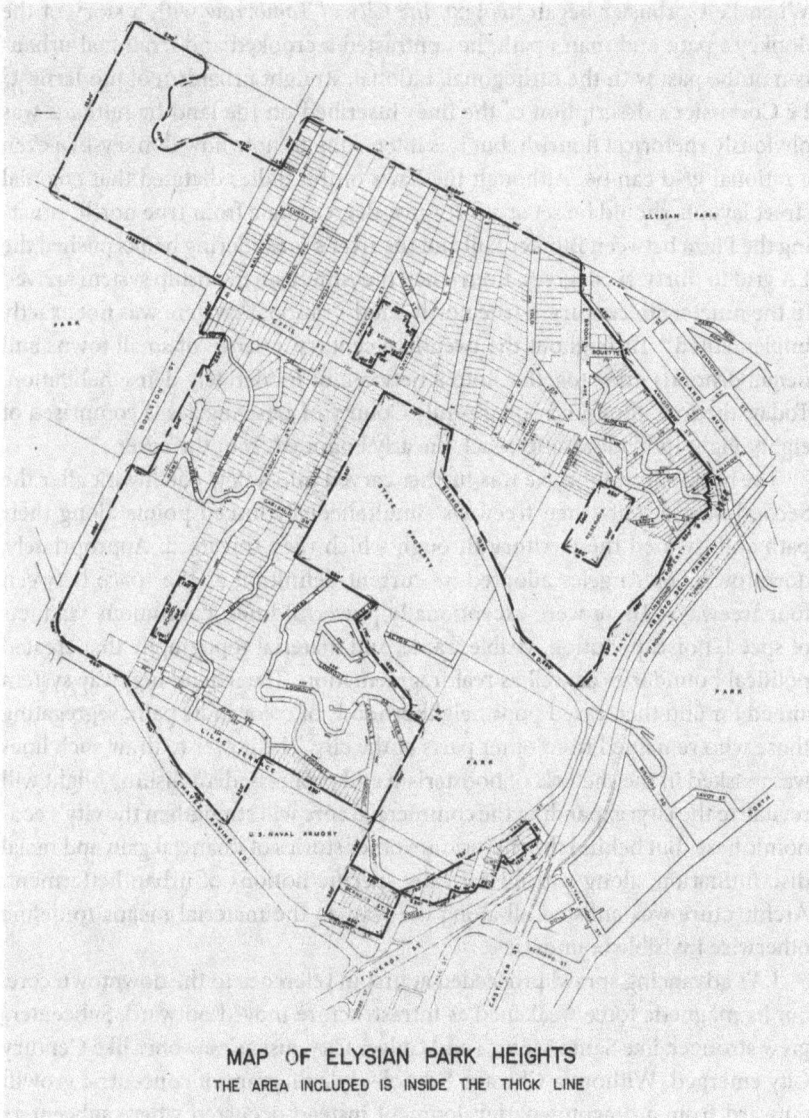

MAP OF ELYSIAN PARK HEIGHTS
THE AREA INCLUDED IS INSIDE THE THICK LINE

FIGURE 10.2. Map of Elysian Park Heights, ca. 1950.
Housing Authority of the City of Los Angeles. Courtesy of Dana Cuff.

Located within a basin framed by the ocean and mountains, Los Angeles'
vast geography cohered in the eighteenth century around a core, and then
around multiple centers. Los Angeles, a city of space according to urban theorist Albert Pope, adapted its Spanish colonial orthogonality to new linearities of
mobility like boulevards and freeways.[2] The eighteenth- and nineteenth-century
gridiron city was followed in postwar urban plans that were rarely orthogonal.

When Le Corbusier began his text *The City of Tomorrow* with a story of the donkey's path and man's path, he contrasted a crooked and irrational urbanism of the past with the orthogonal, rational, straight urbanism of modernity.[3] Le Corbusier's description of the lines inscribed on the land by humans was obviously rhetorical flourish, but it is interesting to note how donkey-like even a rational grid can be. Although the Laws of the Indies dictated that colonial street layouts should be set at a forty-five-degree angle from true north, situating the Plaza between Bunker Hill and the river's meandering banks pushed the LA grid to thirty-six degrees. Even when the American township system arrived in the nineteenth century, a true north-south "rational" system was not exactly implemented.[4] Throughout the twentieth century, a series of small towns and neighborhoods grew together into a network of moderately dense habitation. Today, the four-thousand-square-mile County of Los Angeles is comprised of eighty-eight individual cities, each linearly bounded from the other.

The basin's *terrain vague* was further carved into a new patchwork after the Second World War when freeways simultaneously linked points along their path and divided the territory through which they traversed. Appropriately, downtown Los Angeles adopted its current definition as the space between four freeways. These were exceptionally powerful lines: continuous viaducts of speed, noise, pollution, visible frame, and material topography that created political boundaries as well as real fragmentation. The federal highway system aimed for and then razed poor neighborhoods of color in its path, segregating those who remained from other parts of the city. The power to draw such lines was masked in the rhetoric of boosterism and progress: demolishing blight will revitalize the city; expanding the commercial core will strengthen the city's economic base. But behind the rhetoric are other stories of financial gain and racial discrimination, along with historically specific notions of urban betterment. Architecture was enlisted all along the way, as the material means to define otherwise invisible boundaries.

LA's advancing sprawl proceeded at first in reference to the downtown core, but its magnetic force weakened as infrastructure moved outward. Subcenters grew stronger, like Santa Monica and Culver City, just as new ones like Century City emerged. Without a Chicago School–style diagram of concentric growth outward from a downtown, development instead occurred where subcenters could be delineated to attract development and capital. Parts of the city like Westwood Village in the 1920s or Silicon Beach after the new millennium established boundaries that reinforced identity branding. At the same time, however, further growth congealed along lines linking these subcenters, that is, along LA's characteristic corridors like Wilshire, Olympic, Pico, Hollywood, and Santa Monica boulevards. Even along these passageways, boundaries carve out districts like the Miracle Mile, a one-and-a-half-mile stretch of Wilshire Boulevard planned as a commercial district to rival downtown LA.[5] Thus, Los

Angeles' field-like condition is divided into bounded clusters of identity, if not cities, in their own right. At any point in time, the clusters represent forms of power that have erased, restructured, colonized, preserved, or otherwise over-taken preceding communities of identity.

There is no official count of these clusters, but the best estimate is offered by the *Los Angeles Times*' "neighborhood map" for LA County. Within the county, it tallies 158 cities and unincorporated places and 272 neighborhoods; it counts 114 neighborhoods within the City of LA.[6] These neighborhoods are marked by hundreds of blue signs posted along streets that mark one's entry into or departure from places ranging from Filipinotown and Los Feliz Village to the Furniture and Fine Arts District. Even though there are no official boundaries for those places, the political repercussions of these invisible and moving lines remain. Consider the renaming of South Central to South LA in April 2003 by the LA City Council to rid the community of its negative stigma, or the portion of Compton that rebranded itself as Crystal Park. The name changes were intended "to distance themselves from areas with bad reputations."[7] These are attempts to erase narratives, stained story lines, without necessarily chang-ing anything else. As one councilman said, "It's meaningless and won't really change a thing. What is really needed is a comprehensive program to address crime, unemployment, education and drug abuse."[8] The inarguable truth in

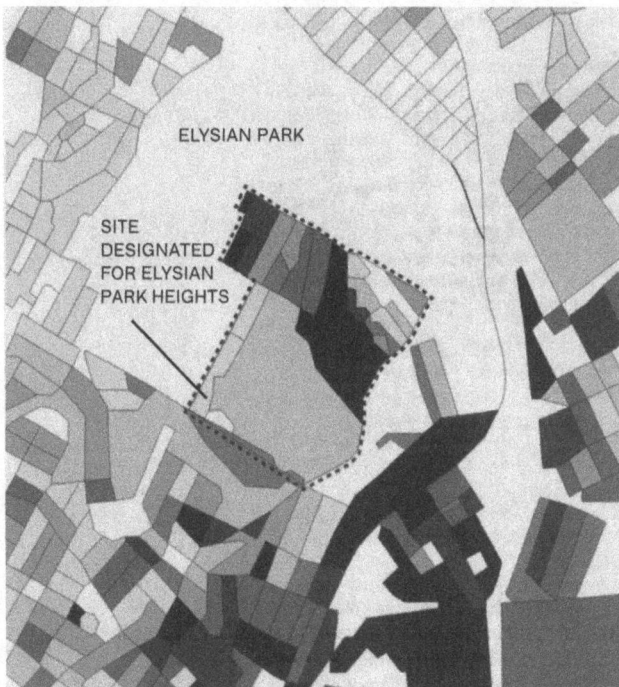

FIGURE 10.3. Condition of Residential Structures Map. This map documents a 1939 survey locating blighted areas for the purpose of public projects and the use of eminent domain. Darker blocks contained more dwelling units needing major repairs (and thus meriting demolition), while lighter blocks had a higher proportion of homes deemed fit for use. White areas contained no residential structures.
Housing Survey, Housing Authority of the City of Los Angeles, August 1939. Archives of the Housing Authority of the City of Los Angeles, Files and Maps. Courtesy of Dana Cuff.

that statement is countered by the historical power of such explicit or implied boundaries, if not the name.

It is not by chance that the hybrid aerial photo-plus-drawing (figure 10.1) was the preferred technique for proposing a major convulsion in Los Angeles in the late 1940s and early 1950s. The Chavez Ravine story was about the land captured by the photograph, which was overlaid with a single boundary line to tell a simple narrative: here is the chosen site. Los Angeles was as much an inhabited *landscape* as a city, and in the ravine, two types of surfaces were patched together so unevenly that nearly three hundred acres of fields and small houses sat within; even the name came from the landform. No other space for development that large existed within a forty-mile radius of downtown. In the late 1940s, photographs of the area in the *Los Angeles Times* showed dirt roads, horses, small grocery stores, and self-built houses, constructing the public imaginary of a rural Mexican village. In fact, more than three thousand people lived in a small portion of the ravine, but all of them would have to move if the city were to pursue its progressive redevelopment agenda. A series of surveys were conducted inside that white boundary, finding about 90 percent of the homes

FIGURE 10.4. Richard Neutra, Elysian Park Heights public housing towers, ca. early 1950s. *Permissions courtesy Dion Neutra, Architect © and Richard and Dion Neutra Papers, Department of Special Collections, Charles E. Young Research Library, UCLA.*

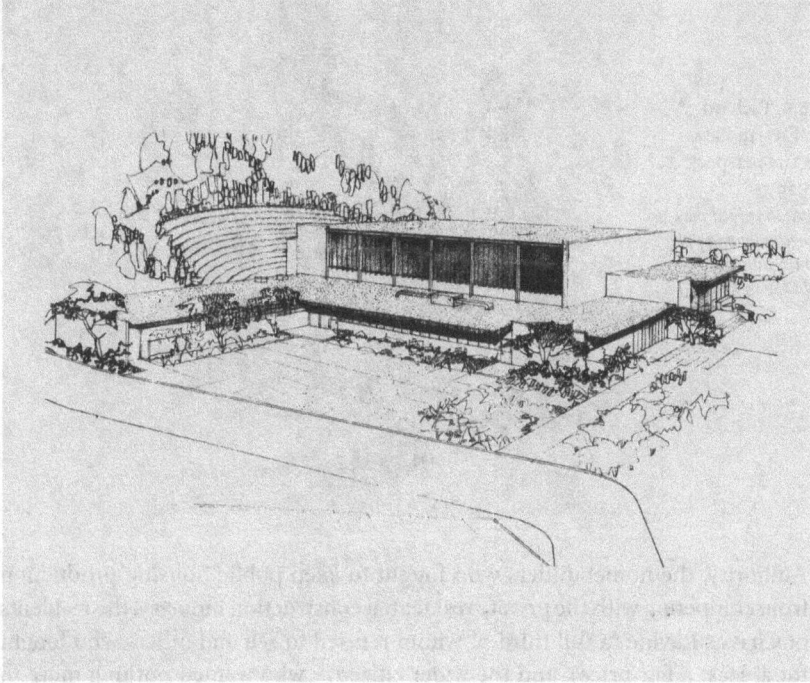

FIGURE 10.5. Richard Neutra, Elysian Park Heights community building proposal, ca. early 1950s.
Permissions courtesy Dion Neutra, Architect © and Richard and Dion Neutra Papers, Department of Special Collections, Charles E. Young Research Library, UCLA.

had at least one basic deficiency (major structural problems or inadequate sanitary facilities) and two-thirds had two or more.[9] The demarcating white line produced a site for Los Angeles, setting the stage for a new narrative: a hillside utopia with 3,360 units of public housing designed by architect Richard Neutra and planner Robert Alexander. Inside the line, the Housing Authority of the City of Los Angeles used eminent domain to purchase every last piece of property, exchanging the rural village for a modern dream.

Henri Lefebvre argues that the representation of urban space abstracts the human body and everyday life to actualize that space for exchange or consumption. "Through its control, the state tends to accentuate the homogeneous character of space, which is fractured by exchange. This space of state control can also be defined as being optical and visual."[10] The line renders urban space, actualizing it for consumption and construction. Here again, Los Angeles' long dominance by real estate speculation would welcome representational techniques that illuminated spatial control. In the case of Chavez Ravine, that drawing laid down the political lines of battle between the City and its Housing

FIGURE 10.6. Richard Neutra, Elysian Park Heights site perspective, ca. early 1950s.
Housing Authority of the City of Los Angeles Photograph Collection, Southern California Library, Los Angeles.

Authority, the homebuilders who fought to keep public housing production from competing with the private residential construction industry, the residents of Chavez Ravine (a full third of whom refused to sell and others who fought for at least a fair price), and the wider citizenry who wanted nothing more to do with low-income housing.

Richard Neutra's site perspective drawing of Elysian Park Heights (figure 10.6) buries the landscape that was visible in the opening aerial photograph. On the razed ground, he portrays building blocks on a hill covered with dense vegetation bisected by roadways. The drawing relies on the outline of the buildings' volumes to delineate the future, "for the outline represents nothing other than the line of demarcation, of separation, the hinge between two surfaces."[11] Hubert Damisch's description applies to the towers and garden apartments in this descriptive view of Elysian Park Heights, whose bold white forms seem to wring themselves out of the dark foliage. The drawing uses the line to hinge each structure upward at right angles from its implied footprint on the ground. While the buildings are transparently speculative, the vegetation erases the past with an opaque ground cover. The way the roadways seem to hover over rather than weave their way through the foliage appears to be an inconsistency in the elegant drawing. However, their treatment is entirely consistent with a reading of the ground plane as an abstraction. Both the aerial photograph and the site perspective obscure the plane of inhabitation, where a lived reality will be violently removed to create a surface for the future. In different ways, both equate the ground's surface with the plane of the representation, be it photo or drawing, to compose what Damisch would call the "projective dimension."

In fact, erasure was the only thing that was real at Chavez Ravine. In the late 1950s, bulldozers cleared the land and its inhabitants, while voters rejected Elysian Park Heights' public housing and backroom politics replaced it with a newly forged, speculative project: Dodger Stadium. The baseball field and its parking lots forget the past that Ry Cooder recalled in the lyrics of his song "Third Base, Dodger Stadium":[12]

> In the middle of the 1st base line,
> got my first kiss, Florencia was kind.
> Now, if the dozer hadn't taken my yard,
> you'd see the tree with our initials carved.
>
> . . . Just a place you don't know,
> up a road you can't go.

One might conclude that power lines do their dirty work in the site plan, and indeed this was the case in postwar Los Angeles. At that time, the city's dominant horizontality was its primary projective dimension: a surface pictured with multiple futures, a plane that begged for limits to demarcate stable

FIGURE 10.7. Dodger Stadium on the Chavez Ravine site where Elysian Park Heights had been planned. From 1962 Fairchild Aerial Survey. *Housing Authority of the City of Los Angeles. Courtesy of Dana Cuff.*

forms, a landscape from which to create places in the field. But the historical specificity of the violent line is no longer the province of plan alone. As Los Angeles begins to grow up rather than out, taking on sectional qualities along with planar ones, a twenty-first-century Los Angeles is finding that erasure as well as vertical growth are both politically embroiled. Instead, current power lines are wedging new programs into forgotten and overlooked spaces, on tight infill sites where every available surface will be deployed. Concomitant forms of violence, including gentrification, extreme densification, and displacement, haunt the architect's speculations. Today, as always, architects hold power in the lines they make, whether rendered or built. It is time to recognize this politically and embodied complexity so that the next generation of architectural city making is cognizant of its power (figure 10.7).

NOTES

The author would like to thank Yang and Joshua Nelson for their able research assistance.

1. The image comes from records kept by the Housing Authority of the City of Los Angeles, which assigned Chavez Ravine the project number Cal 4-11 and the name Elysian Park Heights to the public housing proposed for the site. See Dana Cuff, *The Provisional City: Los Angeles Stories of Architecture and Urbanism* (Cambridge, Mass.: MIT Press, 2000); Don Parson, *Making a Better World: Public Housing, the Red Scare, and the Direction of Modern Los Angeles* (Minneapolis: University of Minnesota Press, 2005).

2. Albert Pope, "From Form to Space," in *Fast-Forward Urbanism*, ed. Dana Cuff and Roger Sherman (New York: Princeton Architectural Press, 2011), 143–75.

3. See Catherine Ingraham, *Architecture and the Burdens of Linearity* (New Haven, Conn.: Yale University Press, 1998); "The Burdens of Linearity: Donkey Urbanism," in *Architecture Theory since 1968*, ed. K. M. Hays (Cambridge, Mass.: MIT Press, 1998), 642–57.

4. D. J. Waldie, "L.A.'s Crooked Heart," *Los Angeles Times*, October 24, 2010, http://articles.latimes.com/2010/oct/24/opinion/la-oe-waldie-maps-20101024.

5. Eric Avila, *The Folklore of the Freeway: Race and Revolt in the Modernist City* (Minneapolis: University of Minnesota Press, 2014).

6. "Mapping L.A. Neighborhoods," *Los Angeles Times*, http://maps.latimes.com/neighborhoods/.

7. Calvin Sims, "In Los Angeles, It's South-Central No More," *New York Times*, April 10, 2003, http://nyti.ms/2ejsSk7.

8. Quote is from then councilman Nate Holden; see Sims, "In Los Angeles."

9. Cuff, *Provisional City*, 272–81.

10. Henri Lefebvre, "Space and the State," in *State/Space: A Reader*, ed. Neil B. Brenner, Bob Jessop, Martin Jones, and Gordon Macleod (Malden, Mass.: Blackwell, 2003), 88.

11. Hubert Damisch, *Noah's Ark: Essays on Architecture* (Boston: MIT Press, 2016), 73.

12. Ry Cooder, W. Garcia, and J. Kevany with BlaPahinui (vocals, guitar, ukulele), "Third Base, Dodger Stadium," in *Chavez Ravine: A Record*, by Ry Cooder et al. (New York: Nonesuch, 2005).

CHAPTER 11

"Downtown Is Not the Heart of the City"

MIKE DAVIS IN CONVERSATION WITH JENNIFER WOLCH AND DANA CUFF

This chapter presents an interview with Mike Davis for *Boom Magazine*. It was conducted during the summer of 2016 by architectural educator and director of UCLA's cityLAB Dana Cuff and dean of UC Berkeley's College of Environmental Design Jennifer Wolch. Chronicler of the California dark side and LA's underbelly, proclaiming a troubling, menacing reality beneath the bright and sunny facade, Mike Davis is one of California's most significant contemporary writers. His most controversial books led critics to label him anything from a left-wing lunatic to a prophet of gloom and peddler of the pornography of despair. Yet much of his personal story and evolution are intimately touched by his experience and close reading of deeply California realities: life as part of the working class, the struggle for better working conditions, and a genuine connection to the difficulties of the region. His most well-known books, *City of Quartz* and *Ecology of Fear*, are unsparing in their assessments of those difficulties. Remaining a central figure of a discipline at the intersection of geography, sociology, and architecture known as the Los Angeles School of Urbanism, Davis is now in retirement from the Department of Creative Writing at UC Riverside. Cuff and Wolch met Davis at his San Diego home to discuss his career, his writings, and his erstwhile and ongoing efforts to understand Los Angeles.

> DANA CUFF: You told us that you get asked about City of Quartz too often, so let's take a different tack. As one of California's great urban storytellers, what is missing from our understanding of Los Angeles?
>
> MIKE DAVIS: The economic logic of real estate and land development. This has always been the master key to understanding spatial and racial politics in Southern California. As the late nineteenth century's most influential radical thinker—I'm thinking of San Francisco's Henry George not Karl Marx— explained rather magnificently, you cannot reform urban space without controlling land values. Zoning and city planning—the Progressive tools for creating the City Beautiful—either have been totally co-opted to serve

the market or died the death of a thousand cuts, that is to say by variances. I was briefly an urban design commissioner in Pasadena in the mid-1990s and saw how easily state-of-the-art design standards and community plans were pushed aside by campaign contributors and big developers.

If you don't intervene in the operation of land markets, you'll usually end up producing the opposite result from what you intended. Over time, for instance, improvements in urban public space raise home values and tend to become amenity subsidies for wealthier people. In dynamic land markets and central locations, nonprofits can't afford to buy land for low-income housing. Struggling artists and hipsters inadvertently become the shock troops of gentrification and soon can't afford to live in the neighborhoods and warehouse districts they invigorated. Affordable housing and jobs move inexorably further apart and the inner-city crisis ends up in places like San Bernardino.

If you concede that the stabilization of land values is the precondition for long-term democratic planning, there are two major nonrevolutionary solutions. George's was the most straightforward: execute land monopolists and profiteers with a single tax of 100 percent on increases in unimproved land values. The other alternative is not as radical but has been successfully implemented in other advanced capitalist countries: municipalize strategic parts of the land inventory for affordable housing, parks, and form-giving greenbelts.

The use of eminent domain for redevelopment, we should recall, was originally intended to transform privately owned slums into publicly owned housing. At the end of the Second World War, when progressives were a majority in city government, Los Angeles adopted truly visionary plans for both public housing and rational suburban growth. What then happened is well known: a municipal counterrevolution engineered by the *LA Times*. As a result, local governments continued to use eminent domain but mainly to transfer land from small owners to corporations and banks.

Fast-forward to the 1980s. A new opportunity emerged. Downtown redevelopment was devouring hundreds of millions of dollars of diverted taxes, but its future was bleak. A few years before, Reyner Banham had proclaimed that downtown was dead or at least irrelevant. If the Bradley administration had had the will, it could have municipalized the Spring-Main Street corridor at rock-bottom market prices. Perhaps ten million square feet would have become available for family apartments, immigrant small businesses, public markets, and the like, at permanently controlled affordable rents.

I once asked Kurt Meyer, a corporate architect who had been chairman of the Community Redevelopment Agency, about this. He lived up Beachwood Canyon below the Hollywood Sign. We used to meet for breakfast because he enjoyed yarning about power and property in LA, and this made him a unique source for my research at the time. He told me that Downtown elites were horrified by the unexpected revitalization of the Broadway corridor by Mexican businesses and shoppers, and the last thing they wanted was a populist Downtown.

He also answered a question that long vexed me. "Kurt, why this desperate, all-consuming priority to have the middle class live Downtown?" "Mike, do you know anything about leasing space in high-rise buildings?" "Not really." "Well, the hardest part to rent is the ground floor: to extract the highest value, you need a resident population. You can't just have office workers going for breakfast and lunch; you need nighttime, twenty-four-hour traffic." I don't know whether this was really an adequate explanation, but it certainly convinced me that planners and activists need a much deeper understanding of the game.

In the event, the middle class has finally come Downtown but only to bring suburbia with them. The hipsters think they're living in the real thing, but this is purely faux urbanism, a residential mall. Downtown is not the heart of the city, it's a luxury lifestyle pod for the same people who claim Silverlake is the "Eastside" or that Venice is still bohemian.

CUFF: Why do you call it suburbia?

DAVIS: Because the return to the center expresses the desire for urban space and crowds without allowing democratic variety or equal access. It's fool's gold, and gentrification has taken the place of urban renewal in displacing the poor. Take Anastasia Loukaitou-Sideris's pioneering study of the privatization of space on the top of Bunker Hill. Of course, your museum patron or condo resident feels at home, but if you're a Salvadorian skateboarder, man, you're probably headed to Juvenile Hall.

CUFF: Would you include architecture in your thinking about real estate? Weren't you teaching a course about this at SCI-Arc [Southern California Institute of Architecture] some years back?

DAVIS: When I was first hired at SCI-Arc in 1988, I confessed to Michael Rotundi [then director] that I knew nothing about architecture. He replied: "Don't worry, we do. Your job is to teach LA. Get the students out into the city." It was a wonderful assignment and over the course of a decade, I participated in a number of remarkable studios and site studies, working with the likes of Michael Sorkin, Joe Day, Anthony Fontenot, and other radical architects.

My own vanity project was demonstrating the feasibility of a community design studio that addressed the problems of older neighborhoods and suburbs. With the support of a leading activist in the Central American community, Roberto Lovato, now a well-known journalist, we focused on the Westlake [MacArthur Park] district just west of Downtown.

I knew the area fairly well, since in the late 1960s I had lived there while briefly managing the Communist Party's bookstore on Seventh Street, oddly near the FBI's old office building on Wilshire. This was right after the final evictions from Bunker Hill and most of its residents had been dumped in tenements near MacArthur Park. Walking to the bookstore I several times encountered the bodies of these elderly poor people on the sidewalk—who knew what dreams had brought them to LA in the 1910s and 1920s?

We finally settled on studying Witmer Street, between Third and Wilshire, because it had an almost complete declension of multifamily building types: a single-family home from the 1890s, a bungalow court from the 1920s, dingbats from 1960, even an old masonry apartment building that was used as a set for Hill Street Blues.

Students divided up into teams, training themselves as building and fire inspectors, and we took the neighborhood apart molecule-by-molecule over two semesters. One group studied fire safety issues and other hazards such as unprotected roofs where small children played. We looked at the needs of home workers, seamstresses, and auto mechanics; studied problems of garbage collection; looked at issues involving gang rivalries and elderly winos. With Lovato's support, we got inside apartments—typically studios for three to five people—and analyzed how families organized their tiny spaces. We researched who owned the buildings, calculated their rental profitability, even visited and photographed the homes of the Downtown slumlords who were living in Beverly Hills and Newport Beach.

The only form of housing that was generally popular, where the tenants had been there for a long time—everybody else was in and out—was the one courtyard apartment complex, with its little gardens and a fountain. The most despised were not the older 1920s tenement fire traps but the dingbats—low-rise six- to twelve-unit apartment buildings with tuck-under parking, built in the fifties and sixties on single-family lots. They were designed to become blight in a few decades and constitute a major problem everywhere in Southern California. The other multiunit types were still durable, but it was hard to imagine any alternative for the stucco rubble other than to tear it down—which in fact developers have done, only to replace the dingbats with four- and five-story "super-cubes" that are just larger versions of the same problems.

Our goal was to bring all our findings together in a kind of Whole Earth Catalog set up as a website, and then invite everybody in the world to write and contribute ideas around generic issues of working-class neighborhoods like trash, play, working, graffiti, gangs, social space, parking, and so on. Our point was not to create a miniature master plan but to build up an arsenal of practical design solutions based on careful, realistic analysis that could help residents frame demands of landlords and the city. We imagined collaborations of architects, artists, and artisans, acting as toolmakers for community self-design and activism. I still believe in the idea, but my own tenure at SCI-Arc ended when our merry prankster and guiding light, Michael Rotundi, left.

CUFF: The idea of toolmaking instead of master planning is useful. A group of urban humanities students at UCLA focused on Boyle Heights, which, like

Westlake, is experiencing development pressure. The tools that the community partners asked for were pretty straightforward, like a manual about how
to turn abandoned spaces into parks. It was an interesting conversation with
the humanities, architecture, and planning students about their own agency.
Could you not deliver what they wanted and still be a socially responsible
partner with community groups? The discussion was interesting because the
agency of the students came into play, from architecture students who are
ready to do something even if they don't have much information, to the humanities students who are reluctant to act since they feel like they don't know
enough or have the right to intervene.

DAVIS: That kind of conscience might be good for some of the senior architects
in LA who regard the city as a free-fire zone for whatever vanity they happen
to come up with, regardless of urban context or history. In *City of Quartz*, I
criticized Frank Gehry for his stealth designs and over-concern with security.
It really pissed him off, because he comes from a social-democratic background and hated my tongue-in-cheek depiction of him as architecture's
"Dirty Harry."

One day, a few years later, he called me in to see him. "Okay, big shot, look
at this." And he showed me the latest iteration of his Disney Concert Hall
design, which had park space wrapped around its non-Euclidean perimeter. "You criticized me for antidemocratic designs, but what is this?" And of
course, it was clever integration of the elitist concert hall with space for local
kids to play and homeless people to relax. It invited rather than excluded residents from the poor Latino neighborhoods like Witmer Street that surround
Downtown. This was more or less unprecedented, and he had to wage a long
battle with the county who wanted the Disney fenced and off-limits. In this
instance at least, celebrity architecture fought the good fight.

JENNIFER WOLCH: Absolutely. However it's an important question particularly for
the humanities students, the issue of subjectivity makes them reticent to make
proposals.

DAVIS: But, they have skills. Narrative is an important part of creating communities. People's stories are key, especially about their routines. It seems to me
that there are important social science skills, but the humanities are important
particularly because of stories. I also think a choreographer would be a great
analyst of space and kind of an imagineer for using space.

I had a long talk with Richard Louv one day about his *Last Child in the
Woods*, one of the most profound books of our time, a meditation on what it
means for kids to lose contact with nature, with free nomadic unorganized
play and adventure. A generation of mothers consigned to be full-time chauf-
feurs, ferrying kids from one commercial distraction or over-organized play
date to another. I grew up in eastern San Diego County, on the very edge of
the back country, and once you did your chores (a serious business in those

days), you could hop on your bike and set off like Huck Finn. There was a nudist colony in Harbison Canyon about twelve miles away, and we'd take our bikes, push them uphill for hours and hours in the hope of peeking through the fence. Like all my friends, I got a .22 (rifle) when I turned twelve. We did bad things to animals, I must confess, but we were free spirits, hated school, didn't worry about grades, kept our parents off our backs with part-time jobs and yard work, and relished each crazy adventure and misdemeanor. Since I moved back to San Diego in 2002, I have annual reunions with the five or six guys I've known since second grade in 1953. Despite huge differences in political beliefs and religion, we're still the same old gang.

And gangs were what kept you safe and why mothers didn't have to worry about play dates or child molesters. I remember even in kindergarten—we lived in the City Heights area of San Diego at that time—we had a gang that walked to school together and played every afternoon. Just this wild group of little boys and girls, seven or eight of us, roaming around, begging pennies to buy gum at the corner store. Today the idea of unsupervised gangs of children or teenagers sounds like a law-and-order problem. But it's how communities used to work and might still work. Aside from Louv, I warmly recommend *The Child in the City* by the English anarchist Colin Ward. A chief purpose of architecture, he argues, should be to design environments for unprogrammed fun and discovery.

WOLCH: We have a completely different question, Mike. One of your books that we like the most is *Late Victorian Holocausts*. It's not about cities or about the West. How did you decide to link up global climate-change history to famine and political ecology? It seems like something of a departure.

DAVIS: After the 1992 riots, I got a huge advance from Knopf to write a book about the city's apocalypse. Through my political activities I had gotten to know the mothers of a number of key players in these events, including Theresa Allison, whose son, Dewayne Holmes, was a prime mover in the Watts gang truce. I also knew Damian Williams's mom—he was the chief villain, the guy who almost beat the truck driver to death at the corner of Florence and Normandie. Through their eyes I had acquired a very different perspective on cause and effect, right and wrong, during the course of the explosion. But at the end of the day, I could not find any real justification for the kind of journalism that makes authoritative claims through selective quotations and portraits of people who generally have no control over the ultimate manuscript. In the 1930s, this kind of social documentation or secondhand existential narrative—Dorothea Lange's photographs or James Agee's *Let Us Now Praise Famous Men*, for example—could claim that it was an integral part of a crusade, the New Deal, or the CIO, that was fighting to improve the lives of the victimized people who were its often unknowing subjects. But now, in our postliberal era, such work runs the danger of simply being sensational and exploitative. Frankly, as much as I wanted to write the book, I couldn't find any real moral license for looting folks' stories and their personal miseries for my greater glory as LA's voice of doom. So I gave the advance back and moved my base of operations to the Cal Tech earth science library and immersed myself in the research on environmental history and disaster that became *Ecology of Fear*.

I also discovered another topic where there was no ethical ambiguity—indeed, a project that perfectly aligned conscience and my zeal for research. Tom Hayden contacted me in 1995 or 1996 and asked me to contribute to a volume he was editing on the one-hundred-fiftieth anniversary of the Irish holocaust. At first I demurred. Brilliant young Irish historians were reinterpreting the Famine, and I had no expertise in this area. But he persisted. "Well, maybe there's something else that happened at the time that you could write about." Then I discovered the famines in China and India during the 1870s and 1890s that killed some twenty million people but had long gone unmentioned in conventional histories of the Victorian era. The result was *Late Victorian Holocausts*, a kind of "black book" of capitalism, about the millions of unnecessary deaths that occurred as European powers—above all, England—force-marched the great subsistence peasantries of India and China into the world market with disastrous results.

WOLCH: We have one last question. Whenever we assign something from *City of Quartz* or another of your disheartening pieces about LA, it's hard not to worry that the students will leave the class and jump off of a cliff!

DAVIS: Gee, you shouldn't be disheartened by my books on LA. They're just impassioned polemics on the necessity of the urban left. And my third LA book, *Magical Urbanism*, literally glows with optimism about the grassroots renaissance going on in our immigrant neighborhoods.

CHAPTER 12

Public Housing in Los Angeles

"Adding Space: The First and Final Frontier?"

JACQUELINE LEAVITT

Los Angeles' twenty-one conventional public housing developments are concentrated in three areas—South Los Angeles (alternatively and more popularly known as South Central), whose population is now more than 50 percent Latino; East Los Angeles, which is primarily second-generation Mexican American; and the San Pedro / Wilmington / Harbor City area to the south of downtown that is mixed but strongly Latino.[1] Two developments are in outlying areas, one in the upscale and primarily white West Los Angeles area and the other in the growing Latino communities of the northeast San Fernando Valley.

The transformation of an unvalued commodity is exemplified best in one of the least marginalized locations in the Los Angeles Harbor City area. About forty acres of land was designated as Normont Terrace in the early forties. Normont now serves as the home to about four hundred mainly Latina with some African American households. In the early nineties the financially broke Housing Authority of the City of Los Angeles negotiated with a developer to lease the property for ninety-nine years, demolish the public housing, rebuild all the units, and initially add eight hundred private market units.[2] The women leaders at Normont Terrace fought to reduce the number of market-rate units and to integrate private and public housing units. The women have not accepted the developer's desire to cluster them in a de facto segregated fashion that may marginalize them more than if all the public housing units were under their control. The outcome of this effort will not be known for many years.

Sometimes women carve a safe space out of more marginalized space, as at Nickerson Gardens in South Central, whose recently ousted leaders had visions for taking control of the entire development.

A few incidents at Nickerson Gardens clarify ways in which acts of resistance take place in the margin/s. The first event concerned the trashing of Nickerson Gardens by a film company that bypassed the all-women resident board.[3] Early one morning, distributing fifty dollars and a pair of sneakers to each willing resident, the film company hung torn clothes and tossed garbage around in order to make a video about rappers, a group strongly identified with young African American men. This video, which clearly labeled Nickerson in its opening shot, was shown on a nationally syndicated television show.

The second incident concerned a 9:30 p.m. visit to the development by a television crew. The crew was searching for a sound bite about crime. Earlier that day, the Housing and Urban Development secretary, Jack Kemp, had come to the development to inaugurate a government-sponsored program. When the crew arrived at the office, the resident leaders were still there reviewing the day's festivities. The women accommodated the crew, hoping to get positive publicity for their ongoing fund-raising for repairing the children's play areas. A young boy was filmed playing in one of the redesigned tot lots that the women leaders had fought for and been successful in getting.

That night, the program ignored the interviews with both the woman president of the board and the more nationally known Bertha Gilkey, who was also present. Instead what was aired referenced a murder that had allegedly taken place at the development, highlighting a young boy's remarks. The reality of this situation, however, was that the murder had not occurred, and the young boy's comment that nothing had improved was taken out of context.

A third incident occurred when John Singleton brought his script, *Boyz 'N the Hood*, to the women leaders to get permission to film part of it at meetings with HACLA [Housing Authority of the City of Los Angeles] and representatives of the media. In general these efforts were not as effective as the direct action by the Nickerson leaders who read Singleton's script and rejected the offer because they believed women were not well represented in the story line.

The attempt to control space at Nickerson Gardens is best seen in the application for funds to transfer ownership of the entire sixty-eight acres from the authority to the residents. With ownership would come the tenants' right to regulate. The vehicle to own would be limited equity cooperatives and a mutual housing association. Opponents of the sale of public housing viewed the Reagan/Bush/Kemp policy from the perspective of a loss of units. Despite the success of national lobbying for legislation of replacement housing as a precondition for sales, on a one-to-one basis, critics doubt cities have either the ability or commitment to achieve this goal. Opponents to sales raise other issues such as housing advocates' fear of losing a permanent stock of public housing for low-income people, politicians' qualms about providing an inferior type of home ownership, residents' worries about inheriting undermaintained capital plants, and housing authority employees' anxiety about losing jobs. The residents would not be moving into the American dream of a detached single-family unit.

Another argument against sales relates to the amount of the subsidy invested in modernizing Kenilworth-Parkside, one showcase complex in Washington, D.C. The total cost per unit was at least $93,202. This expenditure has been described as the equivalent of "above-average, middle-class, detached single-family housing in many cities across the United States."[4] Los Angeles may have houses at this price, but, even in the neighborhood of Nickerson, the second poorest after the Skid Row area, average house prices are closer to $96,000.

A final criticism against sales concerns the low average incomes of public housing tenants and the repercussions for long-term maintenance. Indeed, the average income at Nickerson is below $7,000. Their bid for home ownership rested upon a complex, interlocking package of job creation and federal subsidy. The sales package was tied to an Economic Empowerment Demonstration Program (EEDP) that itself signified an independent action by Nickerson Gardens. The leaders with the help of their consultant, Loren Frelix, received $400,000 from the Department of Health and Human Services (HHS), administered through HUD, initially to be renewable for two additional years. Nickerson applied directly, without prior approval from the authority, and was the only Resident Management Corporation (RMC) in the country to receive funding. As of June 1993, EEDP, which was the catalyst for the security and transportation jobs, as well as training for computers, was virtually closed down because of a lack of refunding, but also because the new board would not allow the old board to lobby for other sources of money.

Omitted from the critique about sales of units, both nationally and locally, are the views of those who wish to buy and who are willing to call home a limited equity cooperative in a townhouse or garden apartment. For example, at Nickerson, forty-eight out of sixty residents in a pilot survey responded positively to the idea of owning their unit and converting to limited equity cooperatives. A planning practice in which the issue is understood not only by standard arguments against or for sales looks to hear the voices in the margin/s. When looked at in terms of transforming space at the margin/s from inside the margin/s by those otherwise considered marginalized, sales may take on a different cast.

In the Los Angeles case, this includes the need to examine the oppositional politics as well. First, what is the reaction of the Housing Authority to losing about 10 percent of its stock? Second, how does the city and HACLA treat the replacement of the over one thousand units at Nickerson? Third, what is the position of powerful political leaders? Fourth, what are the reasons a marginalized group cannot raise sizable in-kind contributions in time to file an application? Fifth, are there internal conflicts within the margin/s on the surface? Such conflict is far more visible among the primarily African American women leaders than between the two racial ethnic groups residing there, that is, the African Americans and Latinos.

Answering these questions can only be speculative but seems to revolve around a complex medley of events which on the surface focused on the crisis in existing leadership and gaps in organizing a constituency. Although the recently elected leaders were openly against home ownership, personal styles of leadership played a role as well as conflicts which were exacerbated by the Housing Authority itself. The new leaders were bolstered by the collaboration within the center—the city, the Housing Authority, and an elected and powerful representative—all of whom did not back the sale. Together they overshadowed those who wanted to buy Nickerson. In terms of outcome regarding spatiality and transformation in the margin/s, the new leaders seem to be withdrawing to the more limited boundaries of the resident leaders' offices, leaving in place a situation where the Housing Authority sustains its institutional power. Again, only time will tell the outcome.

I want to end this chapter with a quote from bell hooks, who clarifies what may have been collectively lost in the valiant but failed bid for limited equity coops at Nickerson. The facts apply only to one development, but hooks connects events that might transform the environment in the margin/s, with repercussions for the center. hooks writes:

> On a fundamental level, when we talk about home we must speak about the need to transform the African-American home, so that there, in that domestic space, we can experience the renewal of political commitment to the Black liberation struggle, so that there in that domestic space we learn to serve and honor one another. If we look again at the civil rights movement, at the Black power movement, folks organized so much in homes. They were the places where folks go together to educate themselves for critical consciousness. That sense of community, cultivated and developed in the home, extended outward into a larger, more public context.[5]

Public housing, because of historic decisions regarding site locations, is a collective space where homes are in the margin/s. These homes are not only for African Americans, but for those whom the White society collectively sees as the "Other." The actions and voices of the "Other" can shape space and do have power to offset hidden values and reclaim the weak, neglected, and wishful values that Kevin Lynch spoke about [in *The Theory of Good Form*]. This is seen in small acts as at Nickerson and Normont and largely invisible to planners. As proxies for the dominant voices in society, planners like myself who work in the margin/s with the marginalized may be able to help shift resources in the center. To do this we must acknowledge differences.

NOTES

This chapter is excerpted from Jacqueline Leavitt, "Adding Space: The First and Final Frontier?," in *Defining Cultural Differences in Space: Public Housing as a Microcosm* (College Park: Urban studies and Planning Program, University of Maryland, 1994), 3–24.

1. Portions of this section appear in Jacqueline Leavitt, "Women under Fire: Public Housing Activism in Los Angeles," *Frontiers* 13 (1993): 109–30.

2. A similar transformation occurred at Columbia Point in Boston when once marginal land became desirable.

3. These incidents are discussed in Leavitt, "Women under Fire" and in "Making Space" (talk, Rutgers University, 1991).

4. "Critics Question Cost of Housing Program," *Washington Post*, August 2, 1992.

5. bell hooks and Cornell West, *Breaking Bread: Insurgent Black Intellectual Life* (Boston: South End, 1991), 18–19.

CHAPTER 13

The City and Spatial Justice

EDWARD W. SOJA

The specific term "spatial justice" has not been commonly used until very recently, and even today there are tendencies among geographers and planners to avoid the explicit use of the adjective "spatial" in describing the search for justice and democracy in contemporary societies. Either the spatiality of justice is ignored or it is absorbed (and often drained of its specificity) into such related concepts as territorial justice, environmental justice, the urbanization of injustice, or the reduction of regional inequalities or even more broadly in the generic search for a just city and a just society.

All of these variations on the central theme are important and relevant, but often tend to draw attention away from the specific qualities and meaning of an explicitly spatialized concept of justice and, more importantly, the many new opportunities it is providing not just for theory building and empirical analysis but for spatially informed social and political action.

My aim in this brief presentation is to explain why it is crucial in theory and in practice to emphasize explicitly the spatiality of justice and injustice, not just in the city but at all geographical scales, from the local to the global. I will state my case in a series of premises and propositions, starting with an explanation of why the specific term "spatial justice" has emerged from literally nowhere in just the past five years and why it is likely to continue to be the preferred term in the future.

Why Spatial? Why Now?

1. Whatever your interests may be, they can be significantly advanced by adopting a critical spatial perspective. This is the premise that lies behind practically everything I have written over the past forty years and is the first sentence in my book *Seeking Spatial Justice*.[1]
2. Thinking spatially about justice not only enriches our theoretical understanding, it can uncover significant new insights that extend our practical

knowledge into more effective actions to achieve greater justice and democracy. Obversely, by not making the spatial explicit and assertive, these opportunities will not be so evident.

3. After a century and a half of being subsumed under a prevailing social historicism, thinking spatially has in the past decade been experiencing an extraordinary diffusion across nearly all disciplines. Never before has a critical spatial perspective been so widespread in its recognition and application— from archaeology and poetry to religious studies, literary criticism, legal studies, and accounting.

4. This so-called spatial turn is the primary reason for the attention that is now being given to the concept of spatial justice and to the broader spatialization of our basic ideas of democracy and human rights, as in the revival of Lefebvre's notion of the right to the city, of particular relevance here in Nanterre. Whereas the concept would not have been easily comprehensible even five years ago, today it draws attention from a much broader audience than the traditionally spatial disciplines of geography, architecture, and urban and regional planning.

5. Thinking about space has changed significantly in recent years, from emphasizing flat cartographic notions of space as container or stage of human activity or merely the physical dimensions of fixed form, to an active force shaping human life. A new emphasis on specifically urban spatial causality has emerged to explore the generative effects of urban agglomerations not just on everyday behavior but on such processes as technological innovation, artistic creativity, economic development, social change as well as environmental degradation, social polarization, widening income gaps, international politics, and, more specifically, the production of justice and injustice.

6. Critical spatial thinking today hinges around three principles:
   a) The ontological spatiality of being (we are all spatial as well as social and temporal beings).
   b) The social production of spatiality (space is socially produced and can therefore be socially changed).
   c) The sociospatial dialectic (the spatial shapes the social as much as the social shapes the spatial).

7. Taking the sociospatial dialectic seriously means that we recognize that the geographies in which we live can have negative as well as positive consequences on practically everything we do. Foucault captured this by showing how the intersection of space, knowledge, and power can be both oppressive and enabling. Building on Foucault, Edward Said states the following:

   Just as none of us are beyond geography, none of us is completely free from the struggle over geography. That struggle is complex and interesting because it is not only about soldiers and cannons but also about ideas, about forms, about images and imaginings.

8. These ideas expose the spatial causality of justice and injustice as well as the justice and injustice that are embedded in spatiality, in the multiscalar geographies in which we live, from the space of the body and the household, through cities and regions and nation-states, to the global scale.
9. Until these ideas are widely understood and accepted, it is essential to make the spatiality of justice as explicit and actively causal as possible. To redefine it as something else is to miss the point and the new opportunities it opens up.

On the Concept of Spatial Justice/Injustice

1. In the broadest sense, spatial (in)justice refers to an intentional and focused emphasis on the spatial or geographical aspects of justice and injustice. As a starting point, this involves the fair and equitable distribution in space of socially valued resources and the opportunities to use them.
2. Spatial justice as such is not a substitute or alternative to social, economic, or other forms of justice but rather a way of looking at justice from a critical spatial perspective. From this viewpoint, there is always a relevant spatial dimension to justice while at the same time all geographies have expressions of justice and injustice built into them.
3. Spatial (in)justice can be seen as both outcome and process, as geographies or distributional patterns that are in themselves just/unjust and as the processes that produce these outcomes. It is relatively easy to discover examples of spatial injustice descriptively, but it is much more difficult to identify and understand the underlying processes producing unjust geographies.
4. Locational discrimination, created through the biases imposed on certain populations because of their geographical location, is fundamental in the production of spatial injustice and the creation of lasting spatial structures of privilege and advantage. The three most familiar forces shaping locational and spatial discrimination are class, race, and gender, but their effects should not be reduced only to segregation.
5. The political organization of space is a particularly powerful source of spatial injustice, with examples ranging from the gerrymandering of electoral districts, the redlining of urban investments, and the effects of exclusionary zoning to territorial apartheid, institutionalized residential segregation, the imprint of colonial and/or military geographies of social control, and the creation of other core-periphery spatial structures of privilege from the local to the global scales.
6. The normal workings of an urban system, the everyday activities of urban functioning, is a primary source of inequality and injustice in that the accumulation of locational decisions in a capitalist economy tends to lead to

the redistribution of real income in favor of the rich over the poor. This redistributive injustice is aggravated further by racism, patriarchy, heterosexual bias, and many other forms of spatial and locational discrimination. Note again that these processes can operate without rigid forms of spatial segregation.

7. Geographically uneven development and underdevelopment provides another framework for interpreting the processes that produce injustices, but as with other processes, it is only when this unevenness rigidifies into more lasting structures of privilege and advantage that intervention becomes necessary.

8. Perfectly even development, complete sociospatial equality, pure distributional justice, as well as universal human rights are never achievable. Every geography in which we live has some degree of injustice embedded in it, making the selection of sites of intervention a crucial decision.

Why Justice? Why Now?

1. Seeking to increase justice or to decrease injustice is a fundamental objective in all societies, a foundational principle for sustaining human dignity and fairness. The legal and philosophical debates that often revolve around Rawls's theory of justice are relevant here, but they say very little about the spatiality of justice and injustice.

2. The concept of justice and its relation to related notions of democracy, equality, citizenship, and civil rights has taken on new meaning in the contemporary context for many different reasons, including the intensification of economic inequalities and social polarization associated with neoliberal globalization and the new economy as well as the transdisciplinary diffusion of a critical spatial perspective.

3. The specific term "justice" has developed a particularly strong hold on the public and political imagination in comparison to such alternatives as "freedom," with its now strongly conservative overtones, "equality," given the impact of a more cultural politics of difference, and the search for universal human rights, detached from specific time and place.

4. Justice in the contemporary world tends to be seen as more concrete and grounded than its alternatives, more oriented to present-day conditions, and imbued with a symbolic force that works effectively across cleavages of class, race, and gender to foster a collective political consciousness and a sense of solidarity based on widely shared experience.

5. The search for justice has become a powerful rallying cry and mobilizing force for new social movements and coalition-building spanning the political spectrum, extending the concept of justice beyond the social and the

economic to new forms of struggle and activism. In addition to spatial justice, other modifiers include territorial, racial, environmental, worker, youth, global, local, community, peace, monetary, border, and corporeal.

6. Combining the terms "spatial" and "justice" opens up a range of new possibilities for social and political action, as well as for social theorization and empirical analysis, that would not be as clear if the two terms were not used together.

A geohistorical look at the concept of spatial justice would take us back to the Greek polis and the Aristotelian idea that being urban is the essence of being political; it would take us through the rise of liberal democracy and the Age of Revolution, and eventually center attention on the urban crises of the 1960s, with its most symptomatic and symbolic moments taking place here in Nanterre. Paris in the 1960s and especially the still understudied copresence of Henri Lefebvre and Michel Foucault, became the most generative site for the creation of a radically new conceptualization of space and spatiality, and for a specifically urban and spatial concept of justice, encapsulated most insightfully in Lefebvre's call for taking back control over the right to the city and the right to difference.

The trajectory of these developments of a critical spatial perspective was both extended and diverted by David Harvey's *Social Justice and the City*, published in 1973. Never once using the specific term "spatial justice" in this book as well as in everything else he has written since, Harvey chose to use the term "territorial justice," borrowing from the Welsh planner Bleddyn Davies, to describe his version of the spatiality of justice. In his "liberal formulations" Harvey advanced the spatial conceptualization of justice and his view would shape all Anglophonic debates on justice and democracy ever since. Despite his recognition of Lefebvre's contributions as a Marxist philosopher of space, Harvey's Marxism moved him away from spatial causality and from a focus on justice itself, and he would rarely mention the term "territorial justice" again, although the notion of the urbanization of injustice would be carried forward and Harvey, very recently, would write again on the right to the city.

The first use of the specific term "spatial justice" that I can find is in the unpublished doctoral dissertation of the political geographer John O'Laughlin, entitled "Spatial Justice and the Black American Voter: The Territorial Dimension of Urban Politics," completed in 1973. The earliest published work I have found using the term in English is a short article by G. H. Pirie, "On Spatial Justice" in 1983, although almost there in 1981 was a book by the French geographer Alain Reynaud, *Société, espace et justice: inégalites régionales et justice socio-spatiale*. From the 1980s to the turn of the century, the use and development of the term "spatial justice" became almost exclusively associated with the work of geographers and planners in Los Angeles . . . and this takes me to my conclusions.

Conclusion

Los Angeles has been a primary center not just in the theorization of spatial justice but more significantly in the movement of the concept from largely academic debate into the world of politics and practice. I believe it can be claimed, although it is almost impossible to prove conclusively, that a critical spatial perspective and an understanding of the production of unjust geographies and spatial structures of privilege have entered more successfully into the strategies and activism of labor and community groups in LA than in any other U.S. metropolitan region. Spatial strategies have played a key role in making Los Angeles the leading edge of the American labor movement and one of the most vibrant centers for innovative community-based organizations. New ideas about community-based regionalism, locational discrimination, electoral redistricting, and environmental justice have propelled such organizations as SAJE (Strategic Action for a Just Economy), the Los Angeles Alliance for a New Economy, Justice for Janitors, and the Labor/Community Strategy Center (one of the leading figures having written on Henri Lefebvre) into the forefront of contemporary struggles over spatial justice and the city.

Perhaps the most dramatic example of the impact of specifically spatial approaches in the search for justice is the Bus Riders Union, an organization of the transit-dependent immigrant working poor that successfully challenged the locational biases of the Metropolitan Transit Authority and their plans for creating a multibillion-dollar fixed rail system that would primarily serve a relatively wealthy suburban population at the expense of the more urgent needs of the inner-city working poor, who depend on a more flexible bus network given their multiple and multilocational job households. A court order was issued in 1996 that demanded that the MTA give first budget priority to the purchase of new buses, reduction of bus stop crime, and improvements in bus routing and waiting times. Similar civil rights cases based on racial discrimination had been brought to court in other cities and failed. In LA, the notion of spatial and locational discrimination, the creation of unjust geographies of mass transit, was added to the racial discrimination arguments and helped to win the case. There are many complications to the story, but the end result was a shift of billions of dollars of public investment from a rail plan that would benefit the rich more than the poor, as is usually the case in the capitalist city, to an almost unprecedented plan that would benefit the poor more than the rich. The bus network today is among the best in the country and is being used as a model of efficiency in other cities.

More recently and of special relevance here, Los Angeles and in particular the Urban Planning Department at UCLA has become the site for the building of a national movement centered on the notion of the rights to the city. Informed by Lefebvre and others espousing a critical spatial perspective, the local movement has been joined at the global scale by the World Social Forum, which in 2005 presented a World Charter of the Rights to the City.

I hope I have been of some help in explaining why, after thirty or so years of relative neglect, Lefebvre's passionate ideas about le droit à la ville have been so actively revived.

NOTES

Paper prepared for presentation at the Spatial Justice conference in Nanterre, Paris, March 12–14, 2008. The article was previously published as "The City and Spatial Justice" (« La ville et la justice spatiale »), translated by Sophie Didier, *Spatial Justice* 1 (September 2009), http://www.jssj.org. We thank the editors for granting us permission to use the text here.

1. Edward W. Soja, *Seeking Spatial Justice* (Minneapolis: University of Minnesota Press, 2010).

CHAPTER 14

Race, Class, and Political Activism

Black, Chicana/o, and Japanese American Leftists in Southern California, 1968–1978

LAURA PULIDO

Among left activists the challenge of balancing race and class in organizing is a long-standing issue. While most progressive organizations seek to promote both antiracist and anticapitalist politics, the histories of these two movements in the United States have often been estranged and contradictory. Indeed, if we consider the degree to which racial ideology and discourse permeate our social and economic structures, then the barriers to building a multiracial left should come as no surprise. Nonetheless, the need to address both racism and class oppression is essential to contemporary organizing efforts, especially given the growing complexity of our racial and class structures. New political strategies are needed to foster a truly democratic and inclusive movement that poses a real alternative to global corporatism. In this chapter, I focus on Los Angeles.

Southern California 1968–1978

My discussion of Southern California begins with the World War II era. Changes triggered by immigration and the military buildup dramatically transformed the region and provide the context to subsequent racial hierarchies. To get a sense of how dramatic the changes were, consider that between 1940 and 1970 the region's population grew from three to twelve million people. In addition to Los Angeles' historic racial diversity, the influx of new arrivals, enhanced employment opportunities, as well as the changing nature of racism all led to changes in the racial/ethnic order. At least four specific changes can be identified: First, post–World War II immigration included a sizable black population, which significantly altered Los Angeles' racial mix.[1] Second, due to their wartime experiences, black and Chicano soldiers returned with a new sense of empowerment and commitment to fight for equality at home.[2] Third, Japanese Americans returned from internment a traumatized and impoverished community, elements of which maintained a low profile in order to avoid hostile attention.[3] Fourth, the rapidly expanding Fordist economy provided many, including Chicanas/os and blacks, an entry into the formal economy.[4]

Whites' privileged position in the racial hierarchy was evident in their economic prosperity, political leadership, domination of cultural and educational institutions, and the extent to which Southern California became equated with the "American dream." The white population's well-being was bolstered not only through legal segregation and the denial of nonwhites' civil rights, but also through preferential policies and practices. Though whites occupied the top position of the racial hierarchy, various communities of color fared differently in Los Angeles.[5]

BLACK LOS ANGELES. The history of black Los Angeles has been a mixed one. While the early part of the century was dubbed a "golden age," blacks faced increased racism, violence, and segregation in the 1920s, resulting in the creation of a black ghetto in South Los Angeles.[6] During World War II, blacks were able to enter the manufacturing economy for the first time; opportunities diminished, however, upon the conclusion of the war, as employers replaced them with whites. Nonetheless, by 1970, the public sector and manufacturing, respectively, were the leading sources of black employment. Ironically, while South Los Angeles was home to the region's greatest concentration of durable manufacturing, including the auto industry, blacks were relegated to the lesser paying light manufacturing sector.[7]

During the 1960s African Americans loomed large in the imagination of Southern Californians. This was due not only to the visibility of the civil rights and black power movements, but also, proportionally, blacks had a greater numerical presence than today in the region. Despite the general prosperity of the time, few blacks shared in this wealth. While some middle-class blacks had begun moving west toward Crenshaw and Baldwin Hills by 1970, low-income blacks remaining in South Los Angeles suffered from 11 percent unemployment, more than double the regional average. In addition, blacks in that community experienced a declining rate of labor force participation, a relative drop in income, and a 25 percent poverty rate. These figures mask considerable variation, however. In Watts, for instance, the poverty rate was an incredible 41 percent, while it was "only" 20 percent in Willowbrook. Such economic conditions, plus the white population's hostility toward desegregation and the historic conflict between the police and black communities, suggest African Americans' position at the bottom of the racial hierarchy. Moreover, they anticipate the Watts rebellion and the militancy of youth who had lost faith in the civil rights paradigm.[8]

CHICANA/O LOS ANGELES. Chicanas/os, who have historically resided on the Eastside, present a distinct economic picture as they were more firmly and evenly attached to industrial employment. World War II offered unparalleled opportunities for Chicanas/os, allowing them to shift out of agriculture and into manufacturing, so that by 1970 Latinos constituted 20.8 percent of all manufacturing workers and were overrepresented in both durable and nondurable manufacturing. A comparison between East and South LA is instructive: while blacks, particularly in South Los Angeles suffered from structural worklessness, Chicanas/os served as low-wage labor and had a slightly higher position in the racial hierarchy.[9]

Chicanas/os, as Almaguer has argued, have historically occupied an intermediary racial position based on class and phenotype.[10] The fact that Chicanas/os are racially marked in numerous ways and that "passing" is a common, if problematic practice precludes any easy characterization of Chicanas/os' racial position.[11] In addition to physical appearance, residential patterns also constituted an important axis of difference. Chicanas/os became highly differentiated depending upon where they grew up (barrio vs. suburb), appearance (*indio* vs. *güero*), and economic status.[12] In addition, however, all Chicanas/os suffered from cultural denigration. The disparagement of all things Mexican was a function of not only racist attitudes toward Mexico, a third world and largely indigenous nation, but also the distinctly working-class nature of Mexican culture, resulting in contempt for Chicano music, family structure, language, religion, and material culture. Hence, it was hardly surprising that many Chicanas/os embraced cultural nationalism in an attempt to reclaim their pride and identity.[13]

NIKKEI LOS ANGELES. Japanese Americans represent yet a third experience.[14] Though having suffered historically some of the most egregious forms of racism, including immigration, employment, property, and housing exclusions, by 1968 whites saw Japanese Americans in a new light.[15] White racism was expressed through the "model minority" construct. Precisely because they were firmly subordinate, both economically and socially, while at the same time had achieved *some* level of prosperity, Japanese Americans, who occupied an intermediary racial position, were rendered models for other people of color. This situation cannot be understood outside of the camp experience and its aftermath.

In February 1942 President Roosevelt signed Executive Order 9066, which led to the wholesale internment of West Coast Japanese Americans. Within a matter of weeks, thirty-seven thousand Nikkei Angelenos were forced into "relocation centers" and held captive until January 1945. The aftermath of this event is still being felt. Previous to World War II, the Japanese American community was characterized by high rates of residential and employment discrimination.[16] Employment exclusions plus an agricultural background led to high rates of self-employment, particularly in the produce market, truck farming, and gardening, which typically paid more than working-class jobs. During internment, however, Japanese Americans suffered enormous social and economic losses. Upon their return they sought to re-create their old enclaves, focusing on Boyle Heights, Sawtelle, and the Jefferson area. Indicative of their racial subordination, Japanese Americans could live only in black and brown spaces. As the Nikkei rebuilt their lives and communities, they gravitated once again toward self-employment, which was most pronounced in highly racialized occupations, such as gardening.[17]

While Japanese Americans responded to the internment in numerous ways, several patterns can be identified. First, there was a general silence regarding the trauma. In order to prevent a recurrence, many sought to assimilate while drawing minimal attention to themselves. This contributed to the beginnings of regional dispersal and exacerbated the decline of community institutions and support. These changes, in turn, set the stage for subsequent social problems, including drug abuse and gang activity. Finally, whites interpreted the behavior of "silent Orientals" as acceptance and quiescence and encouraged other people of color to emulate it. There was no recognition on their part that such behavior was a response to white racism or the degree to which Japanese Americans had internalized the pain of discrimination. This dynamic would be a key ingredient contributing to the political activism of Japanese American radicals.[18]

Race and Revolutionary Politics

George Katsiaficas has identified 1967–70 as a "world-historical movement," as people across the globe mobilized.[19] In the United States, several factors contributed to this counterhegemonic upsurge. First, many African Americans were frustrated by the limited gains of the civil rights movement. After the assassination of Martin Luther King Jr., many were ready to adopt a more radical politics. Second, resistance to the Vietnam War politicized thousands and contributed to a larger culture of struggle. This oppositional culture brought diverse groups together and inspired other movements. Finally, many youth of color were inspired by the revolutionary movements sweeping the Third World. Sympathizing with colonized and racially subordinate populations, Asians, blacks, Latinas/os, and American Indians identified as part of the "Third World." No longer content to seek acceptance from white America, youth of color demanded that they be respected on their own terms. Moreover, through political study many decided that capitalism, U.S. imperialism in particular, was the source of the world's problems.

Thus, over time the civil rights movement was eclipsed by a more radical politics, and with it the geography of political activism shifted from the South to large urban centers, including San Francisco, New York, Chicago, and Los Angeles. Southern California was home to a large number of leftist formations, some of which were multiracial, while others were composed of a single racial/ethnic group. In the late 1960s the third world left began evolving from antiracist and nationalist organizations. By 1978, however, it had largely been destroyed by pressures from within and without, including infighting, sectarianism, changes in the life cycle, and political repression. Despite its brevity, the third world left accomplished a great deal and fundamentally changed the nature of racial politics in the United States.[20]

THE SOUTHERN CALIFORNIA CHAPTER OF THE BLACK PANTHER PARTY. The Southern California Chapter of the Black Panther Party was established in 1968 when Alprentice "Bunchy" Carter, a former member of the Slauson gang, was released from prison and returned to Los Angeles. Carter essentially transformed a vast and diverse army of gangs into one of the strongest chapters of the BPP.[21] The Southern California chapter, which stretched from Bakersfield to San Diego, was unique in several ways. First, it became a testing ground for new ideas and strategies partly because of the diversity of its black population. Los Angeles attracted blacks from the South, Midwest, and North, thus reflecting important regional differences. The chapter developed new programs, including dances, and was in the vanguard of promoting female leadership. Second, the Los Angeles Police Department (LAPD), led by Chief Parker, was notoriously repressive. Parker, a rabid anticommunist, felt that not only was the civil rights movement a subterfuge for communists, but civil disobedience must not be tolerated.[22] The relationship between the LAPD and black Angelenos deteriorated further in the wake of the 1965 Watts uprising. Notwithstanding the growing repression of the LAPD, many blacks felt empowered as they realized that the police could be challenged. As one former Panther explained, "It was like a slave realizing he could be free." The question was *how* to sustain that level of opposition to the police—the BPP was the answer.

The third reason the Southern California chapter was unique was that it had a slightly different composition and orientation relative to other chapters. Not only was it characterized by a large "underground" force, but its membership, more so than other chapters, was drawn from the lumpen proletariat. Membership in the chapter came from three primary sources: gangs, black activists, and self-defense cadre. The latter refers to blacks who had begun arming themselves as a form of self-defense previous to the establishment of the BPP, building on an African American tradition of self-defense.[23]

The Panthers' focus on self-defense cannot be understood outside of the black community's relationship to the police and their position in the racial hierarchy. While police harassment of blacks, particularly black men, is legendary, according to the BPP, the problem was not simply racist cops. Constant surveillance and harassment caused deep anger in the black community, to the point where some could no longer accept such conditions, even if it meant death.

Although many associate the Panthers with guns and violence, of equal significance was its service programs.[24] The Southern California chapter offered a breakfast program, food hand-outs, a school, and prison transport and published a newspaper. These "survival programs" as they were called served several purposes. First, they enabled the Panthers to provide necessary assistance to the community. Second, and relatedly, they generated community support. And third, they highlighted the contradictions of the state, which was crucial to the politicization of the black population: although the state *could* have provided a breakfast program, it did not. This was considered yet another example of the state's disregard for black, poor, and oppressed people and, building upon the teachings of Malcolm X, underscored the need for black self-organization. The BPP's vision was so compelling that it helped to unite the left locally, as seen, for example, in the Panthers' relationship to the Peace and Freedom Party.

Regardless of the innovative nature of the Southern California chapter, it was not able to withstand the police onslaught. One member speculated that approximately half of all BPP murders occurred in Southern California, a number far out of proportion to its membership. Ultimately, the police, with the assistance of the FBI, was successful in destroying the Southern California chapter well before the demise of the larger organization.[25] In addition to infighting and very real class tensions within the Party, the majority of the leadership was eventually imprisoned, murdered, or recalled to Oakland, leaving the Southern California chapter to disintegrate.

EL CENTRO DE ACCION SOCIAL AUTONOMO (CASA). CASA represents a very different expression of left politics. While such distinctions reflect the differential racialization of Chicanas/os, they are also a function of history. The BPP developed approximately six years before CASA, and one of its legacies was the creation of more political space, which encouraged revolutionary organizations. Thus, it is not surprising that CASA, founded in 1972, was explicitly Marxist-Leninist.

CASA evolved from La Hermandad Mexicana Nacional (The Mexican Brotherhood), which Bert Corona and Soledad "Chole" Alatorre brought to Los Angeles in 1968 in order to provide services to immigrant workers and to promote labor organizing.[26] Corona subsequently restructured the organization by creating a series of independent centers (CASAs), united under La Hermandad. Approximately ten CASAs developed, stretching from Chicago to Texas to Seattle to Los Angeles.

La Hermandad and the Chicano movement, or *el movimiento*, were both in full swing in the late 1960s, although with somewhat different constituencies and goals. La Hermandad was rooted primarily in immigrant communities with ties to labor and Chicana/o civil rights groups. *El movimiento*, in contrast, centered largely on young people, especially students, and was far more ideological.[27] Chicana/o youth were struggling with questions of identity, equality, and opposition to the Vietnam War, much of which was expressed through cultural nationalism and the need for self-determination. Indeed, many in the Chicana/o movement, including the prime minister of the Brown Berets, eschewed Marxism as an irrelevant, white ideology that detracted from Chicanas/os' concerns.[28] Nonetheless, a small group of student activists was attracted to CASA precisely because of its work with *Mexicana/o* workers.

Student involvement dramatically changed the organization, particularly when the East Los Angeles group Committee to Free Los Tres joined CASA.[29] The political cultures and goals of the two organizations clashed and generational tensions arose.[30] Corona and Alatorre had essentially created a mass dues-paying service organization with a labor organizing component predicated on reformist politics. The younger generation, however, saw itself as a vanguard and hoped to use the service centers to create a mass movement. Conflict grew until eventually the older generation resigned in 1974. While CASA never succeeded in creating a mass worker movement, it had a major influence on immigration debates, served as a left wing to the more nationalist Chicana/o movement, and trained some of today's most influential Chicana/o labor and progressive leaders.

CASA worked on labor, immigration, and identity issues. Given Chicanas/os' historic role as low-wage workers, the labor focus is not surprising, while the concern with identity reflected their subordinated social status at a time when oppressed groups were challenging what it meant to be a "minority." For Chicanas/os, this process included reclaiming a denigrated racial and cultural identity. One activist summarized cogently the connection between racial and cultural subordination and how Chicanas/os often responded to it: "[My mother] felt that it was even going to be more necessary for us to speak without an accent because we were so dark. She felt that if we had been lighter, then maybe Spanish would have been [okay]. In fact, she used to tell me that it was not uncommon for Mexican women in the 1940s and 1950s to pray for light-skinned babies."[31] Clearly, there was a deeply internalized racism that had to be challenged. But identity was more than just appearance and cultural heritage, it also centered on economic and political subjectivity: If activists sought to build an emancipatory political project, how was Chicana/o subjectivity to be understood? Were Chicanas/os a racially subordinate group? A conquered nation? Or part of the international working class?

CASA responded to this question with the concept of *sin fronteras* (without borders). Most movement activists had adopted a Chicana/o identity and the concept of Aztlán,[32] both predicated on a Mexican American experience. CASA, however, challenged the assumption that Chicanas/os were distinct from Mexicans, arguing instead that Mexicans and Mexican Americans were part of one international working class, *sin fronteras*.[33]

Given CASA's concern with labor, immigration inevitably emerged as a priority. Besides its centrality to Chicanas/os, immigration became a national issue during the 1970s, as seen in various pieces of legislation. CASA assumed the lead in arguing for the rights of immigrant workers and helped establish the National Coalition for Fair Immigration Laws and Practices.[34] It sought to change the terms of the debate through conferences, marches, rallies, and political dialogue with activists and politicians alike. Moreover, it spearheaded the effort to push organized labor, including the United Farm Workers, to begin viewing immigrants as workers instead of enemies.

Despite CASA's impressive work, the organization also suffered from police infiltration and, perhaps more importantly, from a series of internal contradictions that contributed to its demise. A primary problem was the nondemocratic nature of the organization and the concentration of power in one particular family, the Rodriguezes. In addition, the organization was deeply sexist and women occupied a clearly subordinate position. As the contradictions mounted there were a series of mass resignations, including those of prominent leaders, which spelled the end of CASA by 1978.

EAST WIND. East Wind was a revolutionary nationalist organization heavily influenced by the BPP, but because it was Japanese Americans, a distinct political experience resulted. Like CASA, East Wind evolved from previous existing formations. It emerged in 1972 from several initiatives in the Asian American community, including the Garbagemen, Asian American Hardcore, Japanese American Community Services-Asian Involvement (JACS-AI), and the Community Workers Collective.[35] The Garbagemen was the first Asian American left study group to surface in Los Angeles in 1969.[36] From it, two tendencies emerged, Storefront and East Wind. Storefront was a multinational organization in which Asian Americans worked with other racial/ethnic groups, especially African Americans. East Wind was somewhat more nationalist and focused primarily on Japanese Americans. Geographically, it was rooted in Little Tokyo, Boyle Heights, and the Sawtelle area.

East Wind focused its energies on community service, and, similar to CASA, struggled with identity issues. Guided by revolutionary nationalism, activists saw their primary task as preparing the Nikkei population to work with other racial/ethnic groups in building a united front. This required not only lifting the veil of silence that surrounded the community after internment,[37] but also encouraging Japanese Americans to recognize and confront issues of racism, poverty, and the need for community services. East Wind did not readily embrace a working-class politics. While there definitely existed a Nikkei working class, it was relatively small and fragmented. A community focus, in contrast, particularly on the most marginalized, offered a greater set of possibilities. East Wind was well respected for its various campaigns, including its work on redevelopment issues in Little Tokyo, substance abuse prevention and treatment, the establishment of the Pioneer Senior Center, the takeover of Resthaven, a mental health facility in Chinatown, and its extensive solidarity work, including sending a large team to Wounded Knee to support the American Indian Movement.

Responding to the severity of problems experienced by the Japanese community after internment, several individuals began Asian American Hardcore, an early attempt at grassroots drug and gang intervention. Hardcore led to several study groups, including a collective, which eventually resulted in East Wind. East Wind served the community and, similar to Chicanos, struggled with identity issues, which was key to their politicization. Japanese American activists repositioned themselves as "people of color" within the racial hierarchy and directly challenged the "model minority" construct. They did this first by acknowledging the extent to which white racism shaped their experiences and, second, by cultivating a new identity based on pan-Asianness and revolutionary politics. Recognizing the oppressive role of racism was not difficult for politically conscious youth. For instance, most Japanese Americans interviewed had distinct memories of residential discrimination, causing them to identify with African Americans and Latinos. Accordingly, they dismantled the model minority image that activists realized also oppressed other people of color.

In addition to rejecting the model minority image, activists created new, militant, and explicitly leftist identities. Miriam Ching Louie has argued that as Asian Americans became aware of international events, they equated Asia with anti-imperialist and revolutionary politics, which informed their new identities. Aware of the consequences of the model minority image for other people of color, East Wind worked closely with blacks, Chicanas/os, and American Indians.

By the late seventies there was a growing move toward party building within the left.[38] Small organizations like East Wind realized that although they did important community work, their efforts were too isolated to create a revolution. Thus, a period of consolidation began as various groups looked for suitable partners to merge with in order to create viable political parties. East Wind explored commonalities with such organizations as I WorKuen, ATM, and the Revolutionary Communist League, but eventually joined the League of Revolutionary Struggle (LRS), a multiracial organization. The LRS lasted until 1990, at which time it, and the remnants of East Wind, dissolved.

Conclusion

I have explored Los Angeles' third world left in order to underscore the futility of privileging either race or class in left politics. Hopefully, the examples I have chosen demonstrate the extent to which racism and class structures both

inform individual and group experiences, and thus must be addressed in organizing efforts. In addition, we have seen how different racial/ethnic groups are
racialized and classed in distinct ways and how this leads to various positions
within the racial hierarchy. These experiences, in turn, directly inform radical
politics. In the conclusion I would like to consider some of the implications of
this work.

Although I have focused on communities of color, the emphasis on race and
class applies equally to white communities and organizing initiatives. Depending upon local demographics and the regional racial hierarchy, in some places
whites are highly marginalized—which in itself requires close interrogation—
but in most cases where whites constitute a more privileged population, un-
packing white supremacy and/or privilege is the central task.

Some have questioned the overall significance of the third world left, particularly in comparison to the much larger nationalist and antiracist movements
of the time. While it was small, this overlooks its political significance. One of
the third world left's accomplishments was the expansion of political space and
the development of an alternative to more nationalist politics. This not only
led to greater possibilities for interracial solidarity, but also, given their more
radical politics, facilitated the adoption of important reformist measures. For
instance, the appearance of blacks with guns was key to the adoption of affir-
mative action. Likewise, members of East Wind went on to lead the struggle for
redress and reparations, eventually resulting in a formal apology and monetary
reparations. Finally, CASA, as previously noted, was responsible for shifting the
Chicano movement's position on immigrants. Not only is support of immigrant
rights a standard part of contemporary Chicano/Latino politics, but I would
argue that CASA sowed the seeds for the labor movement's recent embrace of
immigrant workers, as many of its members went on to occupy both key labor
and political positions.

This brings up the larger issue of what members of the third world left are
doing today. Most were passionate about their work and have remained politically active. Activists interviewed had carefully evaluated this period of their
lives (most were familiar with self-criticism), and few romanticized it. Most
were critical of the violence, sexism, sectarianism, homophobia, and, in some
cases, racism, which permeated the movement. Equipped with this information, many have sought to contribute to alternative institutions in Los Angeles
that do not repeat the same mistakes. Examples include the Community Coalition Against Substance Abuse and Prevention, the Labor/Community Strategy
Center, the Hotel Employees and Restaurant Employees (Local 11), the Liberty
Hill Foundation, the Coalition Against Police Abuse, and AGENDA. Manuel Pastor has argued that Los Angeles has become a leading site of progressive organizing today, and I believe it is a direct legacy of this earlier activism.[39] Groups
like the BPP, CASA, and East Wind essentially served as a training ground. Not

only did they teach activists specific skills and knowledge, but they also provided activists with a large number of contacts and networks, which are still functioning, albeit in modified form, today. Political activism, specifically, a place's *history* of activism, help shape the political culture of a region.

How to reconcile race and class in political work remains one of the challenges of the left. During the eighties and nineties the United States underwent fundamental political, ideological, and culture shifts, so that while we have made some progress in addressing overt forms of racial discrimination, there has been no comparable progress on poverty issues or structural racism. Today, we face a situation in Southern California where the poor and working class are increasingly composed of immigrants. Precisely because they are not native-born, many feel not only that their poverty is justifiable, but that their racial subordination has nothing to do with the racism that native-born people of color have had to contend with. Yet it is these very contradictions that illustrate the ever-changing nature of the racial hierarchy and underscore the need for new articulations of race and class that can serve as a viable political framework for social change.

NOTES

1. Keith E. Collins, *Black Los Angeles* (Saratoga, Calif.: Century Twenty One, 1980).

2. Kevin A. Leonard, "Years of Hope, Days of Fear: The Impact of World War II on Race Relations in Los Angeles" (PhD diss., University of California, Davis, 1992).

3. Tedsuden Kashima, "Japanese American Internees Return, 1945–55: Readjustment and Social Amnesia," *Phylon* 41 (1980): 107–15.

4. John H. M. Laslett, "Historical Perspectives: Immigration and the Rise of a Distinctive Urban Region, 1900–1970," in *Ethnic Los Angeles*, ed. Roger Waldinger and Mehdi Bozorgmehr (New York: Russell Sage Foundation, 1996), 39–75.

5. Mike Davis, *City of Quartz: Excavating the Future in Los Angeles* (London: Verso, 1990); George Lipsitz, *The Possessive Investment of Whiteness* (Philadelphia: Temple University Press, 1998); Laura Pulido, "Rethinking Environmental Racism: White Privilege and Urban Development in Southern California," *Annals of the Association of American Geographers* 90, no. 1 (2000): 12–40.

6. Collins, *Black Los Angeles*; Lawrence B. de Graff, "The City of Black Angels: Emergence of the Los Angeles Ghetto, 1890–1930," *Pacific Historical Review* 39 (August 1970): 323–52.

7. Laslett, "Historical Perspectives," 64; Edward W. Soja, *Postmodern Geographies: The Reassertion of Space in Critical Social Theory* (London: Verso, 1989).

8. James Paul Allen and Eugene Turner, *The Ethnic Quilt* (Northridge: California State University, Northridge, Center for Geographical Studies, 1997); G. Horne, *Fire This Time* (Charlottesville: University of Virginia, 1995); Bruce Michael Tyler, "Black Radicalism in Southern California" (PhD diss., University of California, Los Angeles, 1983).

9. Laslett, "Historical Perspectives," 65; Allen J. Scott, "The Manufacturing Economy: Ethnic and Gender Divisions of Labor," in Waldinger and Bozorgmehr, *Ethnic Los Angeles*, 215–44.

10. Tomás Almaguer, *Racial Faultlines* (Berkeley: University of California Press, 1994).

11. Cherríe Moraga, "La Güera," in *This Bridge Called My Back*, ed. Cherríe Moraga and Gloria Anzaldúa (Latham, N.Y.: Kitchen Table, 1983), 27–34.

12. *Indio* refers to both an Indian as well as someone with dark skin. *Güero* refers to someone who is light skinned.

13. C. Muñoz, *Youth, Identity, and Power: The Chicano Movement* (New York: Verso, 1989).

14. Nikkei refers to the Japanese American population in its entirety. Issei is the immigrant generation; Nisei is the children of immigrants; and Sansei and Yonsei are the third and fourth generations, respectively.

15. Scott Kurashige, "Transforming Los Angeles: Black and Japanese American Struggles for Racial Equality in the 20th Century" (PhD diss., University of California, Los Angeles, 2000); William Petersen, "Success Story, Japanese American Style," *New York Times Magazine*, January 9, 1966, VI-20; Barbara F. Varon, "The Japanese Americans: Comparative Occupational Status, 1960 and 1950," *Demography* 4 (1967): 809–19.

16. John Modell, *The Economics of Racial Accommodation: The Japanese of Los Angeles, 1900–1942* (Urbana: University of Illinois Press, 1977).

17. Allen and Turner, *Ethnic Quilt*; Kurashige, "Transforming Los Angeles"; Ivan Light and Elizabeth Roach, "Self-Employment," in Waldinger and Bozorgmehr, *Ethnic Los Angeles*, 193–213.

18. Boyle Heights Research Team, "Boyle Heights Study, 1973–74," Working Paper on Asian American Studies, Number 4 (Asian American Studies Center, University of California, Los Angeles, 1975); Roy Nakano, "Them Bad Cats: Past Images of Asian American Street Gangs," *Gidra*, January 1973, 5–7.

19. George N. Katsiaficas, *The Imagination of the New Left* (Boston: South End Press, 1987).

20. Ward Churchill and Jim Vander Wall, *Agents of Repression* (Boston: South End Press, 1988); Edward J. Escobar, "The Dialectics of Repression: The Los Angeles Police Department and the Chicano Movement, 1968–71," *Journal of American History* 79 (1993): 1483–1514; Ollie A. Johnson, "Explaining the Demise of the Black Panther Party," in *The Black Panther Party Reconsidered*, ed. Charles Earl Jones (Baltimore: Black Classic Press, 1998), 391–409; Tyler, "Black Radicalism in Southern California."

21. Elaine Brown, *A Taste of Power* (New York: Anchor Books, 1992); Angela Davis, *Angela Davis: An Autobiography* (New York: Random House, 1974). This section on the BPP benefitted from interviews of the author with Ronald Freeman, June 7, 1999; Roland Freeman, May 16, 2000; and Michael Zinzun, September 15, 2000.

22. Terry McDermott, "Behind the Bunker Mentality," *Los Angeles Times*, June 11, 2000, A1, A28–31; Tyler, "Black Radicalism in Southern California."

23. H. Nelson, "The Defenders: A Case Study of an Informal Police Organization," in *The Black Revolt*, ed. James Geschwender (Englewood Cliffs, N.J.: Prentice Hall, 1971), 79–95; R. Shoats, "Black Fighting Formations: Their Strengths, Weaknesses, and Potentialities," *New Political Science* 21 (1999): 157–70; Akinyele Omowale Umoja, "Repression Breeds Resistance: The Black Liberation Army and the Radical Legacy of the Black Panther Party," *New Political Science* 21 (1999): 131–56.

24. Jo Nina Abron, "'Serving the People': The Survival Programs of the Black Panther Party," in Jones, *Black Panther Party Reconsidered*, 177–92.

25. Huey P. Newton, *The War Against the Panthers* (New York: Harlem River Press, 1996).

26. Mario T. García, *Memories of Chicano History* (Berkeley: University of California Press, 1994).

27. E. Chávez, "Creating Aztlán" (PhD diss., University of California, Los Angeles, 1994); Juan Gomez-Quiñones, *Chicano Politics* (Albuquerque: University of New Mexico, 1990); Ramon Gutiérrez, "Community, Patriarchy and Individualism: The Politics of Chicano History and the Dream of Equality," *American Quarterly* 45 (1993): 44–72.

28. This section benefitted from interviews of the author with K. Bass, Los Angeles, February 8, 2000; M. E. Durazo, Los Angeles, February 24, 2000; B. Gallegos, Los Angeles, May 12, 1999; S. Holguin, Los Angeles, March 29, 2000; C. Montes, June 20, 2000.

29. The Committee to Free Los Tres was a group of young Chicanas/os who supported three activists unfairly charged in the murder of a police officer in East Los Angeles.

30. M. R. Chávez, "Living and Breathing the Movement" (MA thesis, Arizona State University, 1997); D. Gutiérrez, "CASA in the Chicano Movement: Ideology and Organizational Politics in the Chicano Community, 1968–78," Stanford Center for Chicano Research, Working Paper Series 5 (Palo Alto, CA: Stanford University, 1984), 12.

31. R. Santillan, oral history interview, conducted by Carlos Vasquez, UCLA Oral History Program, for the California State Government Oral History Program, Special Collections, University of California, Los Angeles, 1990, 6.

32. Aztlán refers to the mythical homeland of the Aztecs. The concept was reappropriated by Chicana/o activists in the 1960s as part of their identity and larger cultural nationalist politics.

33. D. Gutiérrez, "CASA in the Chicano Movement," 14–15.

34. Ibid., 11.

35. This section benefitted from interviews of the author with C. and M. Masaoka, Los Angeles, November 11, 1999; Mo Nishida, Los Angeles, May 7, 2000; and E. Yoshimura, Los Angeles, February 8, 2000.

36. R. Nakano, "Marxist-Leninist Organizing in the Asian American Community: Los Angeles, 1969–79" (unpublished manuscript, Asian American Studies Center Reading Room, Los Angeles, 1984).

37. Kashima, "Japanese American Internees Return"; Yasuko Takezawa, "Children of Inmates: The Effects of the Redress Movement among Third Generation Japanese Americans," in *Contemporary Asian America*, ed. Min Zhou and James T. Gatewood (New York: New York University Press, 2000), 299–314.

38. Jim O'Brien, "American Leninism in the 1970s," *Radical America* 11–12 (1977–78): 27–62.

39. Manuel Pastor Jr., "Common Ground at Ground Zero? The New Economy and the New Organizing in Los Angeles," *Antipode* 33, no. 2 (March 2001): 260–89.

On Activist Futures in a Dark Age
A Postscript

ROGER KEIL

A puzzling article appeared in the *New York Times* early in 2018 that echoed previous observations about Los Angeles, such as those by Jane Jacobs cited at the beginning of this book. The piece recycled old stereotypes about missing civic elites and who governs Los Angeles.[1] Taking their cues from what they think is normal in New York, the authors bemoan the lack of robust elite governance in the California city, especially that "for all its successes, Los Angeles has not developed the political, cultural and philanthropic institutions that have proved critical in other American cities." The article has led to ridicule and outcry, and this is not the place to enter the debate over its absurd argument and obsolete choice of sources.[2] But it shined a light on the significance this book brings to the conversation. Rather than looking for the missing elites, Don Parson's work pointed us in a different direction. Los Angeles will never be saved by its elites. Perhaps, though, its diverse and multifold masses have a better shot at justice. Parson's work as well as the other sympathetic voices assembled here make the case for a politics and governance from below, and from the periphery. The elites may have failed the center and the region. But there is life in the neighborhoods and projects of the people. In this sense, this book illuminates the popular communities, highlights their contribution to the governance of the region, and contributes to what Pulido, Barraclough, and Cheng have called "recovering and retelling the histories of ordinary people and places."[3]

The significance of this book is mainly in providing a historical perspective on crucial events in Los Angeles (and the United States for that matter) in the mid-twentieth century. Parson's work is the core of this contribution. His fine-grained historical chapters provide nodes in the more granular understanding of historical events and geographical realities that the twentieth century is beginning to be treated to. This book is published roughly one hundred years after the Russian Revolution and fifty years after the global revolts of 1968, two tremendously important events and reference points for the actors and developments that are subject to scrutiny in *Public Los Angeles*. The former stands for the grand revolutionary narratives (and their reactionary countermovements in fascism and McCarthyism) that structured much of the politics of housing, work, and urbanism in Los Angeles and elsewhere and that are subject to Parson's scrutiny above. The sixties revolts on the other hand influenced the generation of authors assembled in this book more directly. Just as much as they famously enticed Henri Lefebvre to voice the "cry and demand" for the Right to the City, they prepared the menu of social struggle and urban change for the most recent decades elsewhere.[4] As we learn from Pulido in her chapter as much as from other voices in this book, the 1960s can be understood as the launching pad from which today's Occupy and Black Lives Matter movements as well as the resistance to alt-right populism critically emerged.

In this sense, this is also a book that gives us advice on how to understand the puzzling contradictions of our time. If we paint the midcentury, between the 1930s and the 1950s, as a dark period, and the 1960s and 1970s as a period of light and opening, we are currently going through another dark period. To bring things around again to Jane Jacobs, perhaps the most influential urbanist of that period, we must note that she wrote in her last book, published shortly before her death in 2006, that there may be "a dark age ahead." Wiser than when she wrote her midcentury masterpiece about the death and life of American cities, and slightly resigned, Jacobs called into question the visions and advances of the twentieth century.[5] While resignation is never a good state to be in, we are admittedly in darker times in Los Angeles or anywhere. Ed Soja remarked that in the 1990s, "without a touch of optimistic exaggeration, it can be said that the spatiality of justice was in the urban air in Los Angeles."[6] Barely twenty years into the new century with its convulsive violence and erratic world politics, who is to quarrel with Jacobs?

Yet this book is a starkly lit signpost that we cannot allow ourselves to be drawn into historical pessimism. Parson's work is a reminder of how regular people, when they organize together and as individuals, when they are courageous, can change the future that seems laid out for them. This book, then, sees its contribution as part of a sustained effort by activists and intellectuals from Los Angeles and beyond to draw on the hope that stems from common histories and geographies. Common is here in the double sense of the word, of course: the everyday and the shared. We see this book, then, as a complement to other guides through the historical geographies of Southern California that have recently been providing much-needed connections of the past and the future, most prominently, perhaps, the magnificent *People's Guide to Los Angeles* by Laura Pulido, Laura Barraclough, and Wendy Cheng. In the introduction to that alternative tour book through the Southland's popular historical geographies, the authors note, "We have thought to uncover and share places that might be overlooked as unremarkable, places where people have nevertheless confronted power and, in doing so, have been transformed by those struggles."[7]

This is the core message also of this book: focus on the small and hidden histories, the buried stories of the everyday, the extinguished but smoldering fires at the grassroots of urban society. But Parson's belief in popular power does not make him a populist. He is a discerning analyst and strategist when it comes to pinpointing the possibilities for change in Los Angeles. When the most devastating political revolt in American history occurred in Los Angeles, in the wake of the Rodney King verdict in April 1992, Parson was somewhat reserved as to what to make of it.[8] At one point, he coolly termed it a consumer riot. In a postscript to an article that he had written before the events but that was published shortly after, he admitted, "Though the Plaza, Pershing Square and the California Plaza were not areas for the staging of the civil disturbances (albeit *cinco de mayo* celebrations at the Plaza were postponed for one month because of the fear of crowds), the riots demonstrated that, in contrast to the postmodern death wish, public spaces are far from dead."[9]

History understood in these critical terms remains crucial to finding our way in these darker times. The history told by Don Parson and others in this book is a history made by humans. It is made with the objective of improving an ever-changing urban environment to create collective economic institutions not entirely reliant on the market, provide more and better—social and public—housing, create social relationships in solidarity, and free from oppression based on class and race relations. The alternative is not an option: a history of dead signifiers, fixed capital, and enshrined privilege. This alternative worldview was on full display at the opening of the new seven-hundred-million-dollar University of Southern California Village at the city's biggest private university in South Los Angeles. At the complex's opening, the university's president, C. L. Max Nikias—now deposed for ignoring the decades-long scandal of student abuse on his campus—referred to the seemingly "eternal" nature of the Village's new collegiate gothic style architecture: "And let's always remember, the looks of the University Village give us 1,000 years of history we don't have. Thank you, and fight on!" As former *Los Angeles Times* architecture critic Christopher Hawthorne observed, the president mistakes both the city of Los Angeles and his own campus as places without a proper history, perhaps no history to speak of at all.[10] Parson's work and the commentary and context provided in this book counteract this view of a history that is empty and has to be performed in architectural form. It rather presents a view of history as made by people for people, by communities for their city. The Los Angeles that comes to life in the work of Don Parson and the other authors in this volume is the city in which its diverse communities can thrive and have a vibrant future rather than a past built in architectural symbolism. It is the city built by and for humanity.

Dark ages are not made to last. Things can be turned around. For that to happen we need to learn from past mistakes without abandoning the project of building a better society. The lessons we learn from Parson's midcentury Los Angeles and from the projects that carried its utopias forward need to be drawn honestly and in a productive fashion. Erik Swyngedouw has reflected on this dark age that, in his words, is also a post-political age, an age with apparently little space for emancipatory politics. The "specter of a once existing but failed communism" of the twentieth century that Swyngedouw describes and the formidable counterrevolutionary forces that helped defeat it are present in the histories of midcentury Los Angeles.[11] Perhaps, then, there is also hope that a revived "communist hypothesis" might be the right recipe for finding a new politics of emancipation: "Communism as an idea manifests itself concretely each time people come together in-common, not only to demand equality, to demand their place within the edifice of state and society, but also to stage their capacity for self-organization and self-management, and to enact the democratic promise, thereby changing the frame of what is considered possible and revolutionizing the very parameters of state and government, while putting tentatively and experimentally new organizational forms in their place."[12] Let us dedicate this hope to the memory of Don Parson, whose belief in a better humankind was the inspiration for this book.

NOTES

1. Tim Arango and Adam Nagourney, "A Paper Tears Apart in a City That Never Quite Came Together," *New York Times*, January 30, 2018, www.nytimes.com/2018/01/30/us/los-angeles-times.html.

2. An excellent embedded summary of reactions can be found in the web links of an article by Christopher Hawthorne, "Los Angeles, Houston and the Appeal of the Hard-to-Read City," *Los Angeles Times*, February 8, 2018, www.latimes.com/entertainment/arts/la-ca-cm-building-type-new-york-times-20180211-story.html.

3. Laura Pulido, Laura Barraclough, and Wendy Cheng, *A People's Guide to Los Angeles* (Berkeley: University of California Press, 2012).

4. Henri Lefebvre, *The Urban Revolution* (Minneapolis: University of Minnesota Press, 2003); Henri Lefebvre, *Writings on Cities* (Cambridge: Blackwell, 1996), 196.

5. Jane Jacobs, *Dark Age Ahead* (Toronto: Random House Canada, 2004).

6. Edward W. Soja, *Seeking Spatial Justice* (Minneapolis: University of Minnesota Press, 2010), 154.

7. Pulido, Barraclough, and Cheng, *People's Guide to Los Angeles*, 13.

8. For an excellent new evaluation of this and other urban revolts, see Mustafa Dikeç, *Urban Rage: The Revolt of the Excluded* (New Haven, Conn.: Yale University Press, 2017).

9. Don Parson, "The Search for a Center: The Recomposition of Race, Class and Space in Los Angeles," *International Journal of Urban and Regional Research* 17, no. 2 (June 1993): 239, https://doi.org/10.1111/j.1468-2427.1993.tb00478.x.

10. Christopher Hawthorne, "Disneyland Meets Hogwarts at $700-Million USC Village," *Los Angeles Times*, August 21, 2017, www.latimes.com/entertainment/arts/la-et-cm-usc-village-review-20170820-story.html.

11. Erik Swyngedouw, *Promises of the Political: Insurgent Cities in a Post-political Environment* (Cambridge, Mass.: MIT Press, 2018), 167.

12. Ibid., 168.

DON PARSON, A SELECT BIBLIOGRAPHY

COMPILED BY B. UYEDA AND JUDY BRANFMAN

BOOKS/DISSERTATIONS

Making a Better World: Public Housing, the Red Scare, and the Direction of Modern Los Angeles. Preface by Kevin Starr. Minneapolis: University of Minneapolis Press, 2005

"Urban Politics during the Cold War: Public Housing, Urban Renewal and Suburbanization in Los Angeles." PhD dissertation, UCLA, 1985.

"Regional Planning, Housing Policy, and Community Action in Northern Ireland." MA thesis, UCLA, 1979.

ARTICLES

"The Decline of Public Housing and the Politics of the Red Scare: The Significance of the Los Angeles Public Housing War." *Journal of Urban History* 33, no. 3 (March 2007): 400–417.

"Injustice for Salcido: The Left Response to Police Brutality in Cold War Los Angeles." *Southern California Quarterly* 86, no. 2 (Summer 2004): 145–68.

"The Burke Incident: Political Belief in Los Angeles' Public Housing during the Domestic Cold War." *Southern California Quarterly* 84, no. 1 (Spring 2002): 53–74.

"'The Darling of the Town's Neo-Fascists': The Bombastic Political Career of Councilman Ed J. Davenport." *Southern California Quarterly* 81, no. 4 (Winter 1999): 467–505.

"'This Modern Marvel': Bunker Hill, Chavez Ravine, and the Politics of Modernism in Los Angeles." In "Land Policy and Land Use in Southern California." Special issue, *Southern California Quarterly* 75, no. 3/4 (Fall/Winter 1993): 333–50.

"The Search for a Center: The Recomposition of Race, Class, and Space in Los Angeles." *International Journal of Urban and Regional Research* 17, no. 2 (June 1993): 232–40. https://doi.org/10.1111/j.1468-2427.1993.tb00478.x.

"Many Histories: Postmodern Politics in Los Angeles." *Science as Culture* 12 (1991): 418.

"Organized Labor and the Housing Question: Public Housing, Suburbanization, and Urban Renewal." *Environment and Planning D: Society and Space* 2 (1984): 75–86.

"Los Angeles' 'Headline-Happy Public Housing War.'" *Southern California Quarterly* 65, no. 3 (Fall 1983): 251–85.

"The Development of Redevelopment: Public Housing and Urban Renewal in Los Angeles." *International Journal of Urban and Regional Research* 6, no. 3 (September 1982): 393–413. https://doi.org/10.1111/j.1468-2427.1982.tb00387.x.

REVIEWS

Review of *City of Promise: Race and Historical Change in Los Angeles,* edited by Martin Schiesl and Mark M. Dodge (Claremont: Regina Books, 2006). *H-Net Reviews in the Humanities and Social Sciences,* October 2006. https://www.h-net.org/reviews /showpdf.php?id=12413.

Review of *Eden by Design: The 1930 Olmsted-Bartholomew Plan for the Los Angeles Region,* by Greg Hise, William Deverell, and Laurie Olin. *Southern California Quarterly* 84, no. 1 (Spring 2002): 80–81.

Review of *Here Comes the Sun: Architecture and Public Space in Twentieth-Century European Culture,* by Ken Warpole. *Science as Culture* 10, no. 4 (2001): 553–58.

Review of *The Terror of the Machine: Technology, Work, Gender, and Ecology on the U.S.-Mexico Border,* by Devon G Pena. *Science as Culture* 7, no. 3 (1998):413–17.

Review of *Variations on a Theme Park: The New American City and the End of Public Space,* edited by Michael Sorkin. *Science as Culture* 4, no. 2 (1993).

CONTRIBUTORS

Judy Branfman, Research Affiliate with the UCLA Institute for Research on Labor and Employment, is a documentary filmmaker, activist, and independent scholar based in Los Angeles. She is working on a documentary, "The Land of Orange Groves & Jails," and book on the precedent-setting court case *Stromberg v. California*. She does outreach and education and project development and coordination with grassroots and other like-minded people and projects.

Dana Cuff is a professor, author, and scholar in architecture and urbanism at the University of California, Los Angeles, where she is also the founding director of cityLAB, a think tank that explores design innovations in the emerging metropolis (www.cityLAB.aud .ucla.edu). She is author, among others, of *Architecture: The Story of Practice*, which remains an influential text about the culture of the design profession, and *The Provisional City*, a study of residential architecture's role in transforming Los Angeles over the past century.

Mike Davis is the author of more than twenty books, including *City of Quartz: Excavating the Future in Los Angeles*. He is professor emeritus at the University of California, Riverside, in the Department of Creative Writing.

Steven Flusty is the nom de plume of Tepan Fyodorovich "Hezârfenzade" İfritoğlu Yoldaş-Paşa, noted metropolographer and founder of the Constantinopolitan aëronautical concern Tophane Çelebifabrikası. In conjunction with the celebrated natural historian, polar expeditionist, and larval vivisectionist Dr. Celeste Tian, he is also co-proprietor of the firm Mahometan & Celestial LLC, a foremost purveyor of modernization to crowned heads the world over since the 18th of October 1860.

Greg Goldin is the former architecture critic for *Los Angeles Magazine* and is a contributor to the *Architect's Newspaper*. He is the co-curator and co-author of *Never Built Los Angeles* and *Never Built New York*. He is currently at work on two new exhibitions, *Never Built Paris* and *Never Built Central Park*.

Roger Keil is a York Research Chair in Global Sub/Urban Studies. He has published widely on urban matters including, *Los Angeles* (Wiley) and *Changing Toronto* (UTP, with Boudreau and Young). His latest book, *Suburban Planet*, was published by Polity in 2018. A former co-editor of the *International Journal of Urban and Regional Research* and the founding Director of the City Institute at York University, he has been the principal investigator of a Major Collaborative Research Initiative on Global Suburbanisms (2010–19).

Jacqueline (Jackie) Leavitt's (1939–2015) research during her decades-long career focused on housing and community development policy, public housing, and the multiple meanings of home, among many other urban and social issues. As a founder of the American Planning Association (APA) Planning and Women Division, she is considered a pioneer in research on gender and community development. Additionally, her work brought to light the ways in which low-resourced populations managed to live, work, and survive in cities and regions across the globe.

Laura Pulido is Professor in Ethnic Studies and Geography at the University of Oregon, where she studies and teaches environmental justice, political activism, racial capitalism, and cultural memory. Among many other publications, she is the author of *Black, Brown, Yellow and Left*, recently co-edited *Black and Brown in Los Angeles*, and co-authored *A People's Guide to Los Angeles*.

Sue Ruddick is a professor and human geographer at University of Toronto. She works at the intersections between geography and philosophy. She publishes in a range of transdisciplinary, geographic, and philosophical journals on questions of urbanization, affect, nondialectical thought, and human-nature relations.

Tom Sitton is a curator emeritus of history at the Natural History Museum of Los Angeles County. He is the author of *John Randolph Haynes: California Progressive, Los Angeles Transformed: Fletcher Bowron's Urban Reform Revival, 1938–1953*, and *The Courthouse Crowd: Los Angeles County and Its Government, 1850–1950*. With William Deverell he is the co-editor of *California Progressivism Revisited* and *Metropolis in the Making: Los Angeles in the 1920s*, and co-author of *Water and Los Angeles: A Tale of Three Rivers, 1900–1941*.

Edward W. Soja (1940–2015) was Distinguished Professor Emeritus of Urban Planning at the University of California, Los Angeles and the author of a series of widely influential books on space and geography, most focusing on Los Angeles. He was one of the most important contributors to postmodern geography, spatial thought, and urban theory.

Jennifer Wolch is William W. Wurster Dean and Professor of City and Regional Planning at the University of California, Berkeley. A scholar of urban analysis and planning, she has authored or co-authored over 125 academic journal articles and book chapters. She was also a recipient of fellowships from the Guggenheim Foundation, Center for Advanced Study in the Behavioral Sciences, the Rockefeller Foundation's Bellagio Study Center, and other prestigious honors.

INDEX

122–24. *See also* anticommunist politics; political activism

social justice, recent trends in, 13, 15–16. *See also* human rights; political activism; revolutionary politics; spatial justice

Social Justice and the City (Harvey), 213

Soja, Ed, 2–3, 5, 10, 21, 161, 182, 209–15, 230; *Seeking Spatial Justice*, 209

Sonoratown, 29, 32, 33–34, 36, 39, 42

Sorkin, Michael, 199; *Variations on a Theme Park*, 176–79

Southern California Library for Social Studies and Research (scl), 96, 157–58, 160

South Gate, Moffatt's career, 96–98, 102, 115

South Los Angeles: African Americans, 12, 38, 48, 217–18; bungalows, 38; employment, 217–18; map, 26–27; Nickerson Gardens, 26–27, 82–83, 85t, 182, 204–7; public housing projects, 70t, 78t, 85t; renamed as South LA, 191; women's resistance in public housing, 204–5, 207. *See also* African Americans; Watts

space, urban. *See* urban space

spatial justice, 2–3, 182, 209–15; agency, 182; everyday life, 2; exchange value of space, 13–14; free speech in public space, 177, 180n10; historical background, 213–14; housing wealth, 14; right to the city, 3, 210, 213, 214–15, 230; social production of spatiality, 210; spatial justice/injustice, 211–12; spatial turn, 210; struggle, 182

Special Subcommittee of the Committee on Government Operations, 127–28

Spring-Main Street corridor, 198

Starr, Kevin, 2, 178

State Commission of Immigration and Housing, California (cscih), 36, 41, 47–48

Stein, Clarence, 56, 60, 88

Stein, Joseph Allen, 71

Steinberg, Henry, 114–15

Stephens, Harrison, 75

Stern, Edith, 152

Sterry, Nora, 39, 51n22

Stevenson, Adlai, 153

St. Louis, 57

Stoddart, Bessie, 29, 31, 33, 41, 166

Storefront, 223

stories, 201–3

Strategic Action for a Just Economy (saje), 214

street speaking, 41

suburbs, 14–15, 168; consumer economy, 153–54; households as social factories, 152–54; incorporated autonomy, 9; Lakewood Plan, 9, 12; nuclear families, 154, 167; owner-occupied single-family homes, 14–15; politics of housework, 152–54; polluted industrial districts, 15; postwar politics of housework, 145–47, *146*; rapid growth, 4–5; weak tax bases, 9, 12. *See also* center and periphery

Subversive Organizations, Attorney General's List of (agloso), 122, 124–25, 128–29, 132, 135–40. *See also* loyalty oaths

sunshine and orange groves trope, 11, 29, 49n1, 51n22, 167, 168

superblocks, 56, 57, 60–61, *61*, 64, 65, 72, 74–75, 83. *See also* modernism

Supreme Court, U.S.: Gwinn Amendment (loyalty oaths), 122, 131, 133–35; Hollywood 10 (free speech), 185; racial covenants, 38

Swyngedouw, Erik, 231–32

Syrians, 33

Taft-Ellender-Wagner bill, 123. *See also* Housing Act (1949)

Taylorism, 147

Tenney, Jack, 104–6. *See also* cuac

theme parks, 176–79

theory, urban. *See* urban studies

Theory of Good Form, The (Lynch), 207

Thousand Oaks, xii, 21, 26–27, 158, 160

towers. *See* high-rises

township system, 98–99, 190

traffic, vehicle and pedestrian: cul-de-sacs, 72, 87; parking in public housing, 62, 63, 65–66; separation in public housing, 71; speeding laws, 99–101; superblocks, 56, 57, 60–61, *61*, 74–75

transit: Bus Riders Union, 11, 15–16, 214; mta network, 12, 15; social status, 16; spatial justice, 214

Truman, Harry, 123, 124, 135

Trump, Donald, 13, 15, 160

unions. *See* labor movement

Union Station, 26–27, 34, 39

Universal CityWalk, 173–75, 177–78

University of California, loyalty oaths, 125

University of California at Los Angeles (ucla), 159, 161–62, 214

University of Southern California (usc), 38, 231

GEOGRAPHIES OF JUSTICE AND SOCIAL TRANSFORMATION

1. *Social Justice and the City*, rev. ed.
   BY DAVID HARVEY

2. *Begging as a Path to Progress: Indigenous Women and Children and the Struggle for Ecuador's Urban Spaces*
   BY KATE SWANSON

3. *Making the San Fernando Valley: Rural Landscapes, Urban Development, and White Privilege*
   BY LAURA R. BARRACLOUGH

4. *Company Towns in the Americas: Landscape, Power, and Working-Class Communities*
   EDITED BY OLIVER J. DINIUS AND ANGELA VERGARA

5. *Tremé: Race and Place in a New Orleans Neighborhood*
   BY MICHAEL E. CRUTCHER JR.

6. *Bloomberg's New York: Class and Governance in the Luxury City*
   BY JULIAN BRASH

7. *Roppongi Crossing: The Demise of a Tokyo Nightclub District and the Reshaping of a Global City*
   BY ROMAN ADRIAN CYBRIWSKY

8. *Fitzgerald: Geography of a Revolution*
   BY WILLIAM BUNGE

9. *Accumulating Insecurity: Violence and Dispossession in the Making of Everyday Life*
   EDITED BY SHELLEY FELDMAN, CHARLES GEISLER, AND GAYATRI A. MENON

10. *They Saved the Crops: Labor, Landscape, and the Struggle over Industrial Farming in Bracero-Era California*
    BY DON MITCHELL

11. *Faith Based: Religious Neoliberalism and the Politics of Welfare in the United States*
    BY JASON HACKWORTH

12. *Fields and Streams: Stream Restoration, Neoliberalism, and the Future of Environmental Science*
    BY REBECCA LAVE

13. *Black, White, and Green: Farmers Markets, Race, and the Green Economy*
    BY ALISON HOPE ALKON

14. *Beyond Walls and Cages: Prisons, Borders, and Global Crisis*
    EDITED BY JENNA M. LOYD, MATT MITCHELSON, AND ANDREW BURRIDGE

15. *Silent Violence: Food, Famine, and Peasantry in Northern Nigeria*
    BY MICHAEL J. WATTS

16. *Development, Security, and Aid: Geopolitics and Geoeconomics at the U.S. Agency for International Development*
    BY JAMEY ESSEX

17. *Properties of Violence: Law and Land-Grant Struggle in Northern New Mexico*
    BY DAVID CORREIA

18. *Geographical Diversions: Tibetan Trade, Global Transactions*
    BY TINA HARRIS

19. *The Politics of the Encounter: Urban Theory and Protest under Planetary Urbanization*
    BY ANDY MERRIFIELD

20. *Rethinking the South African Crisis: Nationalism, Populism, Hegemony*
    BY GILLIAN HART

21. *The Empires' Edge: Militarization, Resistance, and Transcending Hegemony in the Pacific*
    BY SASHA DAVIS

22. *Pain, Pride, and Politics: Social Movement Activism and the Sri Lankan Tamil Diaspora in Canada*
    BY AMARNATH AMARASINGAM

23. *Selling the Serengeti: The Cultural Politics of Safari Tourism*
    BY BENJAMIN GARDNER

24. *Territories of Poverty: Rethinking North and South*
    EDITED BY ANANYA ROY AND EMMA SHAW CRANE

25. *Precarious Worlds: Contested Geographies of Social Reproduction*
    EDITED BY KATIE MEEHAN AND KENDRA STRAUSS

26. *Spaces of Danger: Culture and Power in the Everyday*
    EDITED BY HEATHER MERRILL AND LISA M. HOFFMAN